CU00704126

HUMAN IN VITRO FERTILIZATION

Titles in the series:

A Patient's Right to Know: Information, Disclosure, the Doctor and the Law
Sheila A.M. McLean, University of Glasgow

New Reproductive Techniques: A Legal Perspective
Douglas J. Cusine, University of Aberdeen

Medico-Legal Aspects of Reproduction and Parenthood
J.K. Mason, University of Edinburgh

Law Reform and Human Reproduction
Edited by *Sheila A.M. McLean*, University of Glasgow

Legal and Ethical Issues in the Management of the Dementing Elderly
Mary Gilhooly, University of Glasgow

Legal Issues in Human Reproduction
Edited by *Sheila A.M. McLean*, University of Glasgow

Mental Illness: Prejudice, Discrimination and the Law
Tom Campbell, Australian National University, Canberra and *Chris Heginbotham*, King's Fund College, London

Pharmaceuticals in the European Community
Ken Collins, Member of the European Parliament and *Sheila A.M. McLean*, University of Glasgow

Pregnancy at Work
Noreen Burrows, University of Glasgow

Changing People: The Law and Ethics of Behaviour Modification
Alexander McCall Smith, University of Edinburgh

Health Resources and the Law: Who Gets What and Why
Robert G. Lee, Wilde Sapte and *Frances H. Miller*, University of Boston

Surrogacy and the Moral Economy
Derek Morgan, University College, Swansea

Family Planning Practice and the Law
Kenneth McK. Norrie, University of Aberdeen

Mental Health Law in Context: Doctors' Orders?
Michael Cavadino, University of Sheffield

Artificial Reproduction and Reproductive Rights
Athena Liu, University of Hong Kong

Medicine, Law and Social Change
Leanna Darvall, La Trobe University

Abortion Regimes
Kerry A. Petersen, La Trobe University

All titles are provisional

HUMAN IN VITRO FERTILIZATION
A Case Study in the Regulation of Medical Innovation

JENNIFER GUNNING
Agricultural & Food Research Council

and

VERONICA ENGLISH
Human Fertilisation and Embryology Authority

Dartmouth
Aldershot · Brookfield USA · Hong Kong · Singapore · Sydney

© Jennifer Gunning and Veronica English 1993

All rights reserved. No part of this publication may be reproduced, stored in a retrieval system, or transmitted in any form or by any means, electronic, mechanical, photo-copying, recording, or otherwise without the prior permission of Dartmouth Publishing Company Limited.

Published by
Dartmouth Publishing Company Limited
Gower House
Croft Road
Aldershot
Hants GU11 3HR
England

Dartmouth Publishing Company
Old Post Road
Brookfield
Vermont 05036
USA

British Library Cataloguing in Publication Data
Gunning, Jennifer
  Human In Vitro Fertilization: Case Study
  in the Regulation of Medical Innovation
  I. Title II. English, Veronica
  618.178059

Library of Congress Cataloging-in-Publication Data
Gunning, Jennifer.
  Human in vitro fertilization : a case study in the regulation of
medical innovation / by Jennifer Gunning & Veronica English.
    p. cm. — (Medico-legal series)
  Includes bibliographical references.
  ISBN 1-85521-347-8 : $59.95 (approx.)
  1. Fertilization in vitro, Human—Law and legislation—Great
Britain. I. English, Veronica. II. Title. III. Series.
KD3415.G86 1993
344.41'0419—dc20
[344.104419]   93-24213
                                        CIP

ISBN 1 85521 347 8

Printed and bound in Great Britain by
Hartnolls Limited, Bodmin, Cornwall

Contents

Acknowledgements

As the life of the Interim Licensing Authority drew to a close in the summer of 1991 it was suggested that we might put on record an account of its work. This is what we have attempted to do in this book and to set the Authority's work in its broader context.

We are indebted to the Medical Research Council (MRC) and the Royal College of Obstetricians and Gynaecologists (RCOG) for allowing us access to the relevant files and to Dr Anne McLaren who lent us her private papers. We are also grateful to a number of people who took the time to speak to us and to provide us with insights which we would not otherwise have obtained. Professor Bob Edwards gave us an invaluable account of his work and the early days of IVF. Others who spared us their time included staff at Oldham General Hospital, Sir John Gray and Sir James Gowans (former Secretaries of the MRC), Professor Geoffrey Dawes (former Chairman of the MRC Advisory Group and Deputy Chairman of the VLA), Dr Keith Gibson (the first secretary of the VLA), Dr Joan Box, Sir Malcolm MacNaughton (former Warnock Committee member, President of the RCOG and VLA member), Professor Ian Cooke (former VLA member and now a member of the HFEA), Professor David Whittingham, Dr John Modle of the Department of Health and Professor Peter Braude. Dr Karen Dawson kindly provided information about Australia and interviewed Dr Alan Trounson on our behalf.

It was suggested that it might be opportune to update the Gunning report and the final chapter of the book contains information about international legislation relating to assisted reproduction. Here we are indebted to Sev Fluss, David Shapiro, Derek Morgan, Jan Stepan and Christian Byk for alerting us to new developments. We are grateful to members of the Human Fertilisation and Embryology Authority and its Chief Executive, Flora Goldhill, for help and advice on the Authority's first year's work.

Jennifer Gunning was supported by a small grant from the Nuffield Foundation, SOC/181(2232), and a visiting fellowship in the Centre for the Analysis of Social Policy at the University of Bath. She would like to thank Professor Rudolf Klein for his help and encouragement, Thelma Brown for her assistance and Alison Brady and Frances Bellamy for putting the manuscript in its final form.

On a personal note, our thanks go to Peter and Alexander Gunning and Neil Houston for their continual support and encouragement. Last, but not least, we would like to thank all the members of the Authority for their interest and enthusiasm and in particular Dame Mary Donaldson without whom none of this would have happened.

Jennifer Gunning   Veronica English

Foreword

I am delighted to be invited to contribute very briefly to this case study on human in vitro fertilization.

I found that the facts so lucidly set out by the authors both interesting and fascinating. It is of particular interest that in 1968 Professor Edwards was discussing the formation of just such a body as the VLA and I regret that no international agreement has so far been achieved on many of the problems arising from IVF. With the birth of the first IVF baby in 1978 the race was on between those twin and sometimes conflicting aims, the advancement of scientific research and the relief of infertility.

There is a remarkable similarity between the United States Secretary of Health and Education's reaction to the report of their Ethics Advisory Board and our government's reaction to the findings, some three years later in 1984, of the Warnock Report. The former did nothing, the latter only when forced to take notice by weight of public opinion. On the other hand, the legislation in Victoria, Australia, following the Waller Committee's report has been much criticized for rushing into legislation governing IVF before full exploration of its many facets had been undertaken. The long period of uncertainty and the Department of

Health's 'hands off' approach made our work much more difficult.   Their unwillingness to offer any support either by public recognition or financial aid continued until I presented the then Minister for Health, Mrs Edwina Currie, with the veiled ultimatum that without such support we could not continue.   I will always be grateful for her practical and commonsense approach and for the support which was then forthcoming.   Financially small but great and therefore helpful in terms of public recognition.

In 1985 when I was invited to chair the then VLA I accepted with alacrity and I have never regretted so doing.   I had the privilege, with the cooperation and expertise of so many others, of helping to formulate guidelines for an exciting and fast developing, comparatively new medical science.

Naturally, I had some reservations.   How could such an authority with its apparently disparate membership seek, for the first time in medical history, to control medical clinical treatment? Would those clinicians and others already well established and internationally respected in this field be prepared to accept our findings? Could a non-statutory body with then, as I believed, a two year life span have any real influence or power to enforce such findings? How were we to fulfil our role as 'public watchdog'? Here I would like to pay tribute (a rare event these days) to most sections of the media.

It was recognised very early that initially our only means of public communication would be through these channels.   We therefore resolved that, apart from any matters about which we learned in confidence, there should be complete freedom of communication between ourselves and the specialist journalists.

During our first years I was pleasantly surprised by the cooperation we were given by members of the medical and scientific professions.   It was true that with a statutory authority in the offing anything that they as professionals could do to shape 'things to come' must, as I was told, be in their own best interests.   However, I suspect it must have been something of a shock for them to find themselves, possibly for the first time in their lives, cross examined in some detail by members of the Authority as to their treatment of their patients, their methods and their success rate.   I never, except during the one unfortunate incident involving the removal of a centre's licence, experienced any hostility during our visits to centres. Equally, during Authority meetings our professional members were at pains to ensure that the lay members fully understood the technical and medical approaches to their work.   Similarly the lay members had no inhibitions over questioning all aspects of any treatment undertaken and the ethics governing this.   Save for the question of egg donor anonymity I cannot recall our not arriving at a consensus over any problem.

Medical phrases and usages of technical terms were interpreted not, as we were accused by the pro-life lobby, in attempt to fudge any issue or to blind the public to the reality of any situation but so that they could be more readily understood by the population generally. To this day I cannot understand the furore which arose, during the passage of the bill, over our usage of the term 'pre-embryo' or why the government, save for political pressure, decided to drop what was becoming an internationally accepted term.

During our six years as an Authority our membership remained almost constant. I think it reflects well on the members' enthusiasm and interest in our work and their desire to help resolve so many different issues that we lost only three members and that due to changes in occupation and the extension of our 'sell by date'. I much appreciated the help and advice I received from all members and will always be grateful to Professor Geoffrey Dawes, my vice chairman, for his wise and tactful counsel and his readiness to take on extra duties when necessary.

I would like to draw attention to the vast amount of work which was undertaken apart from our routine meetings and visits. There were the working parties set up to discuss various issues and to report on them to the main meeting. There were papers written by both lay and professional members for a variety of publications. Hours were spent on collating statistics for our annual reports and there were numerous other problems which, as they arose, needed prompt attention.

We were very well served by four successive secretaries. The MRC seconded to us most able people including the authors of this case study. Dr Jenny Gunning joined us at a time when we were developing our work. Her efforts in amassing the incredible amount of paper work, organizing meetings and keeping members fully briefed on any new development has never been fully recognized. She left us to produce a most informative report on IVF internationally. Miss Veronica English worked with her and her successor Dr Jane Frew during the period prior to our receiving government support. I worked very closely with the secretariat and I much appreciated the way Miss English, as our final secretary, took over the task of easing the transition to the statutory body and, together with Professor Thompson, undertook the mammoth task of producing our final statistics.

This was quite the most difficult period of our existence. We had been asked to continue with our work during the nine months overlap and to cooperate with the provisional new authority. This cooperation proved to be mostly one way. Had there been more openness and consultation much unnecessary worry on behalf of the centres could have been avoided, as could some of the pitfalls which emerged such as the two mentioned in the study relating to the storage of embryos and the problem of confidentiality.

Could self regulation in this field have continued to work? Given the goodwill and the cooperation we experienced from the centres, I think that it could. However, with such a lack of resources, our minuscule staff and the ever growing demands on the time of our voluntary members we could not continue to function adequately in this continually expanding field. Furthermore, regretfully it was felt politically that legal sanctions were more acceptable than self regulation.

As I write this, I notice that even further advances are being made with the advent of ovarian transplants. This latest development must be welcomed by many women who cannot produce eggs or whose ovaries, unless they could be removed and replaced at a later date, might be damaged by treatment for other conditions. Should consideration not be given by the HFEA to imposing an age limit for recipients of such transplants? I hope that this technique already falls within its ambit for, as concluded in this case study, can an authority governed by statute move with sufficient speed and flexibility to keep pace with future advances?

Mary Donaldson
March 1993

1 Early Days

Introduction

Medical innovation is a continuous process. It may arise from the scientist's bench, from the adaptation of existing medical techniques or from technologies adapted from outside the medical field. When we require medical attention we expect to have access to the latest treatment and medical technology available. Rarely do we question how this was developed or what are the ethical consequences of its use. The more life threatening the disease, the more radical the treatment we are prepared to accept though often such treatments are costly and someone must decide who should be eligible; doctors or hospital authorities may, for instance, be required to make value judgments about the lives of their patients to determine who should receive dialysis treatment or an organ transplant. Alternatively, the treatments may be so novel that the risk is high yet, while desperate patients may be willing, care needs to be taken to ensure that the benefit outweighs the risk for the individual. Advances in biotechnology are providing evermore sophisticated approaches to the treatment of defects and diseases, particularly at the genetic level, and the sequencing of the human genome is going to pose at least as many questions as provide answers. The aim of this book, however, is not to guess at future medical innovation but to look retrospectively at the development and regulation of a radical new medical technology which brought into question

1

fundamental assumptions about the value of human life. In so doing, we hope to provide a case study which may inform the introduction of technologies to come.

Infertility is not a disease nor is it life threatening. It may arise through disease, genetic or developmental defect or without explanation. Nonetheless it is a condition which may cause great distress and is present in about one in eight couples of reproductive age. In vitro fertilization (IVF) is an accepted method for overcoming this condition and has been available for almost fifteen years yet it still engenders much conscience seeking and moral and ethical discussion worldwide. Some countries have already sought to control IVF by legislation, others are in the process or are still struggling with the concept. Why?

When man becomes involved in creating man in the laboratory and the origins of human life become demystified do we prefer to escape from our discomfort by sticking our head in the sand rather than address it head on? Would our discomfort be less if infertility were a life threatening disorder? How do we balance clinical freedom or the generation of knowledge against the sanctity of human life? We do not necessarily seek to answer these questions but by describing the experience in the United Kingdom, where the innovation was developed, we look at the answers provided by voluntary regulation.

The work of Edwards and Steptoe

Human in vitro fertilization involves the recovery of oocytes (eggs) from a woman's ovaries and sperm from a man - usually the woman's husband or partner - and their culture together outside the body, in the laboratory, until fertilization takes place. The resultant embryos are then cultured further until they consist of two, four or sometimes more cells when they are transferred to the woman's womb via the cervix. All being well, an embryo will implant into the wall of the womb and pregnancy will be achieved. The technique was developed as a treatment for human infertility entirely because of the vision and determination of one man, Robert Geoffrey Edwards.

Bob Edwards trained as a mouse geneticist and reproductive physiologist as a graduate student in the early fifties (1951-1957) at the Institute of Animal Genetics in Edinburgh. He found he had entered a field still full of dogma. His work involved research on reproduction in mice and initially, because his subjects tended to ovulate at night, he was forced to live a nocturnal existence and became known as 'the phantom of the mouse house'. However, by 1957 he had become expert in timing the stages of ovulation by the use of ovulation induction and in maturing mouse oocytes in vitro, the latter being considered by him to be an important step if such techniques were to be applied to the human species. Already at this time, in the USA, studies by Shettles[1] on human oocytes had led to the prediction that in vitro fertilization might provide infertile women with the opportunity of having children.

Between 1958 and 1965 at the National Institute for Medical Research, Mill Hill, the Biochemistry Department at Glasgow University and in the Department of Physiology at Cambridge Bob Edwards extended his work on the maturation of oocytes to species other than the mouse; rabbit, cow, pig, sheep, baboon, rhesus monkey and, finally, human.[2,3,4] In those days wedge resection of the ovary was a common method of treating women with polycystic ovaries and Edwards managed initially to obtain sections of human ovary, from which he obtained oocytes, from Molly Rose, a consultant at the Edgware hospital. In Glasgow oocytes came via Professor Ian Donald, later an opponent of IVF. By 1965 Edwards was finding ovarian tissue difficult to obtain so he secured a Ford Foundation fellowship to work at Johns Hopkins University in Baltimore where he was able to carry out a series of fertilization experiments on human oocytes obtained with the co-operation of Howard Jones.

At this time the limiting factor to fertilization was considered to be sperm capacitation. Edwards, with Jones, therefore set out to mimic the natural conditions of sperm capacitation in order to obtain fertilization. First, sperm were incubated with cervical mucus but this did not lead to capacitation. Then, because fertilization normally takes place in the fallopian tube, matured oocytes were incubated with small pieces of fallopian tube, obtained at biopsy, before sperm were added. Finally, matured oocytes were transferred with human spermatozoa to the fallopian tubes of rabbits and rhesus monkeys. In no case was fertilization confirmed although, in the control experiment, two or more nuclei were observed in one or two of the oocytes, suggesting sperm entry.

The fellowship only lasted six weeks but Edwards was undeterred by the failure of his experiments, realising that he was on the verge of a breakthrough. Shortly after, in an interview for the new journal *World Medicine*,[5] Bob set out his vision for the uses of human IVF - firstly, as a solution for infertility using oocytes obtained from infertile women, or even their close relatives; secondly, by sex selection in vitro, reducing the chance of women at risk having children with sex-linked disorders. The report seems to have raised little comment.

It was not until 1968, when Bob Edwards met Patrick Steptoe, that his research began to take off. At last he had found an enthusiast for the possibilities of IVF and one who had pioneered the technique of laparoscopy which was to revolutionize oocyte retrieval. In February 1969 they were able to report in *Nature*[6] that human oocytes had been fertilized in vitro. This merited editorial comment but elicited scepticism from the establishment which considered their observations insufficient proof of fertilization since neither syngamy nor cleavage had taken place.[7]

Soon Steptoe was obtaining pre-ovulatory oocytes from patients by laparoscopy, that is, matured in vivo and collected from the ovary, with their follicular fluid, through a small incision in the abdomen just before ovulation. These were fertilized and cultured through several cleavage divisions, some up to the 16 cell stage. This work was again reported in *Nature*.[8] However, Edwards and Steptoe received little encouragement from their peers, both being considered somewhat maverick. Steptoe had battled alone for years to introduce laparoscopy as a routine procedure which would be less traumatic for the patient than the usual laparotomy; Edwards' work on human IVF was felt to be intellectually mundane when developmental biology offered more exciting vistas. Tubal surgery was considered to be a more reliable method of treating women rendered infertile because of blocked fallopian tubes, the main indication for IVF.

By the end of 1970 Edwards was culturing embryos to the blastocyst stage.[9] However, work was hampered by the fact that Patrick Steptoe worked in Oldham and Bob Edwards in Cambridge with a four hour drive separating the two. At the beginning of their collaboration eggs would be retrieved from patients in the operating theatre at Oldham General Hospital and the embryology then undertaken in the physiology laboratory at Cambridge. In 1970 the Health Authority in Oldham allocated dedicated facilities to the two pioneers at Kershaw's Hospital in Royton just outside the town. They were allocated two beds, an operating theatre and culture and preparation rooms. Although this meant that embryos could now be cultured on site, lack of funds meant that facilities were barely adequate and Edwards and his assistant, Jean Purdy, were still faced with a four hour journey at short notice when a laparoscopy was due. Edwards and Steptoe decided to apply to the Medical Research Council for support.

An application was prepared for consideration early in 1971. The proposed research programme was divided into five parts, one of which involved the transfer of embryos to patients with the aim of obtaining pregnancies. This was an analysis of implantation in man. Preliminary work had already shown that the uterine conditions in their patients were probably favourable for implantation; they had succeeded in growing human embryos to the blastocyst stage and, although considerable work had been undertaken on the implantation of embryos in mice, little was known about implantation in the human. By replacing embryos into infertile patients Edwards and Steptoe hoped to learn more about this process. Any pregnancies resulting were to be carefully monitored to ensure that development was normal.

Steptoe was using ovulation induction to obtain oocytes from his patients but more needed to be known about the hormonal control of the menstrual cycle and the process of ovulation. Hormonal control of menstruation was usually applied to treat patients who did not menstruate but in ovulation induction for IVF these hormones were being used in patients who were menstruating normally. Research was proposed to analyze follicular fluid from pre-ovulatory and non-ovulatory follicles in order to correlate the levels of steroid hormones with those in blood and urine. Blood and urine steroid levels would also be correlated to the number and size of follicles in the ovary. A better understanding of the process of ovulation would allow methods of its induction to be improved.

Edwards wished also to continue his work on the maturation of human oocytes in vitro in order to understand how chromosomal errors develop. At birth the human female possesses her total complement of oocytes. These mature in the ovary and by a process of reduction division, known as meiosis, reduce their number of chromosomes to half the set found in other body cells in order to accept another half set from a fertilizing sperm cell. This division takes place in three stages: the first division takes place in the fetus at about five months gestation when the primordial germ cells in the fetal ovary divide to become primary oocytes. Only a minute fraction of these survive to puberty. The first meiotic division takes place at ovulation and the second meiotic division at fertilization. Sometimes during this process something goes wrong with the way the chromosomes separate, leaving the egg with too few or too many at fertilization. Trisomy of chromosome 21, that is the presence of three rather than two copies of the chromosome (two from the mother and one from the father), results in the disorder known as Down's syndrome. Observation of maturing eggs in vitro and at fertilization would enable the mechanism and the origin of such errors to be better understood.

Another line of research proposed was to be the study of the fertilization and cleavage of human eggs in culture. First of all, although Steptoe had been able to culture eggs to the blastocyst stage, he had provided no formal proof that these embryos were the result of fertilization rather than parthenogenesis. He needed to provide evidence that the embryos were diploid (had a full set of chromosomes) and to demonstrate that some contained a Y-chromosome; incontrovertible evidence that fertilization had taken place as the Y- chromosome is only carried by sperm.

If the Y-chromosome could be identified by excising a small part of a developing embryo this would enable the sex of the embryo to be determined. This, in turn, would allow women at risk of having children with sex-linked genetic disorders, such as Lesch Nyhan syndrome, to choose only to have female embryos transferred to the womb. Blastocyst manipulation and sex determination formed another part of the proposal to the MRC.

Finally, Edwards and Steptoe wished to examine the role of immunology in infertility, in particular the case where men create antibodies to their own sperm.

The application also sought to resolve the logistical problem of Patrick Steptoe working in Oldham while Bob Edwards was based in Cambridge by suggesting that facilities and a post for Patrick Steptoe be provided; 24 to 30 gynaecological beds in the Cambridge area would be needed, together with outpatient and ancillary facilities. Laboratory space was required close to the theatre for tissue culture purposes and the salaries of two technicians were also requested. Altogether this was an ambitious proposal both scientifically and in its scale which illustrated Bob Edwards' prescience as to where human IVF was going to lead.

The MRC sent the application to six referees for comment after which it was considered by the Council's Clinical Research Board. The Board's views were sought on the scientific merits of the proposed programme, the ethical aspects of the proposed studies, and the scale and period of support requested. The application was declined. The Board accepted that Dr Edwards was an investigator of high scientific standing, energy and originality but the Board and the referees had all had serious doubts about the ethical aspects of the proposed investigation, especially those relating to the implantation in women of oocytes fertilized in vitro. This was considered premature in view of the lack of preliminary studies on primates and the deficiency of detailed knowledge of the possible hazards involved. Reservations were also expressed about the procedure of laparoscopy for purely experimental purposes and about the proposed facilities and arrangements for patient care. It was suggested that Edwards might submit an application for a similar programme of work on primates.

Unfortunately no record of the Board's discussion remains but it is clear, from talking to people concerned at the time, that its members and the referees were more concerned with the safety and well-being of the patients and their potential offspring than the intrinsic moral question of experimenting on the human embryo. Many scientists at that time would not have considered working on the embryo up to the blastocyst stage in any way unethical; the likelihood of congenital abnormalities following embryo transfer was the main subject of discussion. The Chief Medical Officer at the Department of Health and Social Services at the time was quite emphatic from the public health point of view that public money should not be spent on experiments which might produce abnormal offspring. The establishment was more concerned with developing effective methods of contraception than devising novel methods to overcome infertility.

Early ethical discussion of human IVF

One of the few people to consider the ethics of what he was doing was Bob Edwards himself and his views changed with the progress of his research. At the beginning of his work on human oocytes he did not consider it proper at that stage to transfer fertilized eggs to a human recipient. He wrote in an article in *Scientific American* 'If rabbit and pig eggs can be fertilized in culture, presumably human eggs grown in culture could also be fertilized, although obviously it would not be permissible to implant them in a human recipient.'[10]   Nonetheless it was quite clear that his ultimate vision was for his work to be applied clinically. By 1971 Edwards was successfully growing human embryos to the blastocyst stage in culture and there had been a number of reports of the successful transfer of in vitro fertilized eggs in both the mouse and the rabbit, with no observed abnormalities in the offspring.[11-17] In his mind, it was now permissible to attempt embryo transfer in the human.

At the same time, Edwards was fully aware of the social issues surrounding his work. This was demonstrated in a paper, co-authored with an American lawyer, David Sharpe, in *Nature*[18] in May 1971. In this he discusses the possible public unease at work on human embryos and looks at the existing legal framework into which embryo research might fall. It was clear that the law was quite unprepared for the eventuality of embryos developing outside the human body or of their disposal after culture in vitro. The paper upholds the freedom of scientists to pursue their ideas, 'Scientists must maintain their right to exercise their professional activities to the limit that is tolerable by society in order to develop new concepts or discover new facts that could be of great value to our health or understanding'. But it contends that this freedom must be conditioned by some form of public consultation. 'What is to be feared is that if the biologists do not invent a method of taking counsel of mankind, society will thrust its advice on biologists and other scientists and probably in a manner or form seriously hampering science.' However, 'Adverse social judgments have not diverted dedicated doctors and scientists convinced of the value of their own work...'

Edwards and Sharpe considered that regulation by statute would be inappropriate and heavy-handed in that it would be difficult to draft in such a way that it would not restrict future research which might be quite acceptable. They considered a moratorium on human embryology but discounted it as unworkable in the real world. Their solution was '... a simple organization easily approached and consulted to advise and assist biologists and others to reach their own decisions. Such an organization must represent widespread but uncommitted interests and be free of partizan politics. It would frame public debate, act as a watchdog, and yet interfere minimally with the independence of science.' This paper was based on a lecture and discussion held at George Washington University in 1968 nearly 17 years before the Voluntary Licensing Authority was eventually established in the UK.

If the progress made by Bob Edwards and Patrick Steptoe raised little ethical debate in the United Kingdom, the situation was rather different on the other side of the Atlantic. In January 1971 James Watson presented a paper entitled 'Potential consequences of experimentation with human eggs'[19] at the twelfth meeting of the panel on science and technology of the US House of Representatives Committee on Science and Astronautics. He takes a somewhat less sanguine view than Edwards and Sharpe; 'Some very hard decisions may soon be upon us. For it is not obvious that the vague potential of abhorrent misuse should weigh more strongly than the unhappiness which thousands of married couples feel when they are unable to have their own children. Different societies are likely to view the matter differently and it would be surprising if all come to the same conclusion. We must, therefore, assume that techniques for the in vitro manipulation of human eggs are likely to be general medical practice, capable of routine performance in many major nations within some 10 to 20 years'. English cell biology was ahead of its American counterpart in 1971 and Watson links the innovative work of John Gurdon in Oxford on clonal reproduction in frogs with that of Edwards and Steptoe. Action needed to be taken to prohibit human cloning experiments and to consider the consequence of further advances in human embryology. He says, 'This is a matter far too important to be left solely in the hands of the scientific and medical communities. The belief that surrogate mothers and clonal babies are inevitable because science always moves forward...represents a form of laissez-faire nonsense dismally reminiscent of the creed that American business if left to itself will solve everybody's problems. Just as the success of a corporate body in making money need not set the human condition ahead, neither does every scientific advance automatically make our lives more 'meaningful'. He believed that international agreement was the preferred method of control. 'I would thus hope that over the next decade wide reaching discussion occurs, at the informal as well as the formal legislative level about the manyfold problems which are bound to arise if test tube conception becomes a common occurrence. On some matters a sufficient international consciousness might be apparent to make possible some forms of international agreement before the cat is totally out of the bag. A blanket declaration of the worldwide illegality of human cloning might be one result of a serious effort to ask the world which direction it wishes to move.' Of course, such international agreement has never been achieved.

Watson was speaking at the start of a debate which gathered pace soon after and has continued ever since. Paul Ramsey, Harrington Spear Paine Professor of religion at Princeton, writing in the *Journal of the American Medical Association*[20] in June 1971 queries both the validity of the consent obtained by Steptoe and Edwards and the ethics of proceeding to embryo transfer. He reports Edwards as saying to their patients '...your only hope is to help us' and goes on to say, 'Now, I know that there is a spectrum and no clear lines to be drawn between pure experiment, therapeutic investigation and proven therapy. Still one way to make a significant distinction along this spectrum is to suppose one of these women to ask, "Doctor, are you doing this for *me* or am I doing it for you and your research?" The answer to that question to date is that women are undergoing surgery and other procedures for the sake of medical research; and it is a cardinal principal of medical ethics that they should have knowingly consented to that, and not primarily to a therapy they hoped would relieve their own childlessness'. Ramsey considered the consent obtained by Edwards and Steptoe to be defective.

On embryo transfer Ramsey was to repeat the criticisms of the Clinical Research Board of the MRC, 'My point as an ethicist is that none of these researchers can *exclude* the possibility that they will do irreparable damage to the child-to-be. And my conclusion is that they cannot morally proceed to their first ostensibly successful achievement of the results they seek, since they cannot assuredly preclude all damage.' However, unlike the Clinical Research Board he did not consider that work on primates would provide a sufficient guarantee. 'Work in monkeys would enable scientists to describe the risks accurately for monkeys, but not for possible deep injuries in the human case.'

Leon R Kass, from the Committee on the Life Sciences and Social Policy at the US National Research Council, writing later in the same year in the *New England Journal of Medicine*[21] also considers that 'Because the new procedures for in vitro fertilization and laboratory culture of human embryos probably carry a serious risk of damage to any child so generated, there appears to be no ethical way to proceed. One cannot ethically choose for a child the unknown hazards that he must face and simultaneously choose to give him life in which to face them.' However he does suggest that IVF experiments in primates and other mammals should be carried out to assess the 'normality' of the resultant offspring and that, in the meantime, a profession-wide self-imposed moratorium should be implemented to allow interdisciplinary discussion, internationally and in and out of government.

The first IVF baby

Bob Edwards continued to contribute[22-26] to the international ethical debate but at the same time, convinced of the value of what they were doing, he and Patrick Steptoe continued their work on IVF at Kershaw's Hospital. They did not follow the advice to carry out preliminary work on primates. Then, as now, the only species for which there was comprehensive data on the natural rate of embryo loss and on the normal rate of congenital abnormalities, or of inherited disorders, was the human. To establish these data alone would have required a large and lengthy programme of research and the scale of primate colony which would have been required did not exist in the UK. But if it was to be demonstrated that IVF did not incur any increased risk of anomalies before the technique was to be applied to humans, this is what would have had to be done. Edwards and Steptoe decided to carry on using the species they knew best. On the other side of the globe, in Australia, work was also beginning independently on human in vitro fertilization.

In the absence of adequate funding, work proceeded frustratingly slowly. In 1974, prompted by a press enquiry at a press conference held at the release of its Annual Report, the Secretary of the MRC, Sir John Gray, again reiterated that, for the ethical reasons previously given, it would not fund research involving human IVF and embryo transfer and that work on primates should precede work on human fertilization. Some IVF work on rabbits at the MRC's Clinical Research Centre had recently given rise to abnormal offspring. Nonetheless, in 1975, the Council decided to set up a small working group under the chairmanship of Professor R V Short to advise on all aspects of research on in vitro methods of human fertilization and embryo transfer. The group consulted on progress with primate research in the United States. The lack of success with IVF in this species paralleled that in humans. It was thought to be due to lack of synchronization between the fertilized egg and the uterus. However, it was considered that the risks of producing a deformed embryo were not as great as had been feared. The group concluded that there should be no objection to obtaining ova from women for research purposes, provided that there were defined medical reasons for opening the abdomen, and provided that the woman had given her consent and that there should be no objection to the process of in vitro fertilization of human ova obtained in this way. It recommended that there should be no legal or ethical objection to the transfer of in vitro fertilized ova to the uterus. Embryo transfer should only be carried out in patients who had been carefully selected beforehand, and any pregnancy resulting from such a procedure should be carefully monitored by ultrasound, amniocentesis and serial hormone assays; the anonymity of any offspring resulting from embryo transfer should be mostly strictly preserved. Finally, the group concluded that improved techniques of tubal surgery would be likely to be of much more immediate and lasting benefit, and more cost-effective, for the treatment of tubal occlusion than in vitro fertilization and embryo transfer. A report was submitted in draft to the Council's Cell Board where it was noted but no further action was taken.

In 1976 Steptoe and Edwards reported the achievement of a tubal pregnancy following embryo transfer.[27] Although this was frustrating because the pregnancy had to be terminated they had at last proved that it was possible to stimulate women with normal menstrual cycles, to collect and fertilize their eggs, to transfer an embryo cultured to the blastocyst stage and to obtain a pregnancy. With renewed vigour they started to pursue four lines of attack in order to achieve a viable pregnancy. It was considered that one reason for the repeated failure to achieve pregnancies was the fact that the womb might not be receptive following hormonal stimulation of ovulation. Successful live births of mice following the transfer of embryos which had been preserved by freezing had been reported by Whittingham in 1971 and 1972.[28,29] One line of attack was therefore to freeze embryos and return them to patients in subsequent cycles. Two further lines of attack were to try to modify and improve the regimes used for hormonal stimulation and, by measuring luteinizing hormone (LH) in the urine using newly available Japanese kits, to monitor the LH surge more accurately in order to determine the best time to collect eggs. Finally, they would attempt to follow the natural cycle in some patients in order to collect the one egg normally available. In the end it was this last method which was successful and in July 1978 the first IVF baby was born[30] only shortly before Patrick Steptoe was due to retire from Oldham.

As soon as news filtered out that there was an ongoing IVF pregnancy in Oldham both Patrick Steptoe and Bob Edwards and their patients were besieged by the Press, all keen to get an exclusive story. Steptoe and Edwards were concerned about the additional stress being imposed on their patient by the unwelcome attention of the Press whose members were competing against each other to obtain a scoop and who were doing their best to infiltrate Kershaw's Hospital and to get hold of medical records. In the end Steptoe and Edwards advised their patients to accept one offer and issued the following statement. 'For some weeks we have been concerned about the possibility of distress being caused to our patient by the overwhelming attentions of the Press. We have been approached with offers by a number of newspapers, both British and foreign. We advised Mr and Mrs Brown to consider the offers for two reasons - first, to gain financial security for themselves and their children, and secondly because both we and they believed that a contract with one newspaper would be the best means of controlling intrusions by certain sections of the Press. They decided to contract with Associated Newspapers Group Limited.

'We would like to make it clear, in view of uninformed speculation which has appeared, that neither of us has entered into any contract of any sort with Associated Newspapers Group Limited, or any other organization.' The Area Health Authority was forced to employ security officers to keep inquisitive reporters out of Mrs Brown's hospital room.

As the date of the birth approached - a caesarian section was scheduled - the Department of Health, until then having studiously maintained its arm's length approach, on being approached by the Regional Health Authority agreed that a film should be made of the birth and that the Central Office of Information should be employed to make this record. The purpose of the film, subject to the written agreement of the patient and the consultants, would be to assist in the evaluation of the behaviour of the baby at birth and to provide an historic medical record. The film should be available to any persons with a proper interest in showing it.

Medical innovation is always newsworthy but public interest, however sympathetic, inevitably imposes stresses on the patients undergoing treatment and on their relatives. Not only may patients be undergoing invasive therapy but their hospital rooms and operating theatres are invaded by reporters and by television and film cameras. Privacy is difficult to maintain and confidentiality may be breached.

Edwards and Steptoe were forced to cease work in August 1978 because of Steptoe's retirement, though one more of their patients went on to deliver a premature baby. However, the births in the UK were quickly followed by IVF births elsewhere in the world. In November 1978 a 31 year old woman gave birth to an IVF baby in India and in Australia, where work was proceeding based on established techniques developed for farm animal production, success was near. It was quite clear that the use of in vitro fertilization in the relief of infertility would be widely adopted and the Medical Research Council needed to change its policy.

References

1.   Shettles, L. B. (1955), 'Further observations on living human oocytes and ova', *Amer. J. Obst. Gynec.*, **69**, pp. 365-371
2.   Edwards, R. G. (1962), 'Meiosis in ovarian oocytes of adult mammals', *Nature*, **196**, pp. 446-450
3.   Edwards, R. G. (1965), 'Maturation in vitro of mouse, sheep, cow, pig, rhesus monkey and human oocytes', *Nature*, **208**, pp. 349-351
4.   Edwards, R. G. (1965), 'Maturation in vitro of human ovarian oocytes', *Lancet*, **ii**, pp. 926-929

5.   1965, 'Culture of early human embryos is imminent,' *World Medicine*, **1**, **no 6**, pp. 19-21

6.   Edwards, R. G., Bavister, B. D. and Steptoe, P. C. (1969), 'Early stages of fertilization in vitro of human oocytes matured in vitro', *Nature*, **221**, pp. 632-635

7.   Rothschild (1969), *Nature*, **221**, p. 981

8.   Edwards, R. G., Steptoe, P. C. and Purdy, J. M. (1970), 'Fertilization and cleavage in vitro of pre-ovulatory human oocytes', *Nature*, **227**, pp. 1307-1309

9.   Edwards, R. G. and Fowler, R. E. (1970), 'Human embryos in the laboratory', *Sci. Am.*, **223**, pp. 44-54

10. Edwards, R. G. (1966), 'Mammalian eggs in the laboratory', *Sci. Am.*, **215**, pp. 72-81

11. Bedford, J. M. and Chang, M.C. (1962), 'Fertilization of rabbit ova in vitro', *Nature*, **193**, pp. 898-899

12. Brackett, B. G. (1969), 'Effects of washing the gametes on fertilization in vitro', *Fertil. Steril.*, **20**, pp. 127-142

13. Brackett, B. G. and Williams, W. L. (1965), 'In vitro fertilization of rabbit ova', *J. Exp. Zool.*, **160**, pp. 271-282

14   Cross, P. C. and Brinster, R. L. (1970), 'In vitro development of mouse oocytes', *Biol. Reprod.*, **3**, pp. 298-307

15. Mukherjee, A. B. and Cohen, M. M. (1970), 'Development of normal mouse in vitro fertilization', *Nature*, **228**, pp. 472-473

16. Seitz, H. M., Brackett, B. G. and Mastroianni, L. (1970), 'In vitro fertilization of ovulated rabbit ova recovered from the ovary', *Biol. Reprod.*, **2**, pp. 262-267

17. Whittingham, D. G. (1968), 'Fertilization of mouse eggs in vitro', *Nature*, **220**, pp. 592-593

18. Edwards, R. G. and Sharpe, D. J. (1971), 'Social values and research in human embryology', *Nature*, **231**, pp. 87-91

19. Watson, J. D. (1971), 'Potential consequences of experimentation with human eggs'. Presented at the twelfth meeting of the panel on science and technology, Committee on Science and Astronautics, United States House of Representatives, Washington DC, January 28

20. Ramsey, P. (1972), 'Shall we reproduce. The Medical Ethics of *in vitro* Fertilization', *JAMA*, **220**, **no 10**, pp. 1346-1350

21. Kass, L. R. (1971), 'Babies by means of in vitro fertilization: unethical experiments on the unborn?', *N Eng J Med*, **285**, **no 21**, pp. 1174-1179

22.   Edwards, R. G. (1972), 'Judging the social values of scientific advances', World Council of Churches, Geneva

23.   Steptoe, P. C., Edwards, R. G. (1972), 'The research of today and the ethics of tomorrow', BMA Scientific Meeting, Southampton, *British Medical Journal*, **3**, pp. 342-343

24.   Edwards, R. G. (1974), 'Fertilization of human eggs in vitro: morals, ethics and the law', *Q Rev Biol*, **49**, pp. 3-26

25.   Edwards, R. G. (1975), 'Judging the social values of scientific advances', In Birch, C. and Abrecht, P. (eds), *Genetics and the Quality of Life*, Pergamon Press, Oxford. Organised by the World Council of Churches, pp. 41-49

26.   Edwards, R. G. (1976), 'Responsibility and decision making in the orientation and genetic control of human procreation', *Biology and the Future of Man*, Universities of Paris, pp. 377-394

27.   Steptoe, P. C., Edwards, R. G. (1976), 'Reimplantation of a human embryo with subsequent tubal pregnancy', *Lancet*, **i**, pp. 880-882

28.   Whittingham, D. G. (1971), 'Survival of embryos after freezing and thawing', *Nature*, **233**, pp. 125-126

29.   Whittingham, D. G., Leibo, S. P., Mazur, P. (1972), 'Survival of mouse embryos frozen tp -196° and -296ºC', *Science*, **178**, pp. 411-414

30.   Steptoe, P. C., Edwards, R. G. (1978), 'Birth after the replacement of a human embryo', *Lancet*, **ii**, p. 366

2 Birth of a New Ethical Issue

MRC Advisory Group

Early in 1979 it was reported that teams in Australia, India, USSR and Germany as well as one or two groups in the UK, in addition to Steptoe and Edwards, were working on human in vitro fertilization. In March the MRC convened an advisory group to reconsider Council policy on in vitro fertilization. The group was chaired by Dr S G Owen, Second Secretary to the Council, and its membership consisted of experts in gynaecology, paediatrics and fetal physiology and included the Rt Rev the Bishop of Durham (later Archbishop of York). The group drew up its own terms of reference which were 'to consider ethical aspects of research on in vitro fertilization and embryo transfer in humans and to determine on ethical grounds whether or not to advise the Council to proceed with consideration of research proposals in either or both of these areas.'[1] The group agreed that their concern should be only with the ethics of such work, and that it would not be appropriate for them to examine the more specific scientific aspects. The group considered that, should the Council's policy on support for research in this area be revised, the ethical aspects of each proposed investigation would, nonetheless, need to be submitted to the local ethical committee in the usual way.

The group discussed interspecific fertilization in the context of shedding light on the causes of infertility and cancer and in the development of more effective forms of contraception. However they recognized that there were likely to be very deep-rooted feelings and taboos against this sort of research and were anxious to ensure that the product of any interspecific in vitro fertilization could not be transferred to the uterus. Also discussed was human in vitro fertilization with and without subsequent transfer of the embryo to the womb and the need for free and informed consent. It was agreed that it would not be ethical to use sperm from 'sperm banks' for research since the donors of such sperm would not have been aware of the possibility of its use for research. Human ova for research use, where no subsequent transfer was intended, would need to be obtained with informed consent and only in conjunction with some other therapeutic procedure such as, for example, hysterectomy; laparoscopy purely to obtain ova for research purposes could not be regarded as ethical.

Human IVF without subsequent embryo transfer could only be considered as research. It was appreciated that such work brought into question the fate of the fertilized human ovum and raised the difficulty of when human life began but the group concluded that, subject to the provisions of the Human Tissues Act, it would be ethically acceptable for such work to be undertaken when it was relevant to practical problems of clinical medicine.

The group regarded human IVF with embryo transfer as a therapeutic procedure, albeit still an experimental one, and concluded that it was thus covered by the ethics of the normal doctor/patient relationship. It was a procedure which was likely to become increasingly used for the treatment of infertility and the group considered that, in these circumstances, it was important that the Council should support research which would make the treatment safer and more successful and, at the same time provide more insight into the human reproductive process. Work in primates was still considered desirable.

The Department of Health and Social Security (DHSS) was concerned that large numbers of small clinical units offering IVF should not be set up to carry out treatment without supervision. The group agreed that all units offering an IVF service should be under public scrutiny and suggested that the DHSS should establish a register to record not only every pregnancy resulting from embryo transfer, but also every attempt to achieve a pregnancy by this means. A register of this sort would play an important role in research, allowing the success of any improvement in technique to be assessed accurately and assisting in the long-term follow up and monitoring of any offspring.

Recent advances had been made in the use of recombinant DNA techniques in the field of prenatal diagnosis. Such techniques might eventually also be used in the prevention of inherited disease, a field which might become relevant to research on in vitro fertilization. Although it was desirable to try to foresee and safeguard against possible misuses of research procedures in IVF it was not profitable to speculate. Rather, the group considered it was preferable that they should reconvene to re-examine the ethics of IVF and embryo transfer in the light of developments in public opinion in about five years' time; they might be called together earlier should the Council require advice on the ethics of any specific proposal. Five recommendations[2] were made to Council and accepted.

i   Scientifically sound research involving in vitro fertilization, both between human gametes and between human and non-human gametes where there is no intention to transfer the embryo to the uterus, should, on ethical grounds, be allowed to proceed if the aim of the research is clearly defined and acceptable - for example to obtain information about the process of reproduction relevant to clinical problems such as contraception or the differential diagnosis and treatment of infertility.

ii   Informed consent to the research should be obtained in every case from the donor of both ovum and sperm; sperm from sperm banks should therefore not be used unless collected and preserved specifically for this purpose.

iii   Human in vitro fertilization with subsequent embryo transfer should now be regarded as a therapeutic procedure covered by the normal ethics of the doctor/patient relationship. The role of the MRC should be to maximize opportunities presenting themselves to make the procedure safer and more successful, and coincidentally to increase knowledge of human reproductive processes.

iv   The Health Departments should be advised to set up a confidential register to record the number of embryo transfers undertaken and the number of subsequent pregnancies, and should consider the advisability and practicality of monitoring the resulting offspring.

v   The Advisory Group should meet again to examine the ethics of particular studies involving in vitro fertilization and embryo transfer if and when this proved desirable, and should possibly be reconvened to reconsider the general issues in about five years' time.

USA Ethics Advisory Board

In the USA there had been an effective moratorium on research involving human in vitro fertilization and embryo transfer since 1975. In 1973 the Department of Health Education and Welfare (now the Department of Health and Human Services) began to discuss and to draft regulations relating to in vitro fertilization and embryo transfer and finally, in August 1975, these regulations were published (45CFR46.204(D)) stating that 'No application or proposal involving human in vitro fertilization may be funded by the Department or any component thereof until the application or proposal has been reviewed by the Ethical Advisory Board and the Board has rendered advice as to its acceptability from an ethical standpoint'.[3] This meant that without approval from the Ethical Advisory Board no federal funds were available for research and as no Ethical Advisory Board was appointed no research was undertaken.

In 1977 the Department of Health Education and Welfare (HEW) received an application for support for research involving human in vitro fertilization and in September that year an Ethics Advisory Board was eventually appointed. Meeting in May 1978, the Board agreed to review the research proposal, however, following Steptoe and Edwards' success in the field a couple of months later, the Board was asked by the Secretary of the HEW to broaden its remit to consider the scientific, ethical, legal and social issues surrounding human in vitro fertilization and embryo transfer in general. Over the next nine months the Board held a series of eleven public hearings throughout the United States, listening to the views of private individuals, professional societies and public interest groups. Scholars and experts were approached in the fields of reproductive science, ethics, theology, law and the social sciences to prepare reports and to give evidence to the Board. Among the experts invited to give evidence were Steptoe and Edwards; they declined. In a letter to the Chairman and Vice Chairman of the Board (James Gaither, an eminent San Francisco lawyer, and David Hamburg, President of the Institute of Medicine of the National Academy of Sciences) Edwards wrote:

'We feel strongly that any ethical decision about such work should be the responsibility of the patient, the doctor and the funding organization. We are highly diffident about interfering with such a joint decision, especially in another country, by making a presentation to the Board.'

'We have formed our own opinions about the ethical, social and clinical aspects of the work and about the opportunities of future medical advances. We have no doubt about continuing our work to help the infertile. We equally intend to develop our methods for the reversal of sterilization. Tubal occlusion could then be used by women to limit their fertility, relieving them of years of steroidal contraception, in the knowledge that they could conceive another child in the event of remarriage or the death of their family. We strongly believe that funds should be made available for this work in view of its considerable importance both to the patients concerned and for its wider implications in community health.'[4]

They did however offer to send the Board copies of all their papers as they were published and to give advance notice of any lectures dealing with their work. The Board also received over 2,000 pieces of correspondence, all of which were copied and distributed to each of its members. Its report was issued in May 1979.[5]

The Board came to five conclusions. The first was that 'The Department should consider support of carefully designed research involving in vitro fertilization and embryo transfer in animals, including non-human primates, in order to obtain a better understanding of the process of fertilization, implantation and embryo development, to assess the risks to both mother and offspring associated with such procedures, and to improve the efficacy of the procedure.' The Board had received conflicting evidence as to the conclusiveness of the research so far undertaken in animals in assessing the risks associated with IVF and embryo transfer. Although no animal data had demonstrated a higher incidence of abnormal embryos than that associated with the normal reproductive process neither had sufficient data been accumulated to show the absence of increased abnormality following in vitro fertilization. The Board also considered that the effectiveness of the procedures also remained to be demonstrated. It was quite convinced that more research using animal models, particularly non-human primates, would provide a more accurate estimate of the chances of achieving successful pregnancies in patients. The Board suggested that the Department should support such work whether or not parallel human work was in progress.

The second conclusion stated, 'The Ethics Advisory Board finds that it is acceptable from an ethical standpoint to undertake research involving human in vitro fertilization and embryo transfer provided that:

A   If the research involves human in vitro fertilization without embryo transfer, the following conditions are satisfied:

1.   the research complies with all appropriate provisions of the regulations governing research with human subjects (45CFR46);

2.   the research is designed primarily: (A) to establish the safety and efficacy of embryo transfer and (B) to obtain important scientific information to that end not reasonably obtainable by other means;

3   human gametes used in such research will be obtained exclusively from persons who have been informed of the nature and purpose of the research in which such materials will be used and have specifically consented to such use;

4.   no embryos will be sustained in vitro beyond the stage normally associated with the completion of implantation (14 days after fertilization) and;

5.   all interested parties and the general public will be advised if evidence begins to show that the procedure entails risks of abnormal offspring higher than those associated with natural human reproduction.

B   In addition, if the research involves embryo transfer following human in vitro fertilization, embryo transfer will be attempted only with gametes obtained from lawfully married couples.'

The Board carefully stated that this conclusion did not seek to address whether the Department should or should not support such research but to provide general guidance to Institutional Review Boards or other groups who might be asked to review this sort of research and who might benefit from the Board's deliberations. It considered that much remained to be learned about the safety and effectiveness of IVF and embryo transfer before they could be considered standard, accepted medical practice and that research designed to improve the safety and efficacy of these procedures would be ethically acceptable. However the Board considered that embryo transfer should only be allowed for lawfully married couples and that fertilized ova should only be transferred back into the woman from whom they came.

The Board also discussed research involving in vitro fertilization leading to the general advancement of knowledge. Provided that such research was performed as a corollary to research undertaken primarily to establish the safety and efficacy of IVF and embryo transfer, the Board agreed that this would be acceptable from an ethical standpoint.

The Board's third conclusion was, 'The Board finds it acceptable from an ethical standpoint for the Department to support or conduct research involving human in vitro fertilization and embryo transfer, provided that the applicable conditions set forth in conclusion(2) are met. However the Board has decided not to address the question of the level of funding, if any, which such research might be given.' The Board consciously wished to limit its enquiry to the ethical acceptability of IVF research and did not wish to get embroiled in political decisions relating to the allocation of public research funds. It was, the Board agreed, up to the Department of Health, Education and Welfare to make its own decision about the priority such research should be given and that its decision should be made in the larger context where scientific, political, economic, legal and ethical considerations should be taken into account.

In reaching its conclusion about the ethical acceptability of research the Board discussed research involving embryo transfer and research not involving embryo transfer. Both types of research related to the safety and efficacy of clinical IVF procedures were seen as being ethically valid and the Board particularly pointed to clinical trials as being an effective method for evaluating safety and efficacy. While research not involving embryo transfer would also yield potentially valuable information about reproductive biology, the etiology of birth defects and other scientific questions, the Board considered that research applications of this sort should be dealt with on a case by case basis and that it was not appropriate to speculate what sort of research might be sufficiently compelling to justify the use of human embryos.

With regard to the application for support which had led to the appointment of the Board in the first place, the Board recommended that this should be referred back to the National Institutes of Health to determine whether it met the criteria set out in conclusions (2) and (3).

The fourth conclusion stated, 'The National Institute of Child Health and Human Development (NICHD) and other appropriate agencies should work with professional societies, foreign governments and international organizations to collect, analyse and disseminate information derived from research (in both animals and humans) and clinical experience throughout the world involving in vitro fertilization and embryo transfer.' This conclusion derived from the foresight of the Board that IVF techniques would be rapidly taken up and adopted world wide and that sometimes procedures would be performed without the benefit of research design or experimental controls. The Board stated that: 'It would be unfortunate not to have access to the information that might be gained from such clinical experience, notwithstanding the fact that well-designed investigations would be preferable.' The Board was anxious that, wherever IVF and embryo transfer might be carried out, practitioners should not be ignorant of the findings of others.

Fifthly and finally, the Board concluded that: 'The Secretary should encourage the development of a uniform model or law to clarify the legal status of children born as a result of in vitro fertilization and embryo transfer. To the extent that funds may be necessary to develop such legislation, the Department should consider providing appropriate support.' The aim of this conclusion was to clarify any ambiguity that might exist as to the status of children resulting from IVF.

Despite the resources in terms of expense and time and energy that were put into the Ethics Advisory Board and despite the depth of its discussion, the Secretary of Health Education and Welfare took no action on its report. The Board's charter expired in 1980 and it has not been reinstated. The President's Commission for the Study of Ethical Problems in Medicine and Biomedical and Behavioral Research, created by Congress in 1980, endorsed the Board's conclusions but carried out no further analysis and Federal funds remain unavailable for research involving human in vitro fertilization.

MRC guidelines

Following their success in 1978 Steptoe and Edwards had to wait over two years before they could start treating patients again. There was no opportunity for them within the National Health Service as Steptoe had passed retirement age so they had to search for an appropriate property and raise the funds to set up their own clinic. They found Bourn Hall, which they considered the ideal place, but raising funds was more difficult with their first backers pulling out following the report of an abnormal IVF child in the USA. However, their perseverance succeeded and by September 1981 Edwards was reporting that they had established more than 40 pregnancies since resuming work at the beginning of the year.

In the meantime a number of IVF clinics had been established around the world. In Australia where ovulation induction techniques had been pioneered and refined, 52 clinical pregnancies had been achieved by the end of 1981 and this more than doubled in 1982.[7] It was clear that IVF as a treatment for infertility was taking off and fundamental research involving in vitro fertilization had been approved for support by the UK Medical Research Council in 1981. The MRC decided that it was timely to reconvene its Advisory Group to Review Policy on Research on in vitro Fertilization and Embryo Transfer; two years earlier than anticipated.

Chaired this time by Professor Geoffrey Dawes of the Nuffield Institute for Medical Research in Oxford, the Advisory Group met in May 1982. It reviewed research developments since 1979 including advances in genetic manipulation, discussed the ethics of such research and considered a proposal for the international surveillance and monitoring of children born as a result of IVF. Finally, the Group drew up guidelines for research related to human fertilization and embryology.

Since the Group's last meeting research around the world had focused on the application of IVF techniques in humans and much more was now known about their effect in humans than in non-human primates where similar research lagged far behind. Useful work had been carried out in rodents but it was still considered that future advances would require a clear understanding of embryonic development in laboratory animals, especially primates, in order to reduce the risk of abnormalities caused by in vitro procedures. Further animal work was also required to advance knowledge in basic embryology. Nonetheless, it was recognized that extrapolation from animal to human was not always possible and that, even though non-human primates shared with humans many endocrine and morphological similarities during the first six weeks of pregnancy, any primate model would need to be chosen with care. The convoluted cervix of the rhesus monkey, for instance, meant that trans-cervical embryo transfer, the normal method in humans, was not appropriate.

Members of the Group discussed the rapid advances which had taken place in the field of genetic engineering and the possibility that genetic manipulation used in combination with in vitro fertilization might be used to overcome genetic disorders. Those who objected to abortion of fetuses affected by inherited diseases might welcome such an approach. Yet there were many ethical arguments against this form of gene therapy where the germ line would be affected. The Parliamentary Assembly of the Council of Europe had already recommended[8] to the Committee of Ministers that it should amongst other recommendations:

'a. draw up a European agreement on what constitutes legitimate application to human beings (including future generations) of the techniques of genetic engineering, align domestic regulations accordingly, and work towards similar agreements at world level;

b. provide for explicit recognition in the European Human Rights Convention of the right to a genetic inheritance which has not been artificially interfered with, except in accordance with certain principles which are recognized as being fully compatible with respect for human rights (as, for example in the field of therapeutic applications);

and

c. provide for the drawing-up of a list of serious diseases which may properly with the consent of the person concerned be treated by gene therapy (though certain uses without consent, in line with existing practice for other forms of medical treatment, may be recognized as compatible with respect for human rights in the probability of a very serious disease being transmitted to a person's offspring).'

The Advisory Group also discussed the use of human material in interspecific and intraspecific in vitro fertilization in providing useful information on genetic, particularly chromosomal, defects. The former, in addition to providing information on the penetration capacity of sperm from subfertile males, also allowed for the chromosome complement of the sperm to be investigated. The latter, in combination with biopsy at the blastocyst stage, would allow the diagnosis of genetic abnormalities in human embryos before reimplantation. It was agreed that scientifically sound studies in these areas should continue.

Further discussion on the ethical issues surrounding IVF focused briefly on whether there existed an absolute right for a couple to have children; the British Council of Churches had endorsed the argument that there was no such right and that, consequently, childlessness was not sufficient justification for any remedial technique regardless of its consequences. Some members thought that the dividing line was very narrow between 'right' and 'privilege' in this context. The source of embryos for research not involving embryo transfer was also discussed. The freezing of fertilized ova surplus to treatment was beginning to become fairly common practice and it was considered that, subject to obtaining the full, informed consent of both parents, these could ethically be used for soundly based research. Again, ova obtained from women undergoing other clinical procedures, such as sterilization, could be used provided that full informed consent and local ethical committee approval had been obtained.

When, previously, the Group had concluded that scientifically sound research using human embryos would be acceptable, provided that the aims were clearly defined and there was no intention to transfer the embryo to the uterus, the sort of research that they had considered had been related to clinical problems and to the diagnosis and treatment of infertility. Now it was clear that there were opportunities for fundamental research in the fields of embryology and inherited disease where ethically acceptable research involving human embryos might be carried out. The Group attempted to draw distinctions between what might and what might not be ethically acceptable. Research on the gamete up to fertilization would usually be ethical; research on the pre-implantation embryo, provided that the studies were scientifically sound, would also usually be ethical; research on the post-implantation embryo would usually be unethical. However, in order to ensure that the rather dubious premise, that what is scientifically sound must perforce be ethically sound, did not lead to unethical research, the advisory Group recommended that any research applications should be scrutinized not only by the Grants Committees of the MRC but also by its Research Grants' Boards.

Despite the Group's previous recommendation that the Health Departments should set up a register to record the number of embryo transfers undertaken and should consider monitoring the resultant offspring, no action had been taken. This was not serious as relatively few IVF births had occurred, certainly too few to detect any but the most drastic effects. Dr Edwards had provided an outline for a possible international follow-up study of IVF children which would have allowed numbers to be accumulated reasonably quickly but several members expressed doubts about an independent monitoring programme, believing that psychological harm might come to the children if they were made to feel abnormal in any way. In the end it was agreed that further consideration should be given to the matter by the MRC Systems Board which had access to the necessary expert paediatric advice. An international follow-up study was never achieved and statistical data on IVF were later collected independently in Australia, France and the UK.

The conclusions and recommendations of the Advisory Group were published in a statement by the MRC.[9]

Other guidelines in the UK and elsewhere

The Australian National Health and Medical Research Council (NH & MRC) also published in 1982 a statement on human IVF and embryo transfer.[10] This was included in the report of a working party which had been carrying out a general review of ethics in medical research, primarily to revise the Council's existing Statement on Human Experimentation but also to give particular attention to aspects of research which required special ethical scrutiny. The latter included in vitro fertilization and embryo transfer.

In considering IVF and embryo transfer the working party realized that it was not breaking entirely new ground; the ethical debate had, after all, been going on since 1971. However, it considered that statements on the ethical aspects of medical research should be subject to continuing review to take account of advances in technology and changes in public reaction and therefore backed up its debate with a review of the existing literature. The working party then drew up guidelines which did not seek to cover all hypothetical eventualities but to provide a basis from which institutional ethics committees could operate.

It was accepted that infertile couples had a right to seek treatment and to expect that doctors should try to help them no less than they would any other patient. Moreover, progress in infertility treatment had depended on research and it was noted that this research now included studies on gametes and fertilized ova. Nonetheless, the working party considered that uninhibited research on gametes and fertilized ova was not acceptable and attempted to draw up guidelines which would offer infertile couples the best opportunity of happily alleviating their problem without exceeding acceptable ethical boundaries. The working party specifically excluded donor insemination from its deliberations. The resulting guidelines were the first to give comprehensive consideration both to clinical practice and to research and to ensure the keeping of accurate records.

Every centre or institution offering IVF and embryo transfer was required to have all aspects of its programme approved by an institutional ethics committee. This committee was also required to ensure that records were kept of all attempts to achieve pregnancies by these techniques. A register was to be established including for each treatment cycle, details of parentage and the outcome of each stage of treatment from ovum recovery to pregnancy. Summaries for statistical purposes, including details of any congenital abnormalities, were to be available for collation by a national body. This was to be the National Perinatal Statistics Unit in Sydney and, thanks to the foresight of the NH&MRC, Australia has the most comprehensive run of records available on IVF treatment.

Ovum donation was considered acceptable if it was used as part of treatment within an accepted family relationship. Consent was required from both the donor and the recipient couple who should accept the duties and obligations of parenthood. There was to be no element of commerce between donor and recipients. Surrogacy involving IVF was considered incapable of ethical resolution because a legal definition of motherhood in this context was not available.

Research involving sperm, ova and fertilized ova was regarded as being an integral part of safe and effective treatment using in vitro fertilization and embryo transfer and it was recognized that such research could also throw important scientific light on human reproductive biology in general. However, allowing the development of embryos in vitro beyond the normal implantation stage was not considered ethical. Cloning experiments intended to produce multiple genetically identical offspring were also considered ethically unacceptable.

Attention was also given to the ownership of eggs, sperm and embryos. It was considered that gametes should belong to their respective donors and embryos, jointly by the donors of the gametes. The wishes of the donors with regard to use, storage or disposal should be ascertained and respected, as far as possible, by the institution in which they were held. In the case of embryos, where there was any disagreement between donors the institution should be in a position to make decisions.

A time limit of ten years was set for the storage of human embryos as long as this period was not beyond the time of conventional reproductive need or competence of the female donor (the working party did not foresee the treatment of women beyond the normal menopause). It was also stated that storage should be restricted to early undifferentiated embryos.

The guidelines concluded with a clause allowing staff who had conscientious objections to refuse to participate in IVF programmes.

Politically in the UK human in vitro fertilization was seen as rather a hot potato and unlike its counterparts in the USA, which set up the Ethics Advisory Board, and the State of Victoria in Australia, which set up a Committee of Inquiry, both in 1979, the British Government did not hasten into action. When the first IVF baby was born in 1978 a Labour government was coming to the end of its term of office and IVF was an unlikely election issue for either of the two major political parties. On coming to power in 1979 the new Conservative government had other fish to fry. Eventually, in July 1982, the British government responded to growing public concern and established a Committee of Inquiry under Dame (now Baroness) Mary Warnock. Its terms of reference were:

'To consider recent and potential developments in medicine and science related to human fertilization and embryology; to consider what policies and safeguards should be applied, including consideration of the social, ethical and legal implications of these developments; and to make recommendations.'

The Committee was to sit for two years before reporting.

Meanwhile the practice of IVF continued unabated and the number of units offering an IVF service to patients steadily increased. The Royal College of Obstetricians and Gynaecologists (RCOG), the professional body responsible for clinical standards in the treatment of infertility, referred the practice of IVF to its Ethics Committee in order to produce guidance for its members. The Committee's report was published in 1983[11] and although written primarily for the guidance of Fellows and Members of the College it was also aimed at scientists working in the field. Interestingly, the Committee contained no cross membership with the Warnock Committee, which included two Fellows of the College, nor any IVF practitioners though it did take evidence from Robert Edwards and his assistant

Jean Purdy and from the chairman of the College's Artificial Insemination Sub-Committee.

The report covers the social and legal as well as the ethical implications of IVF and starts with definitions of the subject matter with which it deals. Firstly there is set out the definition of medical ethics by Dunstan[12] which sets the tone of the report:

> 'Medical ethics are obligations of a moral nature which govern the practice of medicine... They embody the standards by which each practitioner should inform his conscience, his capacity for moral reasoning and so govern himself and his practice... It is the responsibility of the profession to develop its ethics to accommodate new demands and circumstances not encountered before...'

The Committee also quoted, and supported the view of Edwards[13] that: 'Decisions by professional bodies do not have the force of law, but their collective opinions are a most important contribution to a defence in law or to the maintenance of a programme of medical research.'

It is clear that the emphasis is on the professional responsibility of the individual practitioner while offering guidance which will inform his conscience and provide reassurance for his actions.

A distinction is made between embryo replacement (ER), where the patients' own gametes are used, and embryo transfer, involving the use of donor gametes. Embryo replacement is used where comments may refer to either.

The Committee supported IVF and embryo replacement within marriage and maintained that it should be the responsibility of the practitioner to decide on the suitability for treatment of a couple on medical or social grounds. The practitioner should assess and guide them accordingly. Patients were seen to have no right to any particular procedure if in the practitioner's reasonable judgement it ought not to be provided for them.

The use of donated ova or sperm in combination with IVF treatment was seen as appropriate within a stable heterosexual marriage. While a doctor should have discretion to treat any patient as an individual, the function of medicine was to alleviate the aberrations of nature; in the treatment of infertility, although single parenthood often results from natural conception, the natural situation would be for a child to have two parents. The report states that donation of gametes should be anonymous and that the use of gametes from a sibling or other relative, or known friend, is an undesirable practice and would rarely be justified. The implantation of IVF embryos into surrogate mothers was considered unethical.

The Committee considered that a register of all attempts to produce a pregnancy using IVF should be kept by all institutions providing a treatment programme, including details of the outcome of each stage of treatment. It also recommended that the College should set up a register of every baby born in the UK as a result of this technique with a record of their development up to school age. Little heed was taken immediately of these recommendations.

As within the population as a whole, there was a considerable divergence of views within the College on research involving human embryos. The report contains some discussion on the status of the embryo and the ethics of research - the salient question was not considered to be 'When does life begin?', which was thought to be a physical rather than a moral question, but 'At what point in the development of the embryo do we attribute to it the protection due to a human being?' In the end the Committee decided to support the Medical Research Council statement published the previous year but considered that the limit beyond which embryos should not be allowed to develop in vitro should be 17 days (at the start of early neural development).

Considerable attention was given to legal issues. In the case of multiple embryo transfer leading to multiple pregnancy it was felt that '...a civil action against doctors concerned in IVF and ER would be unlikely to succeed if multiple pregnancy resulted from the implantation of more than one embryo and obstetric or paediatric complications ensued.' It was considered that long years of infertility would lead patients to welcome the possibility of a multiple pregnancy.

The possibility that a child born with an abnormality might in due course be able to sue the doctors and its parents was not ruled out. Although possible under the Congenital Disabilities (Civil Liability) Act 1976, recent rulings in the English courts made such action unlikely. It was considered that '...the fact that an 'acceptable standard' of care has been employed by the doctors and that full informed consent of the parents has been obtained would be a sound defence to any action by the parents and helpful in the defence of any claim by the child when born if the child were subsequently deemed to have a cause of action.'

Stored semen were considered to remain the property of the man, becoming part of his estate in the event of his death. Frozen embryos were deemed to be the property of the parents. It was recommended that a time limit should be set for cryopreservation but no suggestion was made as to what this might be nor was there any discussion of what should happen to stored embryos on the death, or separation and disagreement, of the parents. Ten years on this has been a matter for recent litigation in the United States.

Although the Committee called for legislation it did not consider that 'the question of research on experimentation with early human embryonic material is a matter for the law. That problem is a strictly ethical one, in which it is necessary to be sensitive to public sentiment.' It was also of the opinion that, 'it would be impossible and undesirable to establish legislation to govern techniques of IVF and ER.' The profession was not keen to have legislative interference in matters of professional competence or the doctor-patient relationship, 'means of obtaining redressing situations where "negligent injury" has been suffered already exist, ie by civil action.' What was suggested was legislation which would give the Secretary of State powers of supervision, along the lines of the Midwives Act 1961 and the Misuse of Drugs Act 1971 in the designation of persons, and the Abortion Act 1967 and the Cruelty to Animals Act 1876 in the control of premises. It was suggested that a statutory body should be established to advise the Secretaries of State who should have power to make regulations following that advice. These regulations should cover the licensing and inspection of premises, the registration of directors of institutions undertaking IVF, and the prohibition of IVF and embryo replacement or experiments on human embryos other than by registered persons in licensed premises.

The British Medical Association (BMA) also produced a report on human in vitro fertilization in 1983.[14] The Association had set up a Working Group the previous year with the remit

> 'To consider ethical guidance to the medical profession on the current programme of in vitro fertilization in the United Kingdom, and the social and ethical implications of the future application of this work and other related techniques that may be derived from it in relation to medical practice.'

The Working Group had some cross membership with the RCOG Ethics Committee and with the Warnock Committee. The BMA accepted human IVF in the treatment of infertility as an ethical procedure and considered gamete donation also to be ethical, given the informed consent of all concerned. It considered that before treatment should be offered, a couple seeking IVF should be assessed as to the stability of the family relationship and the sincerity of their intentions to accept the responsibilities of parenthood. The recommendation was made that IVF centres should hold treatment registers and that a central body (the Health Departments) should collate statistical information. Like the RCOG, the BMA accepted the MRC statement on research but, unlike the RCOG, in accepting the need for embryo freezing the BMA recommended that storage should not exceed twelve months. IVF surrogacy was considered unlikely ever to be acceptable.

By the end of 1983, in the UK at least, a number of bodies had begun to issue recommendations or guidelines, not all entirely consistent. More than ten years after the first successful attempt to fertilize a human egg in vitro and five years after the birth of the first IVF child little had really been resolved on the ethical and legal fronts. The debate which had started in 1971 on the status of the human embryo, the freedom of the scientist and the right to reproduce still raged. In the USA Federal funds were not available for research involving human in vitro fertilization but this did not prevent research or treatment being carried out in centres not requiring federal funds and no formal guidelines were available to practitioners. In the UK professional self regulation was seen to be the preferred course of action, the legislation called for by the RCOG merely related to the registration of practitioners and licensing of premises. The MRC was now prepared to consider applications involving human IVF and had issued guidelines which were far from prescriptive. Only in Australia had progress been made in producing guidelines which addressed both research and clinical practice, and in establishing the collection of detailed records. In the State of Victoria a Committee of Inquiry had been set up under the head of its Law Reform Commission but this was yet to produce its final report. Meanwhile around the world the use of IVF procedures increased unregulated.

References

1. 'Minutes of the MRC Advisory Group to review policy on research in in vitro fertilization and embryo transfer in humans', March 1979
2. Ibid.
3. US Federal Register (1975), vol 40 (154), August 8, p.33529
4. Ethics Advisory Board, Department of Health Education and Welfare, (1979), *Report and Conclusions*: *HEW Support of Research involving Human In Vitro Fertilization and Embryo Transfer*, Appendix 12, May 4
5. Ethics Advisory Board, Department of Health Education and Welfare, (1979), *Report and Conclusions: HEW Support involving Human In Vitro Fertilization and Embryo Transfer*, May 4
6. Edwards, R. G. (1981), 'Test-tube babies', *Nature*, **293**, pp. 253-256
7. National Perinatal Statistics Unit, Fertility Society of Australia (1990), *IVF and GIFT Pregnancies Australia and New Zealand* 1988, National Perinatal Statistics Unit, Sydney

 8. Parliamentary Assembly, Council of Europe (1982), 'Recommendation 934 (1982) (1) on genetic engineering'

 9. Medical Research Council (1982), 'Statement on research related to human fertilization and embryology', *BMJ*, **285**, p. 1480

10. National Health and Medical Research Council (1982), 'Ethics inMedical Research': *Report of the NH&MRC Working Party on Ethics in Medical Research*, Australian Government Publishing Service, Canberra

11. Royal College of Obstetricians and Gynaecologists (1983), *Report of the RCOG Ethics Committee on in vitro fertilization and embryo replacement or transfer*, RCOG, London

12. Duncan, A. S., Dunstan, G. R., and Wellbourne, R. B. (1981), *Dictionary of Medical Ethics*, Darton, Longman & Todd, London

13. Edwards, R. G. (1980), Conception in the Human Female, Academic Press, London

14. British Medical Association Working Group on in vitro Fertilization (1983), 'Interim report on human in vitro fertilization and embryo replacement and transfer', *BMJ*, **286**, pp. 1594-1595

3 Committees of Inquiry and the Move to Regulation

The Waller Committee

Two committees of inquiry reported in 1984, the Waller Committee[1] in the State of Victoria, Australia, and the Warnock Committee in the United Kingdom. The former led to immediate legislation, the latter to a prolonged period of consultation.

The Infertility (Medical Procedures) Act 1984,[2] based on the recommendations of the Waller Committee, was the first legislation in the world to regulate in vitro fertilization and embryo research. However, its proclamation in August 1984 was only partial and statutory regulations were not published until 1988. In the interval the Act was subject to amendment in 1987 to allow research involving the micro-injection of sperm but remaining confusion has been the cause of further amendment.

The intention of the Waller Committee and the Act was to allow existing IVF programmes to continue but to control the future direction and development of such programmes, and the undertaking of research, through the establishment of a statutory body, the Standing Review and Advisory Committee on Infertility (SRACI). In fact the provisions of the Act are quite restrictive. The clinical procedure is permitted only for married couples (this includes the case where a woman 'is living with a man as his wife on a bona fide domestic basis although not married to him'). Counselling is compulsory and couples may only enter an IVF programme provided that 12 months have elapsed since investigation by another

33

medical practitioner has indicated IVF to be the appropriate treatment; this is in order to allow time for pregnancy by other means to occur. The procedure may only be carried out in hospitals approved by the Minister; in effect this has meant tertiary referral hospitals.

Research is prohibited unless approved by the Standing Review Advisory Committee. Section 6 of the Act states that

> 'A person shall not carry out an experimental procedure other than an experimental procedure approved by the Standing Review and Advisory Committee.'

where the term 'experimental procedure' is defined as

> '... a procedure that involves carrying out research on an embryo of a kind that would cause damage to the embryo, would make the embryo unfit for implantation or would reduce the prospects of a pregnancy resulting from the implantation of the embryo.'

However, fertilization of ova outside a woman's body is permitted only for implantation. This would seem to allow research on embryos surplus to clinical needs - the report of the Waller Committee had made specific provision for such use - but then requires these embryos to be reimplanted. Something which runs totally contrary to ethical opinion in the UK. Cloning and the fertilization of human by animal gametes are prohibited procedures. However, the fact that the Act failed to define the terms 'embryo' or 'cloning' led to confusion of interpretation which forced the SRACI to recommend amendments.

The membership of the SRACI is set out under the Act. It is composed of eight members as follows:

'(a)   a person holding a qualification in the study of philosophy;
(b)   two medical practitioners;
(c)   two persons representing religious bodies;
(d)   a person qualified in social work;
(e)   a legal practitioner; and
(f)   a person qualified as a teacher with an interest in community affairs.'

These are appointed by the Minister and one of them is appointed chairman. The chairman since 1984 has been Professor Waller, former chairman of the Committee of Inquiry.

The functions of the SRACI are laid down as:

'(a) to advise the Minister in relation to infertility and procedures for alleviating infertility;

(b) to consider requests for approval of and, if it sees fit, to approve, experimental procedures for the purposes of section 6 (3) (of the Act); and

(c) to advise and report to the Minister on any matters relating to infertility and procedures relating for alleviating infertility and any other associated matters referred to it by the Minister.'

In the exercise of these functions it is also required that the Committee:

'(a) shall have regard to the principle that childless couples should be assisted in fulfilling their desire to have children;

(b) shall ensure that the highest regard is given to the principle that human life shall be preserved and protected at all times; and

(c) shall have regard to the spirit and intent of the several provisions of this Act.'

Unfortunately, because it was not clearly drafted, the spirit and intent of the Act became open to interpretation and the SRACI has had to spend much of its time trying to unravel its meaning and drafting definitions. Although the Committee has two doctors amongst its members, neither is an infertility specialist although one has a background in endocrinology. Nor is there any other member with scientific expertise. This has led to a serious lack of understanding of issues relating both to clinical procedures and to research.

There are several examples of confusions that have arisen. The Act appears to encourage research on the freezing of ova:

'Nothing in this Act prevents or inhibits the carrying out in an approved hospital of research on and the development of techniques for freezing or otherwise storing ova removed from the body of a woman.'

But the SRACI, when approached for approval of a project to carry out such research, refused to give permission because to consider such an experiment was outside the Committee's jurisdiction and, moreover, to allow the experiment would be in breach of section 6 (5) of the Act which allows fertilization only for the purposes of implantation. The proposed research required the freezing, thawing and fertilization of ova in order that they might be examined for abnormalities. Animal studies had indicated that although a high percentage of eggs appeared to survive the freezing process it seemed to induce a number of chromosomal abnormalities; the process should not be made available to patients until its safety was guaranteed. Clearly the two sections of the Act were in conflict.

The failure of the Act adequately to define fertilization led to its amendment in 1987[4] in order to allow research on the process of fertilization before syngamy, that is, from the time of sperm penetration until the union of the male and female pronuclei. This arose from an application to undertake research on the microinjection of single sperm into eggs in order to overcome the problems associated with poor sperm quality. Before the procedure could be offered to patients as an alternative to sperm donation its safety had to be proved. Although the amendment sought to allow the specific fertilization of eggs for research up to syngamy some members of the Victorian Parliament interpreted this as setting this time limit for all embryo research. This led to a moratorium on a project to develop embryo biopsy.

The Victorian legislation has been criticized on a number of grounds by patients, clinicians and scientists alike. Patients resent compulsory counselling and consider the requirements for entry into an IVF programme against their best interests. The situation in Victoria exemplifies the mistake of rushing to legislate too quickly on an issue which is complicated medically, scientifically and ethically and which is poorly understood by those outside the field.

The Warnock Report

The Warnock Committee followed the tradition of British committees of inquiry with a broad based membership of expert and lay members, numbering 16 in all, with a lay chairman, the philosopher Dame Mary (now Baroness) Warnock. In terms of interests or expertise the membership of the Committee comprised two obstetricians and gynaecologists, a general practitioner specialising in the sexual problems of the disabled and a leading expert in embryology, all of whom were able to contribute expert knowledge, and an academic general practitioner, a neurologist and a psychologist who had related but not direct medical expertise. The remainder, two social workers, the Director of a trust for social research, a health authority chairman, three lawyers and a professor of social and pastoral theology, was essentially lay.

Given its remit; 'To consider recent and potential developments in medicine and science related to human fertilization and embryology' the Committee decided to consider all those techniques for the alleviation of infertility which could be categorized as assisted reproduction. That is to say, donor insemination, in vitro fertilization, egg or embryo donation and surrogacy. Also considered were the related issues of gamete and embryo storage and embryo research.

Written evidence was invited and was submitted by 22 individuals working in the field of human reproduction or on matters related to the issues being examined by the Inquiry, and by 252 organizations which included, amongst others, the Royal Colleges of medicine, health authorities, university departments, research councils, religious bodies and medical charities. A further 695 letters and submissions were received from the public. Oral evidence was taken from 21 individuals and organizations. This evidence has not been published.

The Inquiry took two years and, as Baroness Warnock says in her introduction to the Committee's report, its task was 'to attempt to discover the public good, in the widest sense, and to make recommendations in the light of that'. In doing so the Committee sought, as far as possible to divide processes designed to benefit the individual (namely the infertile) within society from those concerned with the pursuit of knowledge, which is more likely to benefit society at large. Although it recognized that human in vitro fertilization and embryology were of international concern the Committee made a considered decision not to attempt any unity of approach beyond the UK. The views of members of the Committee were as diverse as the evidence received, particularly where moral issues were concerned, and a consensus was not reached on the subjects of embryo research or surrogacy leading to three expressions of dissent. The result of the Committee's deliberations led to the publication in 1984 of a report[5] containing 63 recommendations.

These recommendations were divided into five broad categories. The first category related to a licensing body and its functions. It was recommended that:

> 'A new statutory licensing authority be established to regulate both research and those infertility services which we have recommended should be subject to control.'

and that

> 'There should be substantial lay representation on the statutory authority to regulate research and infertility services and that the chairman must be a lay person.'

The infertility services to be included for regulation were donor insemination, IVF, egg and embryo donation, and the storage and freezing of gametes and embryos. It was further recommended that all practitioners offering these services, and all premises used for their provision, should be licensed by the authority and that to provide services without a licence should be an offence.

Donor insemination and egg or embryo donation in conjunction with in vitro fertilization were all seen as acceptable methods for the alleviation of infertility. But embryo donation by lavage was not considered appropriate because of the possible risk to the donor. It was recommended that frozen eggs should not be used in therapeutic procedures until further research had been undertaken but that the clinical use of frozen embryos could continue under licence.

By a very narrow majority the Committee agreed to recommend that research conducted on human in vitro embryos might be carried out under licence with unauthorized research being made a criminal offence. There were two expressions of dissent from the members who disagreed. The first group wished for all embryo research to be prohibited and recommended that the human embryo should be afforded special protection in law. The second group, while accepting research on embryos surplus to clinical procedures, dissented from the view that; 'research should be permitted on embryos brought into existence specifically for that purpose or coming into existence as a result of other research'. All were agreed, however, that no embryo should be allowed to develop in vitro beyond fourteen days after fertilization, whether for research or for subsequent freezing and storage. The reference point for this decision was the appearance of the primitive streak, the first indication of the embryo proper. The range submitted in evidence had been from the beginning of implantation (about 6 days after fertilization) to 17 days, at which time early neural development begins. It was further recommended that consent should be obtained as to the use or disposal of spare embryos and, where this involved research, no research should be carried out without the informed consent of the couple from whom the embryo was generated.

Other recommendations in this grouping addressed the use of trans-species fertilization for the diagnosis of subfertility, the need for follow-up studies of children born as a result of the new techniques and the sale or purchase of human gametes of embryos. It was recommended that the use of trans-species fertilization in the assessment of subfertility should be allowed subject to licence and on the condition that any resultant hybrid should be terminated at the two cell stage. It was suggested that the follow-up of children and the maintenance of a central register of all births resulting from licensed procedures should be considered by the licensing body. The lack of any firm recommendation on the collection of statistics or the setting up of a register meant that an opportunity was lost at an early stage for monitoring the long term effects, on patients or their offspring, of the new reproductive technologies. The recommendation that the sale or purchase of human gametes or embryos should be permitted under licence recognized the fact that semen banks, for instance, might justifiably require the reimbursement of their expenses.

The second category of recommendation consisted of those relevant to the principles of provision. In particular, it was recommended that, where donor gametes were used, any third party acting as donor should be unknown to the couple being treated and vice versa, with counselling to be available to both donors and recipients. The Committee recognized that, as far as egg donation was concerned, until eggs could be stored successfully this might not always be possible. It was suggested that the number of children born from the gametes of any one donor should be limited to ten. Openness was recommended to children about their genetic origins with access to be available on reaching their majority to information about the donor's ethnic origin and genetic health.

The recommendation that the use of frozen semen in artificial insemination should continue has been superseded by the advent of the AIDS epidemic. All semen now has to be quarantined, frozen, before use. The Committee also recommended that semen and egg deposits should be reviewed every five years. Ten years was recommended as the maximum limit for the storage of embryos with the right to use or disposal to pass to the storage authority after that time. When one member of a couple dies it was suggested that the right to use or dispose of an embryo should pass to the survivor. If both die, or there is no agreement between the couple as to use or disposal, the right should, again, pass to the storage authority.

It was recommended that, both in the NHS and in the private sector, counselling should be available to all infertile couples at any stage of their treatment.

Six recommendations were made under the heading of service provision. The Committee had been surprised at how few data were available on the prevalence of infertility and on the extent of services available. The first recommendation in this category was therefore that funding should be made available for the collection of adequate statistics. Each health authority was recommended to review its facilities and provision for the treatment of infertility and to provide, at least, for infertility patients to be seen separately from other types of gynaecological patient. It was further recommended that a national working group should be set up, drawn from the health departments, health authorities and those working in infertility to draw up detailed guidance on the organization of services. One of the first tasks of the working group should be to consider how best an IVF service can be organized within the NHS. These recommendations appear to have fallen upon deaf ears and, eight years later, only three IVF clinics exist fully within the NHS.

The next set of recommendations suggested legal limitations which should be introduced with regard to embryo research. It was recommended that the embryo of the human species should be afforded some protection in law so that any unauthorized use of an in vitro embryo would in itself constitute a criminal offence. Other criminal offences would be the handling of or research on a live human embryo derived from IVF beyond 14 days after fertilization; any unlicensed use of trans-species fertilization using human gametes; the placing of a human embryo in the uterus of another species and the unauthorized sale and purchase of human gametes or embryos.

It was recommended that legislation should allow research to be carried out on an IVF embryo, whatever its provenance, up to the end of the fourteenth day after fertilization but no embryo used for research should be transferred to a woman. The recommendation was also made that the proposed licensing body should promulgate guidance on the types of research, other than those precluded by law, which would be likely to be considered ethically unacceptable and therefore would not be licensed.

The final category of recommendations dealt with the legal changes which the Committee considered would be necessary. They dealt predominantly with the status of the child, firstly, in relation to its parents where donor gametes have been used and, secondly in relation to succession and inheritance. It was recommended, in the case of donor insemination, that the child should be treated in law as the legitimate child of the mother and her husband and it should be presumed that the husband has consented to donor insemination unless it can be proved to the contrary. The law should permit the husband to be registered as the father and the semen donor should have no rights or duties in relation to the child. Where egg donation was involved the mother giving birth to the child should be regarded as the mother and, again, the donor should have no rights or obligations. Where succession and inheritance were concerned, it was recommended that any child not in utero at the date of the father's death should be disregarded for these purposes. For the purposes of primogeniture, the date of birth and not the date of fertilization should be the determining factor.

Three recommendations addressed the question of surrogacy, the practice whereby one woman carries a child for another with the intention that it should be handed over after birth. Here, the Committee was unable to reach agreement. It was recommended that legislation be introduced to render criminal the creation of surrogacy agencies, to render criminally liable the actions of professionals who knowingly assist in the establishment of a surrogate pregnancy and to render illegal, and therefore unenforceable, all surrogacy agreements. Two members of the Committee disagreed strongly enough to make an expression of dissent. They considered that it would be a mistake to prevent surrogacy being offered as a treatment for childlessness believing that there might be rare occasions when surrogacy might be beneficial to couples as a last resort. They suggested that surrogacy should come within the remit of the licensing authority which should have the power to license agencies. Access to a licensed agency could only be by referral from a consultant gynaecologist and anyone making surrogacy arrangements for a couple without a licence to do so would be committing an offence.

Reactions to Warnock

The Warnock Report generated much heated discussion in and out of Parliament but the government was in no hurry to act on its recommendations. The only issue on which the government saw fit to take action was surrogacy. The practice had been growing in the United States where a number of commercial agencies had been established. It was reported in the press that American agencies were planning to operate in the UK and early in 1985 a British woman, Kim Cotton, achieved notoriety by acting as surrogate mother to an American couple. With all party support, emergency legislation was piloted through Parliament resulting in the Surrogacy Arrangements Act 1985 which banned commercial agencies and the advertising of or for surrogacy services.

After its publication in July 1984 the Report had a mixed reception. It was welcomed by the Medical Research Council, the Royal Society, the British Medical Association and the Church of England and many other organizations but it was vociferously condemned by the Society for the Protection of the Unborn Child (SPUC), LIFE and the Roman Catholic Church, and by a small number of leading clinicians such as Sir John Peel and Professor Ian Donald. The government invited comments on the Report by the end of the year and, in October, the MRC recalled its Advisory Group to do so, with a view to the Group's recommendations being considered by the Council of the MRC at its meeting on 29 November. While commenting favourably, the MRC Group expressed concern at the definition of research within the Warnock report which stated 'we exclude from the concept of research what we have called new and untried treatment undertaken during the attempt to alleviate the infertility of a particular patient'. The Group felt that this could create a rift between clinicians and scientists by seemingly allowing a relatively free hand to clinicians while restricting the freedom of scientists to carry out similar research. The Group welcomed the recommendation that a statutory authority should be established and, on the suggestion of its chairman Professor Dawes, proposed that in view of the necessity of maintaining strict standards, in this field of research some interim arrangement might be instituted until such time as the Warnock provisions could be implemented. It was suggested that these arrangements might include a licensing body, with its membership drawn from the MRC and RCOG, with whom all persons involved in human IVF and embryo research might register.

In Parliament the Warnock Report was first debated in the House of Lords on 31 October 1984. It was not well received. In fact, it was castigated by many speakers and a number called for a moratorium to be imposed on human embryo research until legislation was enacted. The President of the RCOG (also a member of the Warnock Committee), Professor Callum MacNaughton, attended the debate and was concerned by the strength of feeling expressed. As a result he also approached the Secretary of the MRC, Sir James Gowans, to suggest that their two organizations should, as quickly as possible, mount a joint initiative to set up an independent licensing body. This added force to the recommendation of the MRC Advisory Group but the proposal still had to be sanctioned by the ruling councils of the two organizations.

Government ministers were also unsettled by the course of the House of Lords debate, in particular the calls for a moratorium on research. The Department of Health was quite aware, as its observers sit on all MRC committees, of the proposed initiative to set up a non-statutory licensing body and it approached the MRC with a view to referring to this initiative at the beginning of the House of Commons debate on 23 November. Sir James Gowans, Secretary of the Council thought it improper that an announcement about a non-statutory licensing authority should be made in the House of Commons before the proposal had been sanctioned by his Council. Moreover, he felt that it might well be counter productive for the Secretary of State for Social Services to make such an announcement until the proposals for the authority were more fully developed and he therefore wished MRC public relations to remain low profile until this was the case.

The debate in the House of Commons was another confused and emotive affair. The Minister for Health, summing up at the end, noted the polarity of views expressed by Members of the House but offered no indication of future government action. Subsequently a number of MPs decided to take the issue into their own hands. The Rt Hon J Enoch Powell had won fifth place in the ballot for Private Member's Bills and decided to use the opportunity to present a bill 'To make provision relating to human embryos produced by in vitro fertilization, and for connected purposes.' This was the Unborn Children (Protection) Bill which was introduced on 5 December 1984 and received its Second Reading on 15 February 1985.

The bill sought to prohibit human in vitro fertilization except for the purpose of embryo insertion and, in so doing, to prohibit embryo research. The fertilization of a human ovum in vitro was to be allowed only with the authority of the Secretary of State. The possession of a human embryo produced in vitro other than for insertion into a patient would be a criminal offence. Moreover, the Secretary of State was to oversee all IVF treatment giving specific authority in each case with such authority to expire at the end of four months, although this was renewable for a further two months provided renewal was sought before the expiry date. The bill was unique in requiring a government minister to give permission for a medical procedure and in effectively requiring a woman to be licensed in order to have a baby. The impact of the bill, if enacted, would have been Draconian. Nonetheless, the bill received considerable support in the Commons and, at its second reading in February 1985, commanded a majority of 172. It only failed to become enacted because it ran out of time at the Report stage due to filibustering by those Members who supported the Warnock recommendations.

Setting up the Voluntary Licensing Authority

The proposal to establish an interim licensing body received approval from the Councils of the MRC and RCOG and discussions took place between the two organizations as to the form and the remit of the new body. Its establishment became urgent with the advent of the Powell Bill and it needed a name. The Genetic Manipulation Advisory Group, a non-statutory body reporting to the Health and Safety Executive (HSE) on genetic engineering projects was seen as a possible model and the HSE was approached for advice on a suitable name. It was strongly advised that the expression 'Voluntary Licensing Body' should be avoided. To grant a licence suggested that the body had government authority to issue such a licence, which it would not, yet the term voluntary suggested no obligation whatsoever to seek a licence. The title suggested was 'The Joint MRC/ RCOG Advisory Committee on Human in vitro Fertilization and Embryology'. This was considered to be equally, if not more, ambiguous and the title finally decided upon was The Voluntary Licensing Authority for human in vitro Fertilization and Embryology.

It was agreed that the Authority should have a distinguished lay chairman and a strong lay membership covering a wide range of experience in order that there should be public confidence in its independence. It was suggested that the total membership should number 12 or 14 with four to be nominated by the MRC and four by the RCOG with the remainder to be chosen by joint consultation. The General Medical Council (GMC), the Health Departments and the Department of Education and Science were invited to appoint observers; all declined. The President of the GMC wrote explaining that, in view of the Council's statutory responsibilities, it would be wiser if it were not to be associated in any way with the proposed licensing body, even in an observer capacity. The GMC had no wish to find itself compromised in the event of any possible judgement on the profession which it might be required to make in the future. The government departments also declined to advise on the selection of the chairman or members of the Authority and proceeded to keep themselves at a great arm's length from the entire initiative.

It was thought that the chairman should probably be an eminent lawyer or philosopher and a list of some dozen suitable candidates was drawn up including lawyers, philosophers, university vice-chancellors and other persons notable in public life. The President of the RCOG suggested that Dame Mary Donaldson be considered. She was a former Lord Mayor of London, had a notable record of public service and was interested in health issues. Sir James Gowans approached Dame Mary about the chairmanship and she indicated her willingness to take on the job.

It then remained to select the other members; a list of over 50 possibilities was drawn up including the names of both expert and lay people from many walks of life. The RCOG nominated four of its members, Professor M C MacNaughton, the President of the College and a former member of the Warnock Committee; Dr J D O Loudon, Chairman of the RCOG Ethics Committee; Professor R W Shaw, Professor of Obstetrics and Gynaecology at the Royal Free Hospital and Professor W Thompson, Chairman of the RCOG Fertility Committee. The MRC nominees were Sir Douglas Black, a former Chief Scientist at the Department of Health and Social Security; Professor Geoffrey Dawes, who had chaired the MRC Advisory Group on IVF; Dr Anne McLaren, Director of the MRC Mammalian Development Unit and also a former member of the Warnock Committee and Dame Cicely Saunders, founder and Medical Director of St Christopher's Hospice. Five lay members were selected in consultation with Dame Mary Donaldson. These were Sir Cecil Clothier, a lawyer and former Health Services Commissioner; Professor the Revd G R Dunstan, Emeritus Professor of Moral and Social Theology in the University of London; Miss Susan Hampshire, the actress and Dr Penelope Leach, a research psychologist and child care specialist. Dame Cicely Saunders was forced to resign for personal reasons during the first year and was replaced by two lay members, Mrs Alwyne Cox, a magistrate and Miss Patricia Lamburn, Editorial Director at IPC Magazines. Thereafter this membership remained virtually unchanged for the life of the Authority although it was increased in number as the work load increased. Full details of the Authority's membership are given in Appendix 1.

It was envisaged that government legislation would be enacted within a couple of years so that the main tasks of the Voluntary Licensing Authority would be to register and approve centres undertaking IVF and to consider and approve proposals for research in preparation for handing over to a statutory authority. The following remit was therefore drawn up:

1. To approve a Code of Practice on research related to human fertilization and embryology.
2. To invite all centres, clinicians and scientists engaged in research on in vitro fertilization to submit their work for approval and licensing.
3. To visit each centre prior to its being granted a licence.
4. To report to the Medical Research Council and The Royal College of Obstetricians and Gynaecologists.
5. To make known publicly the details of both approved and unapproved work.

It was anticipated that the Authority would need to meet about six times in its first year and to undertake about 15 site visits (12 IVF centres were known to be in existence but this number was likely to increase). It was thought that site visits could be delegated to subcommittees of the Authority. The MRC agreed to provide the Secretary and administrative staff for the Authority. The MRC staff would be responsible for all the arrangements for the Authority's meetings and the preparation and circulation of papers. It was agreed that meetings of the Authority would be held at the RCOG. The costs of the Authority would be shared jointly by the MRC and RCOG.

A press conference was held on 29 March 1985 to announce the establishment of the Voluntary Licensing Authority. Although the Authority was generally well received the occasion was noticeably low key. It was rather overshadowed by parliamentary activity on Enoch Powell's Unborn Children (Protection) Bill. The Authority had, in fact, held its first meeting three days before; it urgently needed to draw up guidelines and procedures and to demonstrate to the general public that it would be a force to be reckoned with in the regulation of human in vitro fertilization and embryo research.

References

1. Committee to Consider Social, Ethical and Legal Issues Arising from In Vitro Fertilization (1984), Report on the disposition of embryos produced by in vitro fertilization, Parliament of the State of Victoria, Melbourne, Australia

2.   *Infertility (Medical Procedures) Act 1984*, Parliament of the State of Victoria, Melbourne, Australia

3.   Dawson, K. (1987), 'In vitro fertilization: legislation and problems of research', *BMJ*, vol 295, pp. 1184 - 1186

4.   *Infertility (Medical Procedures)(Amendment) Act 1987*, Parliament of the State of Victoria, Melbourne, Australia

5.   *Report of the Committee of Inquiry into Human Fertilization and Embryology* (1984), Cmnd. 9314, HMSO, London

4 The Voluntary Licensing Authority

By the time the Voluntary Licensing Authority was established in March 1985 almost every major city in Europe, Australia, Japan and the United States would have had an infertility centre specialising in the application of IVF. Worldwide about 1,000 children had been born as a result of IVF and the technique had become an established method in the alleviation of infertility. Yet its success rate was still very low and more research was needed both to improve the technique and to increase the understanding of infertility. In Britain, Enoch Powell's private member's bill had reached the committee stage and it seemed likely that IVF treatment would be strictly curtailed. It was important that public confidence be restored. It was essential, therefore, that the new Authority should establish its presence and draw up and publicise guidelines and conditions of licence. One of the Authority's first acts was to provide Members of Parliament with explanatory information about human in vitro fertilization and to inform them about its role. In the end, the Powell Bill was talked out and failed to become law. The VLA, having established the criteria by which it would work, got on with the business of licensing centres and approving research projects.

When it started work the Authority believed that it was setting standards for legislation to come within about two years. In fact, it was to regulate human IVF and embryo research in the UK for six years. What may have been seen as a disadvantage, that the Authority had no statutory powers and so could not work with the backing of the law, was, in fact, one of the reasons for its success. Not having its terms of reference or code of practice decreed by statute, the Authority had the flexibility to react to changes in practice and to new ethical issues as they arose. Practitioners were keen to demonstrate that they had won a public seal of approval and so were encouraged to seek a licence.

Terms of reference

The terms of reference of the Authority were initially laid down by its parent bodies the MRC and RCOG (see Chapter 3). In drawing up the terms of reference account was taken of the fact that it was research involving human embryos that was of most public concern and that, at the time, clinical treatment involving IVF was largely experimental and being carried out by relatively few innovative practitioners. By 1988, however, the situation had changed. The majority of centres seeking approval from the VLA offered a clinical service only and most new developments were occurring in the clinical context. The Authority found itself becoming more and more concerned with matters of developing clinical practice. The political situation had also changed. The government had published, first, a consultation paper and, then, a White Paper. It looked as though legislation was in the offing and the Authority wished to have a clear remit to participate in the inevitable debate. It was plain that its existing terms of reference were no longer appropriate. With the agreement of the MRC and RCOG the Authority's terms of reference were amended to the following:

1. To approve a Code of Practice for research in human embryology and for related medical procedures in the treatment of infertility; and to amend the Code from time to time in the light of consultation and experience.
2. To invite all centres, scientists and clinicians engaged in pre-embryo research or developmental practice in in vitro fertilization, GIFT or other such procedures to submit work for approval or licence.
3. To visit each centre before the grant of licence and to return for review visits as necessary.
4. To report to the Medical Research Council and to the Royal College of Obstetricians and Gynaecologists.
5. To publish information on centres and work approved and not approved.
6. To contribute as expedient to the relevant public debate and legislative process.

Guidelines and Conditions of Licence

One of the Authority's most important tasks, if it was successfully to license centres and laboratories, was to draw up a sound code of practice. This it did in its Guidelines for both Clinical and Research Applications of Human in vitro Fertilization. Initially in drawing up its guidelines the VLA drew on the recommendations of the Warnock Committee, the MRC statement on research related to human fertilization and embryology, the report of the RCOG Ethics Committee[1] and the expert advice of those of its members who worked in the field. Later, in the light of experience, the guidelines were changed to take account of developments in clinical practice. The full guidelines indicating the changes and when they occurred may be found at Appendix 2.

Initially research applications were to the fore and, in preparing its Guidelines, the VLA started from the premise that scientifically sound research involving human embryos was ethically acceptable, provided that its aims were clearly defined and acceptable and provided that there was no attempt to transfer the embryo to the uterus. Acceptable aims were those outlined as relevant to clinical problems such as the diagnosis and treatment of infertility or of genetic disorders, or the development of safe and more effective measures of contraception. Unacceptable research was stated to include modification of the genetic constitution of an embryo, the placing of a human embryo in the uterus of another species for gestation, cloning by nuclear substitution, and growing an embryo beyond fourteen days after fertilization. This was the limit recommended in the Warnock Report and was based on the fact that the primitive streak, which heralds the development of an individual embryo, appears at about this time.

The donation of gametes for research involving fertilization was considered acceptable but only if appropriate consent was obtained. The same applied to embryos surplus to therapeutic need. The Authority wanted donors to be fully aware and willing for their gametes or embryos to be used for such research. For this reason it did not condone the use of sperm from sperm banks for research projects unless donors had an opportunity to object. All research applications were required to have local ethics committee approval before they were submitted to the VLA.

By 1985 one or two centres were beginning to use cryopreservation techniques to store embryos for future use; this is now commonplace. It was clear to the Authority that, while the technique had considerable clinical advantages, it also raised ethical dilemmas which needed resolution. These dilemmas, which primarily related to the ownership and use of frozen embryos, had already been considered by the Warnock Committee. This had recommended in its Report that storage should be allowed for a maximum of ten years 'after which time the right to use or disposal should pass to the storage authority'. The Warnock Report recommended that rights to use or disposal should also pass to the storage authority in the case where both partners of a couple storing embryos had died or where there was any disagreement between partners as to the use of their stored embryos. Where one of a couple died, the right to use or disposal should pass to the survivor. However, such rights could only be embedded and enforced in law and the guidelines of the VLA could have no statutory basis. The Authority, therefore, recommended the ten year storage limit suggested by Warnock but subject to review in the interim, initially after a period of two years. The issue of use was to be covered in consent procedures.

It was clear that a better answer to surplus egg collection was to freeze and store unfertilized eggs. Fewer ethical problems surround banks of gametes than banks of embryos. However, eggs are much more difficult to freeze. They are amongst the largest cells in the body and because they can only be retrieved as single cells their components are much more susceptible to damage during the freezing process. Early embryos are formed from the cleavage of the fertilized egg without any change in volume and all the resultant cells are totipotent, ie they each have the potential to develop into a human being. In this way, if one or two cells are damaged by the freezing process the remainder can continue to develop normally. This is not the case with the freeze damaged egg. Research was being undertaken on the storage of eggs at low temperature for clinical use but, while the Authority approved such research, it forbade the transfer to the uterus of previously frozen eggs fertilized in vitro until such time as scientific evidence was available as to the safety of the procedure. Frozen embryos were not allowed to develop beyond the 14 day limit.

In more than a quarter of cases infertility is due to male factors. Interspecific fertilization is one method of diagnosing whether a partner's sperm have fertilizing capacity. In this case a hamster egg is used but, although a human sperm can penetrate the egg and cause it to cleave, species differences mean that it is unable to develop further into a viable hybrid organism. However, the debate on the Powell Bill had raised the possibility of the creation of hybrid monsters in the public imagination. The Authority therefore drew up a guideline which would allow this diagnostic test but would meet public concern by forbidding continued development in vitro. In fact, the test is now rarely used.

The appropriate disposal of human embryos, either surplus to clinical requirements or following research, was also addressed in the VLA guidelines. The Authority was aware that public sensitivity was likely to exist with regard to the fate of embryos which were not returned to the uterus. While it was unreasonable to expect full obsequies to be performed over something which was only potentially a human being, neither was it appropriate for human embryos in vitro to be left lying about the laboratory. Each centre was required to have a policy for disposal, the method depending on the use of the embryo. Human embryos require special culture conditions to develop normally in vitro and will degenerate quickly if exposed to air, water, alcohol or heat. The Authority recommended that exposure to one of these should be included in any disposal policy.

The guidelines discussed above related mainly to research applications and they worked well. No centres were found to be carrying out research that was unacceptable and these guidelines remained virtually unchanged, apart from the tightening up of their phraseology, during the lifetime of the Authority.

The remaining guidelines addressed considerations which should be taken into account when establishing clinical or laboratory facilities for in vitro fertilization. Firstly, it was required that each centre should have access to an ethics committee to ensure that only acceptable work was being carried out at the centre in question. Most early IVF programmes were being carried out in, or in conjunction with, university medical schools and it was expected that centres would have recourse to their local research ethics committee. However, as more IVF clinics became established in the private sector, this was not always possible and centres were expected to set up their own ethics committees. In doing so they were referred to the Royal College of Physicians of London's Guidelines on the Practice of Ethics Committees in Medical Research of 1984. This led to some confusion where clinics had no research programme and eventually led to the Authority drawing up its own guidelines for ethics committees. These are dealt with separately later in the chapter.

Clinics and laboratories were required to have appropriately trained staff and proper facilities and to keep detailed records of treatments and experiments. Clinics, in particular, were asked to provide detailed records of all children born as a result of IVF to Dr Valerie Beral who was carrying out a follow-up study funded by the MRC. In 1983 Dr Beral had set up a national register of IVF births at the London School of Hygiene and Tropical Medicine and the MRC provided the funds to follow up the first 1,000 children born as a result of the technique.. The outcome of the study was published in the British Medical Bulletin in 1990[2] and provided an analysis for 1581 births arising from IVF and GIFT during the period 1978-1987. The size of the study was too small to provide sufficient statistical power to detect deviations from the norm in terms of congenital malformations but it was demonstrated that the high frequency of multiple births was the main determinant of the outcome of pregnancy and the health of children at the time of birth. Subsequently for the period 1989-1991 details of IVF and GIFT births were collected for the Authority by the Office of Population Censuses and Surveys (OPCS).

Statistics about the volume and success of IVF and GIFT treatments were collected and published annually by the Authority.[3-8] Collecting data to provide statistics about treatments and outcomes from individual clinics was a sensitive issue. Clinics did not wish to be identified and were only willing to supply data provided that their anonymity was maintained. The Authority was often criticised on this account, being told that it was doing patients a disservice by not providing a league table according to success rates. As far as the Authority was concerned, not having a legal mandate, it was a matter either of having no data to provide public information or of respecting the wish of clinics not to be identified. While the MRC study was being carried out only rather simple data were collected but, even so, the VLA secretariat found it notoriously difficult to extract the required data, with centres having to be chased continuously. There were other reasons for not publishing a league table such as the widely differing selection procedures imposed upon patients by different clinics; the success rate of a clinic which imposed no selection criteria on its patients could not be compared with a clinic which limited treatment to patients aged 35 or under with tubal problems. In addition, new centres often had not completed many cycles of treatment in their first year and statistics showed that there was usually a learning curve.

The difficulty in collecting data from centres forced the Authority to make the provision of annual returns a condition of licence. This became more important from 1988 when the VLA needed to collect more complex data, taking over where the MRC study left off. Since more comprehensive information was being collected it was considered that centres would prefer to supply data to a disinterested third party; the OPCS was approached and agreed to handle data which were now to be collected from the clinics, treatment by treatment, on a prospective basis. The new data sheets were designed by the Authority and agreed in consultation with the centres. Although each record would be anonymous, not holding details of a patient's name, it had been hoped to collect the NHS numbers of women receiving treatment in order to facilitate future longer term studies of any morbidity or mortality associated with assisted conception. However, clinicians refused to collect this data on the basis that most people did not know their NHS number and it would be an unwarranted intrusion on their privacy to attempt to do so. This was therefore abandoned.

The year 1987 saw a number of changes to the Authority's guidelines following its experience in visiting clinics over the previous two years and the development of other techniques involving the collection and transfer of human gametes such as GIFT (Gamete Intra Fallopian Transfer) and POST (Peritoneal Oocyte and

Sperm Transfer).   At the time, laparoscopy was the dominant method of egg collection for IVF and a number of district general hospitals were being persuaded by one of the pharmaceutical companies providing the necessary hormonal preparations that GIFT was a cheaper and easier option as there was no requirement for an embryology laboratory.   Ovulation is induced and eggs retrieved as for IVF but the gametes are returned to the patient's fallopian tubes for fertilization to take place.   By 1987 well over 2,000 patients were undergoing GIFT treatment.   Since it involved the same methods of ovulation induction and egg collection and the same risks of multiple pregnancy following multiple gamete transfer, the Authority was concerned that technique should be subjected to the same standards as IVF.   It therefore brought GIFT within its remit and invited clinics providing GIFT treatment to register with the Authority.   By 1991 some 42 centres offering GIFT had registered.   In addition a number of licensed IVF centres were also offering GIFT.

Multiple embryo transfer was a feature of IVF treatment since it gave a greater likelihood of success.   In its first report the VLA had recommended the replacement of up to three or four.   However, its statistics collected subsequently showed that, while this was true up to three, replacing four or more embryos did not generally contribute to any greater success.   Moreover, the higher the number of embryos replaced, the greater the likelihood of multiple pregnancy.   It also became apparent that a number of clinics were replacing more than four embryos and, where GIFT was being undertaken, in some cases considerably more than four eggs.   The Authority did not consider that this was best practice, nor was it in the patients' best interest, and decided to introduce a new guideline limiting the number of eggs or embryos transferred to three, allowing four in exceptional circumstances.   The Humana Hospital Wellington refused to conform and had its licence withdrawn until it agreed to abide by the new guideline.   This was a trial of the VLA's influence as the Humana was one of the largest infertility centres in the country and the fact that the hospital capitulated gave the Authority greater strength in enforcing its conditions of licence.   The clinic did not give up without a fight.   It circulated questionnaires eliciting support to practitioners around the country and to patients.   A number of these were returned to the Authority, rather than to the clinic, with expressions of dissent or with complaints from patients.

Another problem to arise with the increase in the number of private clinics was the qualification of the directors.   Where clinics were associated with university or other National Health hospitals, directors had professorial or consultant status but, as more independent clinics were established, a number of directors were either not medically qualified or did not have accredited consultant status.   The Authority considered that it was in the best interest of the patients that clinical matters should be overseen by a fully accredited consultant obstetrician and gynaecologist. A new guideline was added to the effect that, where the director did not have accredited consultant status, or the equivalent, or was a non-clinician, full clinical responsibility must be assumed by a Consultant Adviser who took an active role in overseeing the centre's treatment protocols and emergency procedures.

A continuing problem was that of counselling. Infertile couples are under a considerable amount of stress; this is exacerbated by treatment and more so when treatment is unsuccessful. The Authority was keen that, when contemplating and undergoing IVF treatment, infertile couples should have access to good independent counselling to help them to decide whether to continue with treatment or to come to terms with treatment failure. Clinicians were expected to explain the implications of treatment and nursing staff to deal with day-to-day anxieties but counselling was considered best undertaken by properly trained third parties. A guideline was drawn up to this effect. However, there continued to be confusion about the definition of counselling, with many clinicians interpreting it as merely the giving of information regarding procedures rather than helping couples come to a better understanding of themselves as well as the treatment. The Authority continued to find the quality of counselling variable. In some clinics counselling was undertaken by nursing staff who had been trained to do so; in others the National Association for the Childless provided infertility counselling and in others it was someone with religious training. The VLA was powerless to do much about the situation because of both the shortage of qualified counsellors and the shortage of training available. In addition, patients travelled many miles from home to obtain treatment which meant that counselling was not always readily accessible when most needed.

The screening of gamete donors for Human Immunodeficiency Virus (HIV) and hepatitis B was also an issue that arose after the establishment of the Authority. By 1987 the screening of semen donors was required by the Department of Health and Social Security.[9] Although the preparation of sperm for IVF and GIFT purposes greatly reduced the risks of contamination, the VLA considered that, nonetheless, clinics should be encouraged to use only quarantined frozen semen. If fresh semen was used, then the risks had to be explained to the patients and the choice given to them as to how to proceed. It was also thought important to screen for those at high risk from developing AIDS when recruiting semen donors to the extent of including a question about homosexuality in the instruction sheet given to recruits. Donors were expected to sign that they had read and understood this material. The Authority, following discussion, decided that patients entering an IVF programme should also be tested for HIV and hepatitis B antibodies. In the Netherlands a number of patients contracted hepatitis B following the contamination of culture fluid by serum from an infected patient. Guidelines were included requiring the testing of donors and patients. Clinics, however objected to the testing of patients complaining that this would be an added burden. Problems such as the use of contaminated serum could be avoided through proper laboratory practice. The authority retreated from its position on patients but continued to require both donors and recipients to be tested for HIV and hepatitis B whenever donor gametes were to be used.

Conditions of licence

Centres engaged in or proposing to undertake the practice of IVF and embryo transfer or research involving human in vitro fertilization were invited to apply to the Authority for approval. They were expected to complete a written application form providing full details of the clinical service to be offered or research to be undertaken and, where IVF or GIFT treatments had already been completed, details of the numbers of egg collections, numbers of transfers and any known outcomes. For all senior clinical, laboratory and nursing staff curricula vitae were required, together with details of the membership of the local ethical committee. The Authority also required to see any literature provided to patients, including any consent forms used. The clinical director and/or senior researcher were required to sign declarations that they would abide by the guidelines of the Authority and an authorized representative (usually the chairman) of the ethics committee was required to declare that the programme of the centre had been considered by the committee and discussed in the context of the guidelines.

Once it had an application form and all relevant information to hand, the Authority would send a group of members to inspect the facilities and speak to the director and staff. The group would then report back to the Authority on the suitability of the centre for approval. Approval was given subject to the following conditions.

'1.   The centre is required to follow the "Guidelines for Clinical and Research Applications of Human In Vitro Fertilization", published by the Authority.
2.   The centre is required to notify the Authority immediately of any changes in the information provided by it in the application for Approval. This is particularly important where changes in staff or in the nature of the work described or the services offered are concerned.
3.   The centre is required to make available to the Authority its records for inspection whenever requested, including the provision of annual returns.

4.   The centre is required to allow the Authority to visit its premises for the purpose of inspecting its clinical and laboratory facilities whenever requested.

5.   Each centre must have access to a local ethical committee and research proposals must be approved by it before they are submitted to the ILA (VLA). Each research proposal at an approved centre will be considered on a case by case basis.

6.   Approval may be withdrawn at any time should a centre cease to follow the Authority's Guidelines or to observe any of the conditions which may be attached to the approval, or should there be a change in the nature of the research or the services provided which does not satisfy the Authority's requirements.'

Failure to observe these conditions of licence would lead to withdrawal of approval although, as it had no statutory force, the Authority could not prevent a clinician or scientist from continuing to practice IVF or to undertake embryo research. It is to the Authority's credit that it was forced to withdraw approval only once when a clinic director declined to observe the guideline limiting the number of eggs or embryos to be transferred. In this case a combination of peer pressure and the commercial interests of the hospital in which the clinic was sited appeared to bring the centre back into line. The private hospital was probably unwilling to have its position in any possible action for negligence jeopardized by its failure to conform to a recommended code of clinical practice. This isolated case, however, does not imply that all other clinics obediently met all conditions of licence. Much of the time of the Authority's secretariat was taken up with chasing centres for details of changes of staff or services offered or trying to extract statistics. On one occasion the chairman of a local ethics committee was forced to contact the VLA through concern that the clinic director was not keeping his committee or the Authority informed about a number of procedures. But, on the whole, slowness to comply with the conditions of licence was due to pressure of work rather than to the arrogance of the practitioner.

Consent

The Warnock Report had made a number of recommendations on consent both in relation to treatment for infertility and to the use of spare embryos. Legally a patient cannot be treated or examined without a valid consent, unless there are exceptional life or death circumstances. In practice the form of such consent varies from the tacit or verbal to signed written consent. Where in vitro fertilization is concerned the issues may be so complex, with the possible involvement of third parties as well as the patients, that formal consent in writing was seen as essential. The VLA therefore recommended in its First Report that signed consent should be obtained not only for routine IVF treatment but also for the use of embryos donated for research. The Authority stated that signed consent was important because;

'(a) Copies of the consent form can be kept by the patients. Given that patients often wait a long time for their treatment, even after having been assessed as suitable, the form is a useful document to remind them of the exact terms of their consent.'

and

'(b) The form provides evidence that the clinician has explained what the treatment involves. Whilst it is appreciated that it is also important that the doctor writes an appropriate note in the patient's records stating what he has said, the consent form does provide an additional security.'

Steptoe and Edwards had been criticised early on for obtaining defective consent[10] and the VLA found a wide variety of forms of consent being used in the centres it visited. It was in the interest of both patient and clinician that any consent was clearly set out and understood. To this end, the Authority drafted a model consent form which could be used by all centres. Initially one form was drafted to cover both consent to treatment and the donation of spare embryos for research. However, following advice from the General Medical Council (GMC), consent for the two purposes was separated. Also on the advice of the GMC, the form for the latter stated that couples had been allowed a delay of at least 24 hours to consider the use of their spare embryos. Copies of the specimen consent forms produced by the Authority may be found at Appendix 3.

The pre-embryo

The VLA was established at a time of emotional parliamentary debate about human embryo research. However, it was also a time of general public ignorance about human reproduction and development; an ignorance which still persists. One of the Authority's first acts was to provide an explanation for Members of Parliament about human in vitro fertilization which avoided the rhetoric of the current debate.

The term 'test-tube baby' emblazoned across the pages of the tabloid newspapers served to reinforce the Huxleyan vision of fully formed fetuses in glass tubes. The Warnock Committee and the Authority itself recommended that licensed research should be allowed up to 14 days after fertilization. In order to explain why, a clear definition of this stage of development was needed. Scientists had a number of terms for the stages of development from fertilization to the appearance of the embryo proper such as zygote, for the fertilized egg, morula, when the clump of dividing cells after about three days resembles a mulberry and blastocyst for the tiny, fluid-filled sphere of cells which is formed at about five and a half days. But all these terms are confusing for the layman as is the term conceptus which classical embryologists had also used to describe these stages. Unfortunately, clinicians and embryologists working in the field of IVF had dropped into the habit of calling what had always been recognised as a pre-embryonic phase by the generic term 'embryo' which should properly be applied to the phase when the organs such as heart, gut, eyes, etc develop. The VLA decided to use the definition 'pre-embryo'. In the words of one member of the Authority, the Reverend Professor Gordon Dunstan,

> 'For upwards of 2,000 years embryo has been used to denote the growth of the organism in the womb from the time of the first formation of the body parts until their completion followed by the fetal stage in which the completed baby grows to viability. Now that science has revealed a vital pre-embryonic stage of cellular activity before organogenesis can begin an appropriate name should be given to it. Pre-embryo seems a proper name to describe this stage in development'

Embryo transfer is usually carried out about two days after fertilization, when it consists of four or eight cells, and research is allowed up until 14 days when a structure known as the primitive streak is formed. In order to clarify the term 'pre-embryo' the Authority based its description on natural events following fertilization in vivo. First of all, it explained, fertilization does not produce an embryo; it stimulates cell division. Fertilization normally takes place in the fallopian tube and the fertilized egg travels down the tube to the womb, dividing as it goes. This takes about three days during which a cluster of about eight cells will have been formed (the stage chosen for embryo transfer in an IVF programme). The cluster of cells is about 0.1 millimetres in diameter and invisible to the naked eye. No one cell is different from another, each could go on to form an embryo, or none. If conditions in the womb are not ideal the cells will continue to divide for a few more days and then be shed during the woman's menstrual period. If conditions in the womb are suitable, the cell cluster may begin to embed itself into the lining of the womb and some of the cells at its centre will begin to differ from the others to form a structure known as the 'embryonic plate'. Any embryo that develops will develop from these cells; the remainder will form the placenta and the sac in which the embryo and fetus will develop. Whether or not an embryo will develop is determined by the appearance of the primitive streak in the embryonic plate. If there are two primitive streaks, twin embryos will develop; if no streak appears the cluster of cells become what is known as a blighted ovum and is either shed as a miscarriage or reabsorbed. Occasionally, the cells may proceed to form a growth known as a hydatidiform mole.

The Authority therefore considered that its choice of the term 'pre-embryo' was both logical and consistent. In order to make its reasoning clear to the public, the VLA published an explanation of the term in its First and Third Reports.[4,11] This was prepared by one of the Authority's lay members, Dr Penelope Leach. Later, the American Fertility Society independently arrived at the same definition.

However, the term was not picked up by the British Government in drafting legislation nor did it become fully endorsed by the profession. During the debates in Parliament much criticism was levied at the definition. It was described as 'designed to dehumanise the human embryo' and 'a cop-out, a way of pretending that the public conflict about IVF and other innovations in human embryology can be made to go away by means of an appropriate nomenclature'.[12] Because the term was not incorporated into the Human Fertilization and Embryology Act it has fallen out of use.

Ethics committees

One of the first requirements of the VLA was that any centre applying to the Authority for approval of its clinical or research programme should also have the approval of a local ethics committee. The ethics committee was expected to keep a watching brief over the activities of a centre and the director of a centre was expected to inform the ethics committee of any changes in procedures offered or new research undertaken and to use the Committee for advice on ethical matters related to treatment. Centres were expected either to make use of an existing local hospital ethics committee or to set up a committee especially for the purpose. The objectives of this requirement were primarily to protect the interests of patients and of any children resulting from the use of assisted reproduction but also to protect the interests of society in general, in terms of respecting societal relationships and the traditional family structure. By ensuring that a centre maintained appropriate ethical standard the ethics committee provided both reassurance for the public and protection from criticism for the centre.

Originally, centres were referred to the Royal College of Physicians (RCP) of London's *Guidelines on the Practice of Ethics Committees in Medical Research* (revised 1984) for advice on the setting up and conduct of such committees. These guidelines related to the conduct of research on human subjects and were based on the protection of human rights provided through the guidelines proposed by the World Health Organisation[13] and the Council for International Organisations of Medical Sciences.[14]   Some centres regarded IVF as a routine clinical service and did not consider that it was necessary to seek ethical approval for their work. But the Authority took the view that, as IVF was a relatively new and still a highly sensitive procedure, local ethical approval was necessary. However, by 1989, IVF could no longer be considered an experimental procedure and the RCP guidelines had become inappropriate. Ethics committees were beginning to question their role and turned to the Authority for guidance. This resulted in the drawing up of *Guidelines for Ethics Committees for Centres Offering Assisted Reproduction* (the full guidelines are at Appendix 4), which set out advice on the conduct and structure of ethics committees.   In doing so, the Authority was treading on extremely delicate ground which could be seen as infringing professional freedom.

With regard to research, the Authority was concerned that it should be demonstrated that information could not be obtained from animal models or that the appropriate animal work had already been undertaken and, further, it wished to be assured that there was no intention to replace any embryo resulting from or used for research. The Authority had had to refuse approval for a project whereby it was intended to inject single sperm into eggs to achieve fertilization and then to replace the resulting embryos into patients. The aim was to overcome infertility caused by poor sperm in the male partner. At the time the successful use of this technique in mice had been reported from Australia but the results were far from clear cut and the mouse work needed to be repeated before it could be applied to patients. In addition, the Authority wished to be assured that embryos resulting from this technique were morphologically and chromosomally normal to avoid the transfer of defective embryos. The embryologist concerned merely went and carried out his experiments in Italy where ethical standards were more lax. This sort of problem is not, of course, resolved by legislation unless some sort of international agreement is reached.

With regard to clinical practice, the Authority wished to be assured that its guidelines were being obeyed and that, where there was any departure from the guidelines, the proposed departure was approved by the ethics committee and reported to the Authority. In approving any departure the ethics committee was to assure itself that no alternative procedure existed for the case in question (the fact that a clinic had difficulty in meeting the guidelines was not sufficient); that the patients had been fully counselled; that the interests of the potential offspring had been taken into account also the interests of any third party such as a donor; that the wider interests of society in terms of its norms and obligations had been taken into account and that any implications for after-care had been considered. A case had been notified to the Authority where the nursing staff in a clinic had become concerned that a teenage Asian girl was to be used as an egg donor for her mother; the ethics committee had not been consulted and it was not clear that the daughter's best interests were being taken into account. This was a situation to be avoided. Advice was also given on membership which it was said should include those with medical and scientific expertise and a nurse in active practice. It was also recommended that there should be not less than two lay members and that there should be women amongst the membership. Generally, Health Authority or university research ethics committees met these requirements, however, the Authority found that these were often heavily male dominated and that lay representation was poor. On qualification for membership the Authority stated that,

'It is not necessary that those who become members of the Committee are experts in moral philosophy or in particular disciplines; they need to be reflective people of good will, with a high regard for the human personality, for truthfulness and for the continued advance of reproductive medicine and medical science. Those who are totally opposed to work involving the human pre-embryo should be left to attack the system from outside; but neither should individuals be included who are acquiescent and likely to give automatic approval. Of the medical and scientific members there should be a majority who are employed in providing clinical care. It is also important that there will be individuals who will look at applications critically from the patient's point of view.'

It was suggested that the Committee should elect its own chairman, preferably from amongst the lay members, and that the chairman should have no financial interest in the centre concerned. This had, on occasion, been found to be the case. The Authority required details of the ethics committee, including the names and occupations of its members, to be provided with each application for approval. On one occasion the director of a centre and the chairman of his ethics committee refused to divulge any information about the committee members saying that, like members of a jury, they should remain anonymous. It was pointed out that this analogy was not appropriate and, in fact, juries are identified several times in court. After some prolonged correspondence the relevant information was provided.

It was recommended that an ethics committee should meet at least twice a year and that the chairman and some of the members should visit the centre for which they were responsible. In the course of its work the Authority had come across ethics committees who, despite having approved its work, had never set foot in the centre for which they were responsible.

The Authority also provided advice on the mode of working and business of ethics committees. It was suggested that business should be conducted at meetings and not only by post or by telephone, as had been found on occasion to be the case. The Authority also discovered that one ethics committee had met in haste in a hotel bar. In addition, it was recommended that there should be a quorum, whose composition should be defined as well as number, so that important decisions should not be taken in the absence, for instance, of a lay member. The importance of preserving confidentiality in the Committee's proceedings was emphasized, in order to avoid any damaging publicity which might affect patients, nonetheless, the Authority requested that records of business should be kept and made available to it on request. Where Committees found projects or procedures unacceptable they were advised to make this known to the director in writing or, if they found themselves in some uncertainty, to refer such issues to the Authority. Having approved a project or procedure, Committees were expected subsequently to monitor them. It was realised that detailed follow-up would not be practicable but it was suggested centres might be requested to provide an annual report. If a Committee discovered that its advice was not being heeded or that the Authority's guidelines were being infringed it was asked to report such facts to the Authority. Finally, Committees were asked to keep themselves well informed on issues related to assisted reproduction, both ethical and technical, and to circulate among members relevant publications, such as Government consultation documents or guidelines from the Royal Medical Colleges.

Generally IVF centres came to value having an ethics committee and frequently sought their advice on clinical issues such as whether or not to offer treatment to certain individuals, whether or not known donors should be used and on other issues of concern. However, in its *Code of Practice*,[15] the Human Fertilization and Embryology Authority now only requires embryo research projects to be referred to a local research ethics committee up to a third of whose members may be employed by or have a financial interest in the centre concerned. All other activities are left to the concern of 'the Person Responsible' as defined in the Human Fertilization and Embryology Act 1990 section 16(2)(a). This can be, and generally is, the clinical director who thus may have complete autonomy within the limits of the law.

Licensing clinics and laboratories

The Voluntary (later Interim) Licensing Authority met, on average, every other month. At these meetings reports from visits to clinics and laboratories would be discussed and decisions made whether or not to give approval. Applications for research were also discussed and approved, or not, as the case may be. A total of 79 research projects received approval during the lifetime of the Authority. Some time was also given to discuss matters arising from correspondence with members of the public or with clinics which could not be dealt with solely by the secretariat. Considerable time was spent discussing ethical issues such as egg donation or the selective reduction of pregnancy (these will be treated in depth in Chapter 5). The Authority was keen to keep abreast of developments abroad, mainly ethical and regulatory, and received regular reports at its meetings on activities in, for instance, the Council of Europe and the French National Ethics Committee. It was also essential for the Authority to be well-informed on the latest clinical and scientific developments in the field of IVF and, at each meeting, a clinical or scientific member of the Authority would be delegated to report on the latest literature and to explain the implications of these developments for the benefit of the lay members. Press coverage of human IVF was also monitored and cuttings provided at every meeting.

Certain activities were delegated to sub-groups of the Authority. These included drafting the annual report or responses to government consultation documents and visiting clinics and laboratories. These groups would report back to the full Authority.

Visiting groups consisted of not less than three members of the Authority and comprised one clinician, one scientist and one, or more, lay members. The group was generally, but not always, chaired by the clinical member and would be attended by a member of the secretariat. For the first two years visits were only made to new applicants for approval. However, when it became clear that the government was unlikely to make an early move to legislate, the Authority decided to review approved centres on a regular basis. A centre would be reviewed every two to three years or when it moved to new premises or changed medical director. Visits would also be made if there was concern that the Authority's guidelines were being infringed. On average 11 visits were made each year though the load was greatest in the Authority's first and last years and least in its second year of existence. By the time the Authority handed over to the HFEA 53 centres had been approved, 3 of which carried out research only and 30 of which offered a clinical service only.

New centres were required to complete an application form for approval of their activities and to submit curricula vitae for all senior staff. Copies of any information leaflets given to patients before or during treatment, specimen consent forms, specimen laboratory or clinical record forms and clinical data for all IVF and GIFT treatment cycles were also required. For centres being reviewed, copies of all current documentation and the latest clinical data were requested. A visit would then take place when a centre had been in operation for three to six months in order to allow it to be fully operational and to have its procedures and protocols established.

Visits to centres followed a set pattern. On arrival at the centre the group would have a private discussion in order to identify from the papers any special matters which warranted detailed investigation. Members were also provided with a check list of routine issues which they needed to cover. This was followed by a meeting with the medical director and senior staff of the centre and, whenever possible, the chairman or another representative of the local ethics committee. The visiting group would then tour the clinical and laboratory facilities before having a further private meeting in which it would formulate its recommendations. Finally, the group would again meet the director to tell him of their findings.

The visiting group would look at the standard of the clinical and laboratory facilities, the privacy and quality of counselling afforded to patients, the expertise and attitude of staff and the emergency equipment and procedures. The clinical facilities encountered ranged from the sublime to the ridiculous; from sumptuous suites in private hospitals to a curtained-off alcove in a corridor. Laboratory staff skilled in human embryo culture were, and are, in short supply and it was not unusual to come across embryologists moving from centre to centre at ever increasing salaries. While thought had generally been given to the physical and psychological comfort of the women undergoing treatment the same could not often be said about their partners who tended to be offered rather primitive facilities in which to produce their semen samples, generally a lavatory. At one clinic, where the hapless male partner could only access the lavatory provided by passing a row of other patients in the waiting room, a member of the visiting group suggested that this might be rather inhibitory and could be improved. On the Authority's next visit a special room had been provided with soft lights, sweet music and stimulating literature.

Emergencies were usually well catered for with up-to-date resuscitation equipment on hand. However, on one early visit when a director was asked what he would do in the case of an emergency, he paused and answered 'Dial 999'. Areas where centres were frequently asked to make improvement were in maintaining the confidentiality of patient records and in the quality of patient information literature. Patient records were often left out or in accessible positions. The Authority required that these should be kept in locked cabinets in an office which was locked when not occupied. Patient information varied considerably ranging from glossy 'sales brochures' at some private clinics to rather perfunctory notes at others. Lay members of the Authority, as non-specialists, were asked particularly to comment on this literature. They were often critical of the jargon employed, which could be confusing to patients, and the inclusion of ill-defined or unsubstantiated success rates. The Authority tried to provide constructive criticism to centres on their patient literature and generally this was welcomed. The aim was to persuade clinics to provide material that was written simply, intelligently, consistently and capable of being understood by patients at all levels of intellect, without being patronizing. On one occasion, a new clinic, confident of approval, had already claimed in its literature that it was VLA approved. This was looked at somewhat askance.

Clinical and laboratory facilities and procedures were carefully scrutinized. In the early days of IVF, eggs for fertilization were retrieved by laparoscopy and, where this was possible, laboratories would be sited next to the theatre where the operation was performed. However, the advent of vaginal ultrasound and the possibility of retrieving eggs without a general anaesthetic meant that a laboratory/theatre complex was no longer necessary. It is essential to the success of in vitro fertilization that the eggs are maintained at body temperature. Where the laboratory was not sited next door to the retrieval room, eggs would be transported from one to the other in a thermostatically controlled 'hot block'. In some cases the laboratory would be sited in a different building some distance away and some ingenuity was shown in methods of transport; a 'hot block' which plugged into a car cigarette lighter was one solution, another centre used the cleavage of one of the female members of its staff. Early on laboratories were dissuaded from using fluorescent lighting but this turned out to be unnecessary precaution. However, other factors were found to affect the success of in vitro fertilization such as a change in the detergent used to clean glassware and fumes from newly painted laboratory walls. Clinics were asked not to keep organic solvents in their laboratories.

The Authority also looked at the way clinical IVF centres were funded and became more and more concerned at the lack of provision within the National Health Service. By 1991 only three centres were funded wholly within the NHS, the majority (28) were entirely within the private sector. The remainder were able to make some use of NHS facilities but few were able to offer a free service to patients and those that did had long waiting lists and restricted the number of treatment cycles available. Some of these centres were eventually forced to charge patients in order to be able to continue to offer a service. Other centres operated on a non-profit making basis and some ran a 'Robin Hood' system whereby paying patients subsidized those who could not afford to pay. A number of centres were dependent on funds raised by patient support groups in order to buy essential equipment such as ultrasound scanners. Initially the geographical distribution of IVF centres was very much skewed towards London and the South East of England; latterly this has improved. The Authority was concerned that access to treatment was being limited by the ability to pay.

As well as being an essential part of the licensing process visits were particularly important in enabling members of the Authority to meet all the staff at centres. Centres equally came to value visits as members of the Authority were able to pass on tips that they had picked up on their visits to other centres. On early visits both the visiting group members and IVF centre staff were a little uneasy and uncertain of each other, both coming to terms with a novel form of regulation, but the Authority usually received a courteous welcome and centre staff were generally helpful and interested.

Meetings for IVF centres and ethics committees

As part of an aim to allow a two way exchange of information between itself and its licensed centres the Authority held an annual meeting for IVF centres where speakers addressed topics of interest and clinic directors could speak informally to members of the Authority over a buffet lunch. This was later extended to include a special meeting for members of ethics committees and, from 1990, directors of centres offering a GIFT service only were invited to attend.

These meetings allowed the Authority to discuss with centres matters which had arisen from its business over the past year and to take on board the views of practitioners in the field. Experts were invited to speak on special topics and a broad range of issues was covered during the life of the Authority. A paediatrician spoke on the problems resulting from high order multiple pregnancy, both in terms of the effect on special baby care units in NHS hospitals, where the sudden arrival of quads may take up a facility for many weeks or even months, and in terms of the types of morbidity likely to affect the babies. Developmental problems could persist and often there was a profound effect on social relationships within the family. Clinicians practising in the field spoke on advances in using patients' natural ovulatory cycles for IVF treatment and on intra vaginal embryo culture, a method introduced from France whereby eggs and sperm could be cultured in a small vial held in place in the patient's vagina by a contraceptive cap. A member of the Office of Population Censuses and Surveys talked about the practicalities of data collection and a sociologist addressed the question of the involvement of close relatives in gamete donation, focusing on experiences with donor insemination.

Lawyers were invited to speak about the legal position of centres undertaking the selective reduction of pregnancy and about the Human Fertilization and Embryology Bill. This included consideration of GIFT and whether it should be included in regulations, counselling, confidentiality and genetic screening, and the role and liability of members of ethics committees. Specialist members of the Authority spoke on practical and ethical problems related to IVF for lay members of ethics committees, on guidelines for ethics committees and on changes in data collection. Scientific members spoke about the implications of a ban on human embryo research.

In the Authority's final year, the Minister for Health, Mrs Virginia Bottomley, addressed the meeting and announced that the Human Fertilization and Embryology Authority would assume full responsibility on 1 August 1991. Professor Colin Campbell, Chairman of the HFEA, gave a report on its activities.

Primarily the VLA benefited from its lack of legal standing which enabled it to recognise where it had made an inept or erroneous judgment and to change its view. There was by no means total agreement within the Authority on all issues although it always strove to reach consensus before imposing its view. It tried to make discussion as open as possible and its meetings with centres and ethics committees allowed it to take account of the opinions of others. On one occasion where it was having difficulty in reaching a consensus, on the issue of egg donation, the Authority expanded the debate and organized an open meeting with an independent chairman and drew in experts from related fields. The result is reported in the next chapter.

References

1. Royal College of Obstetricians and Gynaecologists (1983), *Report of the RCOG Ethics Committee on in vitro fertilization and embryo replacement or transfer*, RCOG, London
2. Beral, V., Doyle, P., Tan, S. L., Mason, B., Campbell, S.(1990), 'Outcome of pregnancies resulting from assisted conception', *British Medical Bulletin*, **46**, 3, pp. 753-768
3. Voluntary Licensing Authority (1987), *The Second Report*

4. Voluntary Licensing Authority (1988), *The Third Report*
5. Voluntary Licensing Authority (1989), *The Fourth Report*
6. Interim Licensing Authority (1990), *The Fifth Report*
7. Interim Licensing Authority (1991), *The Sixth Report*
8. Thompson, W.T. and English, V. (1992), *Statistical Analysis of the United Kingdom IVF and GIFT Data 1965-1990*, Human Fertilisation and Embryology Authority, London
9. DHSS AIDS Booklet 4, *AIDS and Artificial Insemination - Guidance for Doctors and AI Clinics* (CMO(86)12)
10. Ramsey, P. (1972), 'Shall we reproduce. The Medical Ethics of *in vitro* Fertilisation', *JAMA*, **220, 10**, pp 1346-1350
11. Voluntary Licensing Authority (1986), *The First Report*
12. Hansard, House of Commons, 23 April 1990, Cols. 104 and 105
13. World Medical Association (1985), *The World Medical Association Handbook of Declarations*
14. WHO/CIOMS (1982), *Proposed international guidelines for biomedical research involving human subjects*, WHO, Geneva
15. Human Fertilisation and Embryology Authority (1991) *Code of Practice*, HFEA, London

5 The Ethical Minefield

The new reproductive technologies bring their problems: the conflict between clinical freedom and the need for regulation; the use of close relatives as gamete donors or as surrogate mothers; sterilization in exchange for eggs; multiple births and the selective reduction of pregnancy; freezing embryos; access to treatment limited by ability to pay; therapeutic research. The Voluntary Licensing Authority had to address all of these problems which from time to time brought it into conflict with individual centres which seemed too often only prepared to focus on the immediate problem of resolving infertility without considering what the long term effects of treatment might be. This chapter will address some of these problems and the recommendations made by the Authority.

Selective reduction of pregnancy

Selective reduction of pregnancy may be defined as reducing the number of embryos or fetuses implanted in a multiple pregnancy, usually by means of the selective injection of air or potassium chloride, leaving others to continue development. The technique was originally developed to allow the survival of a normal fetus in the case of twin pregnancies where the other fetus suffered from a chromosomal or developmental abnormality.[1,2] In 1987, it was reported to the Authority that certain IVF centres were carrying out selective reduction of high order multiple pregnancies resulting from infertility treatment in order to avoid the maternal complications and poor perinatal outcome that often accompany such pregnancies. However, the procedure itself is not without risk and may result in defects in the surviving fetuses or the loss of the pregnancy altogether.[3] The Authority was concerned about both the ethical and legal implications. Following discussion, the Authority agreed that it was unethical to replace more embryos than necessary and then to use selective reduction to deal with the consequent multiple pregnancy. On the legal aspects the Authority took advice from a specialist in medical law, Dr John Keown of the University of Leicester. He subsequently gave a paper on the subject at a meeting for IVF centres. This was later published.[4]

Clinics carrying out selective reduction claimed that they did not need to be registered under the 1967 Abortion Act since they were not undertaking termination of pregnancy. The point of selective reduction was that pregnancy should continue. Keown rebutted this by saying that, while the 1967 Abortion Act sets out the grounds and prescribes the formalities to be observed if section 58 of the Offences Against the Person Act 1861 is to be neutralized, doctors undertaking selective reduction still fell foul of the act. Section 58 makes it a criminal offence to use any instrument or to administer any noxious substance to a woman, whether pregnant or not, with intent to procure her miscarriage. While it might be argued that the word 'miscarriage' presupposes the expulsion of the fetus from the womb and that this does not happen with selective reduction of pregnancy or that selective reduction is not undertaken with the intent to procure the miscarriage of the woman but to ensure better carriage of the remaining fetuses, these arguments are not consistent with the established interpretation of miscarriage. In law 'miscarriage' is interpreted sufficiently broadly to include any fatal interference with the fetus. That is, it is the taking action to cause fetal death which is the criminal offence, not simply causing the expulsion of the embryo or fetus.

Selective reduction cannot be undertaken until after the fetal heart is detectable by ultrasound, about six weeks after conception, and the procedure is usually carried out between the eighth and fourteenth weeks of pregnancy. This means after most or all of the fetal organs have formed. At this stage, rather than being absorbed by the uterus, the fetal sac will collapse and the remains of the aborted fetus become attached to the placenta to be expelled from the uterus after the delivery of the remaining fetuses. So that even the argument that miscarriage requires the expulsion of the fetal parts is eventually met.

Keown's advice to IVF clinics wishing to undertake selective reduction of pregnancy was to comply with the 1967 Abortion Act to render the procedure lawful. Nonetheless it was not clear that the Act would necessarily provide protection since section 1(i) of the Act stated that protection was afforded when 'a pregnancy is terminated' and, following selective reduction, the pregnancy continued. Later, the anti-abortion organization LIFE reported an IVF clinic, known to have undertaken selective reduction, to the Director of Public Prosecutions but no prosecution followed.

The Government, recognizing the ambiguity in the law, decided eventually to bring selective reduction within the ambit of the 1967 Abortion Act by including an amendment to the Act in the Human Fertilisation and Embryology Act 1990 (section 37(5)). Section 5(2) of the Abortion Act now reads:

> 'For the purposes of the law relating to abortion, anything done with intent to procure a woman's miscarriage (or, in the case of a woman carrying more than one foetus, her miscarriage of any foetus) is unlawfully done unless this is authorised by section 1 of this Act and, in the case of a woman carrying more than one foetus, anything done with intent to procure her miscarriage of any foetus is authorised by that section if -
>
> (a)   the ground for the termination of the pregnancy specified in subsection (1)(d) of that section applies in relation to any foetus and the thing is done for the purpose of the miscarriage of the foetus, or
>
> (b)   any of the other grounds for termination of pregnancy specified in that section applies.'

Subsection (1)(d) refers to the risk that if the child were born it would suffer from serious handicap.

Therapeutic research

Drawing a line between the doctor's right to clinical freedom and the need to impose regulations for the benefit of patients is extremely difficult. Therapeutic research, where a doctor may undertake novel or untested procedures for the benefit of individual patients, is an extremely grey area and one which the VLA was, on the whole, powerless to address. The area of reproduction is one where medical intervention has often been introduced without rigorous evaluation. As the epidemiologist Archie Cochrane said in his Rock Carling lecture in 1972, 'G & O stands for gynaecologists and obstetricians, but it could also stand for GO ahead without evaluation!'[5]   This is particularly true in the field of assisted reproduction in the UK where treatment is primarily undertaken in the private sector and clinicians are often unwilling to admit uncertainty or to submit patients to a research programme.

The VLA introduced its guideline limiting the number of eggs or embryos transferred on the basis of the statistics it had collected, which indicated that multiple pregnancies more frequently followed the transfer of four or more embryos. There were clinics which objected to this restriction on the grounds that it discriminated against their older patients. The Authority said that it would be quite happy to approve a relevant, properly controlled research project and to revise its view if this showed that older patients were more likely to have a successful pregnancy when more than four eggs or embryos were transferred. No applications were received; clinicians said that they could not expect paying patients to take part in a trial. Who should decide which attitude is in the patients' best interest? The VLA was not in a position to force clinics to undertake research. The best it could do was to expect ethics committees to monitor the activities of the clinics for which they were responsible.

The powerlessness of the Authority in influencing therapeutic research has already been illustrated by the case where micro-injection experiments were undertaken in Italy when not approved for clinical application in the UK. In this case, because the relevant embryo research was not undertaken the patients became the experimental subjects. This would have been the result of Enoch Powell's Unborn Children (Protection)Bill which would only have allowed the fertilization of a human egg in vitro for the purpose of reimplantation. The problem of where to draw the line in therapeutic research without hindering clinical freedom is not peculiar to assisted reproduction, it applies to the development of many novel procedures. But it is, perhaps, exacerbated where desperate patients are willing to undergo almost any procedure and, perhaps because they are paying, believe that they must be getting the best treatment. However, the approach to the problem is not best met by legislation or formal regulations but from within the medical profession itself.

Egg donation

For women with dysfunctional ovaries for example, who have undergone premature menopause, or who have had their ovaries removed, the only way to achieve a pregnancy is through the use of a donor egg or embryo. When sperm are donated for infertility treatment they are generally held in a sperm bank and the donor remains anonymous. But there are no egg banks and donor eggs are in short supply. The tendency was for clinics to suggest to patients that they ask friends or relatives to act as egg donors for them. Although it agreed to discourage the practice, the question as to whether this was acceptable greatly vexed the Voluntary Licensing Authority which found itself unable to come to a consensus. The Authority therefore decided to hold an open meeting with an independent chairman to discuss the issue. This was held in conjunction with the King's Fund Centre in London in September 1988. The aim of the meeting was to bring together not only those involved in the mechanics of egg donation, the clinicians and their patients, but also those who might have to deal with the outcome, sociologists, social workers, psychologists and lawyers in order to look at the broader implications of egg donation.

The meeting was chaired by Mr Robert Maxwell, Director of the King Edward's Hospital Fund for London and the introductory talk was given by a clinical member of the Authority, Professor William Thompson. He outlined the indications for egg donation and the possible sources of donor eggs. The VLA limited the number of embryos transferred in any one cycle to three or, exceptionally four, but generally excess of this number was collected. This therefore represented a potential source of donor eggs. However, it was usual for all eggs to be fertilized with the husband's sperm and for those embryos not used to be retained and frozen for use in a later cycle. Another acceptable source would be eggs collected from consenting women undergoing other gynaecological operations such as laparoscopic sterilization of hysterectomy. Donors recruited by public appeal might seem an obvious source but it seemed unwise to replace altruistic motives by monetary gain. A further source would be the friends or relatives of infertile couples. In these circumstances the donation would not be anonymous and, furthermore, it would be difficult for doctors to ascertain that consent for such a donation had been freely given without undue pressure from within the family circle. Professor Thompson then set out the Authority's dilemma about whether or not the anonymity of egg donors should be maintained, the sort of counselling which was required and the need to establish legal definitions of maternity and paternity. Parental definitions have since been addressed by the Human Fertilisation and Embryology Act 1990 (sections 27 and 28).

The consumer's perception

Dr Virginia Bolton from the Assisted Conception Unit of King's College Hospital, London, reported the results of a survey of patients eliciting views on egg donation.[6] Questionnaires were given to couples receiving egg donation (25 out of 28 couples responded) and a sample of patients undergoing IVF treatment (87 out of 104 men and 94 out of 108 women responded). The questionnaire was devised in such a way that patients were asked to respond to a random series of statements about egg donation indicating their level of agreement or disagreement or their uncertainty. Not surprisingly, the egg donation patients had a more positive attitude towards egg donation than the IVF patients but a consistent and interesting trend was that the male partners of the egg donation patients were more reserved in their responses.

The majority of all patients felt that egg donation is a treatment that should be both widely available (95%) and offered routinely to everyone who needs it (92%). Opinions, were more divided, however, on the question of whether recipients should be subjected to a screening process. While a small percentage of patients remained uncertain, the remainder were divided approximately equally in both the IVF and the egg donation groups. Though in the latter, more men (44%) than women (32%) agreed that couples should be screened very carefully. Indiscriminate use of the technique was not wholly condoned.

The questionnaire contained a number of statements to test patients' anxieties about egg donation. None of the egg donation patients agreed that egg donation would inevitably lead to problems though 20% of their male partners were uncertain. The IVF patients were less confident with a small percentage agreeing that problems would inevitably arise from egg donation. Curiously, for a section of the population which one might expect to be well informed about such things, nearly a third of all patients were uncertain as to whether egg donation increased the chances of having an abnormal child. Ignorance was greater among the male partners where a small percentage agreed that egg donation would increase the chances of having an abnormal child. These findings illustrated the importance of providing potential recipients with proper information and counselling. The great majority of patients agreed that potential donors and recipients should be counselled before donation was undertaken though there were marked differences of opinion about the continuation of counselling after a pregnancy had been established. While 24% of the men and 32% of the women egg donation patients felt that further counselling was unnecessary, 68 and 56% respectively agreed that continued counselling would be beneficial. This might suggest an element of concern among egg donation patients that unforeseen stresses might arise as a result of their treatment.

Perhaps the most interesting results of the survey were those which revealed patients' attitudes towards donors and their relationship with the child resulting from their donation. Patients were reasonably evenly divided about whether donors should be friends or relatives of the recipients but there was more uncertainty among IVF patients as to the acceptability of relatives as donors. There was an interesting difference between the male and female partners of egg donation patients on this point, with 60% of women agreeing that donors could be relatives compared with 44% of the men while 52% of the men disagreed compared to 28% of the women. There was much less certainty about telling the child that it had been conceived using donated eggs with a large majority of all patients being uncertain or disagreeing.   Feelings were even stronger about allowing a related donor maintaining contact with the child. Of the egg donation patients, none of the men agreed that a relative who donated eggs should be allowed to keep in touch with the child while only 16% of the women agreed.

Dr Bolton argued for a flexibility of approach toward egg donation but her survey served to underline the complexity of the issue and the inconsistency of attitude among patients.

Implications for the donor

Professor Janet Finch, Professor of Social Relations at the University of Lancaster, spoke about the implications for relatives who might donate eggs. She spoke from the background of her research on family obligations rather than as an expert in assisted reproduction.   Although her research had not specifically covered reproduction it had, nonetheless, revealed relevant information about the giving of assistance within families; how it operated, between whom and what kinds of obligation were felt.   It seemed that, even between quite close relatives, the principle of reciprocity was the foundation of such activities. There was a strong need to pay back what was given although the paying back need not be either direct or immediate.

Her research had investigated attitudes to kinship and obligations. In a survey this had revealed divided opinions about obligations, even between parents and children, where 57% of the sample believed that children had an obligation to look after their parents in old age but a significant 39% did not. But when questions were asked about reciprocity the answers were clearer. There were strong indications that, where people had a history of mutual support, this created an obligation to continue; where there was no such history the obligations were less clear. The principle of reciprocity, it seemed, over-rode all others in family relationships. Indeed, a series of 120 in-depth interviews, a sub-sample of the survey population, revealed that the principle of reciprocity was particularly strong between people of the same generation, of whom siblings are the prime example. Although many people are usually willing to give rather minor types of assistance to any sibling - lifts in the car or help with decorating - more major commitment will occur only where siblings have built up a relationship of direct mutual aid. If this was not the case it would be considered 'too much to expect'. The only situation where family relationships could bear a one-way form of support was the case where older generations give support to younger, especially parents to children.

Looking at this evidence about kinship, it was clear that a number of dilemmas would present themselves to a sister who is asked to donate eggs. First of all, she is being asked to give a gift which is well beyond the normal types of assistance which sisters give to each other, even if they do have a history of mutual support. Then the provision of the gift would involve her in medical procedures entailing both risk and discomfort. Finally, she is not only giving to her sister but also, by implication, to her brother-in-law. This is a particularly difficult element because of the ambiguity, within British kinship, about whether in-laws are really members of the family. Asking a sister to donate eggs to another infertile woman, a procedure used by some clinics to maintain donor anonymity, does not entirely circumvent these problems. She is still being asked to give a substantial gift to enable *her* sister to become pregnant. Beyond the act of egg donation, further dilemmas present themselves in terms of long term obligations. Is the donor sister expected to form a special relationship with the child or become involved in its care? What if the child is handicapped? Alternatively, she might be required to forgo any special relationship with the child, whatever her feelings.

Dr Finch suggested that egg donation between relatives constituted a gift of such magnitude that it could never be reciprocated. This derived from both its short term and its long term consequences. It could not be a once and for all gift because its consequences live and grow to be part of family, a constant reminder. In this way it was a different sort of gift to blood or bone marrow where the gift may be made to save a relative's life. Dr Finch emphasized that her findings related to the white majority in British society but she pointed out the British population is very varied in ethnic and racial terms and that kinship traditions from other cultures might be very different. However, she warned that formulating guidelines to suit the whole population would be immeasurably complex and to encourage donations between relations would be a public statement about the nature of kinship which did not align with most people's expectations and experiences and might have some unanticipated consequences.

Implications for the family

Professor Jean La Fontaine, a social anthropologist, suggested that anthropology had two points to contribute to the debate about in vitro fertilization: it can draw attention to the underlying conceptions of parenthood, putting them in a comparative perspective; and it can add further understanding of the English family system by drawing on our knowledge of systems of relationships. She drew attention to the distinctions between paternity and maternity and the fact that each role has a different relationship to the reproductive process. Because of this, although a child is believed to be equally the child of both parents, the principles which apply to donor insemination cannot simply be applied to egg donation in in vitro fertilization.

Professor La Fontaine pointed out that the existence of illegitimate children makes clear that the biological and social elements in fatherhood are separable. Children are often described as fatherless but this is a social not a biological description. Paternity is not a matter of genetics but, rather it depends on the man's marriage to the woman who bears the child. Marriage ensures that the children born to a married woman can be assumed to be the genetic children of her husband; hence the emphasis in the past on a wife's duty of fidelity and the double standards which exist about adultery. The physical relationship is less significant than the social one. In some societies if a man proves infertile he may ask a brother to sleep with his wife to beget a child which will be his, not that of the begetter. However, the fact that the begetter is a brother ensures that the child is of the right lineage and also ensures that the wife is not alienated from her lawful husband. In some societies the marital right to a woman's children may persist even after her husband's death. In British society donor insemination fulfils the same need and anonymity of the donor is accepted as the best means of preserving the husband's relationship with his wife.

Maternity cannot be separated from its biological elements. Pregnancy is a patently visible process and childbirth is an exclusively maternal function. Conception is far less significant socially in this context. Society generally accepts that the woman who carries a child to term and gives birth to it is its mother. This has now been enshrined as a principle in the Human Fertilisation and Embryology Act 1990. It is also clear that women value the process as one which legitimizes their status as mother. Childbirth marks the achievement of adult status for women in many societies; the demand for in vitro fertilization indicates that the same may be true in our own. It is questionable therefore whether a woman, whether related to the potential recipient or not, should be allowed to jeopardize her own chance of children to donate eggs. The suggestion that related women might act as egg donors arises primarily from a shortage of supply. There is also an argument that stresses the biological component of maternity which claims that it is superior to have a known donor; the fetus is less 'alien' and if the donor is a close relative the gift is a symbol of strong affection which related women are expected to have for one another. But if the donor remains childless difficulties may arise. Donors who were young at the time of the gift or were junior to the recipient might later come to resent what they came to see as a sacrifice extracted rather than a gift freely given. The gift may even become a weapon whereby to demand more than would be considered normal between two related women.

There are also possibilites for other disturbances in the family system arising from the linking through physical parentage of a couple who are not married and the potential claims of two women on one child. In fact five relationships may be involved: between donor and recipient, between the husbands of these two, between the donor and the recipient's husband and between the recipient and the donor's husband. Some of these relationships may be affected more than others.

If the donor and recipient are related there is the additional factor of what is expected of that relationship normally. If the donor is the sister of the recipient, the nature of the relationship between her and her brother-in-law needs to be considered. This is a relationship about which there is considerable ambiguity; she is identified with the wife but defined as a sister. It took 60 years for the ban on marriage to the deceased wife's sister to be lifted and considerable ambivalence about the idea still exists. But now that the wife's sister is marriageable, she has become rather more wife than sister. The possibility of a man's coming to see her as the mother of his child and becoming too close to her might cause his wife to feel jealous and cause difficulties in the donor's own marriage. Jealousy might also arise between the two husbands. The relationship between the recipient and the donor's husband is probably the least likely to generate problems but it may suffer the repercussions of difficulties in the other relationships.

An unacceptable relationship for egg donation is that between mother and daughter. The older generation generally has authority over the younger and maternal authority might be used to pressure a daughter into giving eggs. Alternatively, a woman who gives her daughter an egg might be more inclined than normal to use her authority to interfere in the child's upbringing and her relationship with both her daughter and her son-in-law might be affected as a result. The older generation might have a useful function as arbitrators in the cases of sister to sister donation where difficulties have arisen between the sisters and/or their husbands.

The generation of the child also needs consideration. The child resulting from IVF using a known donor and the donor's other children is important but may be less often discussed. Socially speaking, the relationship between these children will be that of first cousins but genetically they will be half-siblings. The law bans marriage between half-siblings but not between cousins. Dr Bolton demonstrated that the tendency was for IVF patients not to want to tell their children about their origins but not to do so might involve the parents conniving at incest. The precedent from adoption would seem to indicate that a child should be told of its genetic origins when there is IVF using an egg from a closely related donor.

Implications for the child

Professor Michael Freeman of University College London, a specialist in Family Law, addressed the legal implications of egg and embryo donation. At the time of the meeting, the Family Law Reform Act 1987 had made the provision that children born to married women as a result of donor insemination could be treated in law as legitimate, provided that their husbands had consented to the procedure, but this principle had not been extended to egg or embryo donation. As the husband of the gestational mother was now treated as the father of the child the need for consistency seemed to dictate that there should be a presumption in favour of regarding the gestational mother as the mother rather than the egg donor. This was the solution favoured in the Warnock Report (para. 6.8)[7] and, eventually, the solution arrived at in section 27(1) of the Human Fertilisation and Embryology Act 1990. The Act makes provision for this definition to be waived in the case of adoption in section 27(2) and in the case of surrogacy in section 30 which requires the genetic parents to apply within six months of the child's birth for an order to be treated legally as its parents. Section 28 of the Act extends section 27 of the Family Law Reform Act 1987, with regard to paternity, to infertility treatments other than donor insemination except where a man's sperm have been used after his death to create an embryo. This makes a child legally fatherless in the case where a woman chooses to be inseminated with her husband's sperm after his death.

Professor Freeman also addressed the legal principles which might be applied to 'ownership' of embryos. The law does not recognize general property rights in human bodies or tissues. The control of human tissues remains with the possessor and once tissues or organs are removed from a person, that person has no legal right of recovery over them. At common law, therefore, individuals or couples whose gametes or embryos are frozen and stored in a bank have no property rights over them. The V/ILA made provision for the subsequent use of stored embryos through consent procedures; the matter is treated in a similar way by the Human Fertilisation and Embryology Act 1990.

The probity of egg donation between sisters is a social issue which is not covered by the law. Professor Freeman suggested that concern about the pressures on sisters or the effects on the child was based purely on speculation and that it behoved those who wished to interfere with freedom to adduce a strong moral case to do so. It was a practice which should be carefully monitored and a matter on which open and informed debate should and would continue.

Dr Jill Hodges, a child psychiatrist, spoke extrapolating from her studies of adopted children since there were no long term studies of children resulting from egg donation on which to draw. She started from the assumption that the child would be told of its origins although she acknowledged that with donor insemination this often was not the case. While this omission is generally to protect the husband or may stem from the wish of both parents to feel that the child is theirs rather than to aknowledge difference it is recognized that family secrets can exercise a very disruptive effect upon the relationships and the individuals involved.

In adopted children it has been shown that there are qualitative shifts in children's understanding of adoption with age. Pre-school generally do not understand the information they have been given although they may acquire a 'working adoption vocabulary'. By six/seven years of age, most have made a clear distinction between adoption and alternative ways of entering a family and have accepted that adoption is a permanent arrangement. Between eight and 11 years children begin to understand the uniqueness and some of the complications involved in adoptive status. It is only when they reach early to middle adolescence that children achieve something of an adult understanding of adoption as a legally based permanent arrangement. Adoption is relatively simple to understand compared to egg donation yet it only becomes understood when childhood is all but over.

At the emotional and psychological level children see adoption as a matter of rejection and acceptance and many adopted children, and adults, have an intense wish to know what their biological parents were like and will fantasize about their biological parents. Adoption agencies now generally feel that it is helpful for the adopted child's sense of identity and self esteem to have a full description of the biological parents and, of course, legislation now allows access to birth records at 18. The adoption example demonstrates that, not only may the biological facts present the child with an additional cognitive task in understanding its origins, but that what is understood of the biological facts also has an emotional meaning.

Using the adoption model as an example the situation arising from egg donation seems relatively simple. The child is born of its mother. It does not have to contend with the emotional problems of rejection. It is, genetically, its father's child. If the egg is donated by the mother's sister the child even has some genetic similarity to its mother. However, difficulties may arise because the mother and donor are related not only genetically but psychologically and emotionally. Their relationship to each other and their relationships with the child have emotional meanings both for themselves and for the child.

References

1. Kerenyi, T., Chitkara, U. (1981), 'Selective birth in twin pregnancy with discordancy for Down's syndrome', *N Engl J Med*, **304,** pp. 1525-27

2. Rodeck, C. H., Mibashan, R. S., Abramowicz, J., Campbell, S. (1982), 'Selective feticide of the affected twin by fetoscopic air embolism', *Prenat Diagn*, **2**, pp. 189-94

3. Evans, M. I., Fletcher, J. C., Zador, I. E., et al. (1988), 'Selective first trimester termination of octuplet and quadruplet pregnancies: clinical and ethical issues', *Obstet Gynaecol,* **71**, pp. 289-96

4. Keown, J., (1987), 'Selective reduction of multiple pregnancy', *New Law Journal,* **137, no 6335,** pp 1165-66

5. Cochrane, A. (I 972), *Effectiveness and Efficiency: random reflections on health services,* Nuffield Provincial Hospitals Trust

6. Bolton, V., Golombok, S., Cook, R. et al (1991), 'A comparative study of attitudes towards donor insemination and egg donation in recipients, potential donors and the public', *Journal of psychometric Obstetrics and Gynaecology,* **12,** pp. 217-228

7. *Report of the Committee of inquiry into Human Fertilisation and embryology* (1984), Cmnd 9314, HMSO, London

6 The Interim Licensing Authority

The Consultation document

The Government was slow to take action after the publication of the Warnock Report. On 10 December 1986, a consultation document was published entitled: 'Legislation on Human Infertility Services and Embryo Research';[1] many felt this was a way of delaying any action, particularly since a general election was looming and the issues concerned were bound to be controversial. However, the Government's position, as stated in the document, was that: 'the range and complexity of the issues raised by the Warnock Report and the strength and diversity of opinion expressed make it desirable that there should be a further period for consultation before any legislation is drafted'.[2]

The consultation document itself contained a brief account of the main infertility treatments considered in the Warnock Report, namely: IVF, donor insemination, egg donation, embryo donation and surrogacy. The development of gamete intra-fallopian transfer or GIFT, was mentioned as one of the developments since the Warnock Report was published; this technique involves the collection of eggs and sperm and placing them together directly into the fallopian tubes. The first pregnancy resulting from this technique was reported in 1984. Other developments since the Warnock Report which were mentioned in the consultation document were the passing of the Surrogacy Arrangements Act in 1985 to prevent the development of commercial surrogacy agencies in Britain; the setting up of the Voluntary Licensing Authority and the introduction of three Private Members' 'Unborn Children (Protection)' Bills aimed at prohibiting human embryo research, of which one was introduced by Enoch Powell MP and two were introduced by Ken Hargreaves MP; all of these attempts failed to complete their passage through the House of Commons due to insufficient time being available. Since the Warnock Report was published there had been other advances in IVF both in the UK and overseas. The most notable of these were the improved techniques for preserving human embryos by freezing to allow their transfer in a future cycle and the injection of sperm directly into the eggs where there was severe male factor infertility, to allow the creation of embryos; the latter of these had not yet been used in clinical practice. In the two years since the Warnock Report major developments had been made in IVF and this emphasized the need for some guidance for the scientists and doctors working in the field.

One recommendation of the Warnock Report on which there was very little disagreement was that there was a need for some form of regulation of IVF. Those involved with the work welcomed the opportunity of having a regulatory body to protect them against claims of unethical behaviour and those who were against the work considered that, if it were to be continued, it should be under the control of a regulatory body so that the scientists and doctors were not given a completely free hand. The consultation paper set out and sought views on three options for the control of infertility services.

Option A   The establishment of a statutory licensing authority to regulate certain types of infertility treatment, as recommended by the Warnock Report.

Option B   Direct control of certain treatments by the Secretary of State, as suggested in the Private Members' Bills which had been presented to Parliament.

Option C   Voluntary professional self-regulation in the way that the Voluntary Licensing Authority regulated IVF and the Royal College of Obstetricians and Gynaecologists governed the provision of donor insemination.

The most controversial issue raised in the Warnock Report was that of research on human embryos. The majority view of the Warnock Committee was that research involving human embryos up to 14 days after fertilization should be allowed to continue, provided that certain controls were in place to ensure that the human embryo was afforded some protection in law. The consultation paper set out the main arguments advanced in favour of and against embryo research and came up with a novel approach whereby Parliament would be offered alternative sets of draft clauses, one clause following the recommendations of the Warnock Report and the other, the suggestions in the Unborn Children (Protection) Bills. The Government had decided at any early stage that it should take a position of neutrality during the parliamentary and public debates on this issue and, following the long-standing tradition, Members of Parliament were to be given a free vote on the issue which was ultimately a matter of conscience.

In addition to these two main issues, the consultation paper also sought views on issues such as: the legal status of children born as a result of donation of sperm, eggs or embryos; how such donations should be recorded and what, if any, information should be made available to the child; the availability of counselling for infertile couples; whether surrogacy arrangements should be made unenforceable by law etc. Around 200 replies were received to the consultation document and, on most issues, there was a clear response; for example, 70% of those who responded supported option A, the establishment of a statutory licensing authority to regulate infertility treatment. The issues on which opinion was sharply divided were embryo research and the information which should be made available to children born as a result of donation.[3] The VLA's response supported option A; it had always been intended that the voluntary regulation of IVF would be an interim measure until a statutory authority was established and this view was reiterated in the VLA's response to the consultation document. The VLA agreed with the recommendations in the Warnock Report on the research issue and these were reflected in the guidelines currently being used by the VLA. The Authority also followed the Warnock recommendation that only basic information about the donor's ethnic origin and genetic health should be made available to children born as a result of donation. The Authority stressed the importance of maintaining anonymity of donors, for fear of discouraging donors as appeared to have happened in Sweden when anonymity was withdrawn. It was felt that this could have serious implications for the provision of donor insemination in the country. The consultation document had used the term 'embryo' throughout, whilst acknowledging that the term 'pre-embryo' was preferred by some.

The White Paper

Almost exactly 12 months after the consultation document had been published the Government, in November 1987, released a White Paper: 'Human Fertilisation and Embryology: A Framework for Legislation'.[4] This expanded on the information in the consultation document and reflected the views received from those consulted; the issues on which there was most disagreement were left open for further discussion in Parliament. The White Paper set out the proposed remit, function, composition and licensing powers of the new statutory licensing authority; it also set out the criteria for licensing which were to be debated at length at later stages of the legislative process; these were:

'1. any [research or] treatment involving human embryos created in vitro, or procured from the womb of a woman (eg by lavage)';

2. treatments involving the use of donated gametes (eg AID) or donated embryos;

3. the storage in an arrested state of development of human gametes or embryos for use at a later stage. (This is currently achieved by freezing using cryo-preservatives);

4. the use of diagnostic tests which involve the penetration by human sperm of an animal ovum.[5]'

The effect of these criteria was that new treatment techniques such as GIFT, which had been developed since the Warnock Report, would only be a licensable activity where donated gametes were used. These criteria were used by the Government to justify their strong resistence to including GIFT within the legislation, although the way in which these criteria were chosen and whether the criteria excluded GIFT, or whether the decision to exclude GIFT moulded the criteria, is a matter of debate. In its response to the White Paper, the VLA expressed its support for the inclusion of GIFT and expressed the view it was to repeat many times, that its exclusion was inconsistent since both IVF and GIFT required gamete preparation and handling and both raised the same issues about the number of gametes or embryos to be replaced in single cycle. The VLA also disagreed with the use of the term 'embryo' in the legislation since, biologically, it argued, the term embryo is only correct after the development of the primitive streak at around 14 days; the introduction of sperm and eggs stimulates cell division which may or may not result in the formation of an embryo, more likely it will not. The VLA preferred to use the term 'pre-embryo' for the period up to 14 days after fertilisation although, in view of the accusations made against the Authority for using this term as a way of disguising its true nature, it is not surprising that the Government, which was determined to remain neutral, did not accept this. One of the reasons given by the Government was that the term embryo was used in the Warnock Report; Dr Anne McLaren, the well renowned biologist, who was a member of the Warnock Committee, has put on record that, with hindsight, she regretted not pursuing this point more strongly at the Committee's early discussion.[6] Another issue on which the VLA disagreed with the proposals in the White Paper related to the costs of funding the new SLA. The White Paper proposed that 'Provision will bemade for contributing towards the costs of the SLA from public funds, although it will be expected to meet a large proportion of its expenditure from fees collected in connection with its licensing activity'.[7] The VLA was concerned that the majority of patients, who were treated in the private sector, would have the licence fees passed onto them and that any fees charged to NHS centres would further reduce the already extremely limited provision of NHS treatment for infertility. It was feared that many centres, which were already operating on a shoe string budget, would be forced to close down if licence fees were payable.

The Warnock Report had recommended that certain types of research, such as cloning and techniques aimed at modifying the genetic constitution of an embryo, should be prevented through guidance from the new authority about research which was unlikely to be considered ethically acceptable under any circumstances. The Government decided to take this one step further and proposed, in the White Paper, a complete prohibition on certain types of research within the legislation, thus making any breach of the prohibition a criminal offence. Should new developments make any of the prohibited research appropriate, an affirmative resolution from Parliament would be required.

In view of the sensitive nature of the issues covered, time was made available for debate in both Houses of Parliament in the early part of 1988. In introducing the White Paper in the House of Commons, Tony Newton MP, the Minister for Health, stated that the principles behind the White Paper were: 'that due respect must be given in law to the presence of human life, the desire not to cut off hope unnecessarily from infertile couples and others who may be helped by the new development and that the welfare of children born as a result of such treatments must be of paramount importance'.[8]

Official recognition

After the third round of consultation, the Warnock Report, the consultation document and the White Paper, it was largely expected that the long awaited Human Fertilisation and Embryology Bill would be introduced into the 1988/89 session of Parliament; in the event this was not the case. This left the VLA in a difficult situation. It had originally been set up for 18 months to two years, and funding from the Medical Research Council and the Royal College of Obstetricians and Gynaecologists had been agreed on that basis. Times were hard and the MRC was turning down much good research, through lack of funds. It was becoming more and more difficult for the MRC to justify its expenditure on regulating clinical practice rather than on research. The RCOG was also having difficulties, having been badly affected by the stock-market crash of October 1987, and subsequently was forced to reduce its contributions to the costs of the VLA by three-quarters. The President of the RCOG made it clear that this in no way reflected any lack of support for the work of the Authority and was merely a financial consideration. The Authority was housed within an office at the MRC Headquarters in Park Crescent, which was already overcrowded; when the Chairman needed to work at the Authority's office, it was on a borrowed chair and at the corner of a desk. The Authority had three staff all of whom had other considerable responsibilities and duties within the MRC. The Authority had no dedicated secretarial support and had to rely on the MRC's typing pool which frequently caused long delays in processing work because of other pressures on this facility. In addition to these practical administrative difficulties members of the Authority, who had agreed to give up their time for the work of the Authority, were finding it increasingly difficult to give an ad infinitum commitment and three of the members, who had increasing other commitments, were forced to resign. The Authority decided that if it was to continue with its work, it needed to know how long it was likely to be in existence and to have some formal recognition from the Government, including financial support, to enable the Authority to maintain the high standards it had set itself. Without adequate resources serious consideration needed to be given as to whether the Authority could continue.

The Chairman of the Authority met Mrs Edwina Currie MP, the then Junior Health Minister, to discuss these and other issues. Following this meeting a number of changes took place within the Authority. In line with the White Paper, the Government were insistent that licence fees should be charged but the Authority fought this strongly on the following grounds:

1.   The Authority had no statutory right to charge licence fees; if a licence was withdrawn it was because the centre was not abiding by the Authority's guidelines or was not functioning in line with best practice. Centres were therefore anxious not to lose their licence. If a licence was withdrawn merely for non-payment of fees, the Authority would not have the same moral force.

2.   If a fee were to be charged the question arose of the level at which it should be set. To charge a token fee would be costly to administer and would be unfairly weighted against the smaller centres and those treating NHS patients. The alternative would be to charge only those centres treating private patients but this could endanger the frail structure of those centres which provided a service for NHS patients by ploughing back the fees obtained from private patients.

3.   A precedent for a body such as the VLA, which was set up in anticipation of legislation, not charging fees, was set by the Advisory Committee for Animal Research which set the standards for the Animals (Scientific Procedures) Act 1986.[9] Licence fees were only introduced after the passing of legislation. The Authority still disagreed in principle with the idea of charging licence fees for the regulation of infertility treatment.

Finally, these arguments were accepted and an announcement was made in the House of Commons on 16 December 1988[10] that a contribution of around £45,000 would be provided towards the Authority's running costs; this was to cover the costs of secretarial support, word-processing equipment and the short fall caused by the reduced contribution from the RCOG. Having originally wanted nothing to do with the Authority, the Government finally gave recognition to the VLA.
In order to reflect this and to remind those concerned that the VLA was only ever meant to be a temporary measure, the word 'voluntary' was removed from its title. This, it was believed, conjured up images in the minds of some of well-meaning, ill-informed volunteers seeking to control this very difficult medical field. The Authority decided to change its name to the Interim Licensing Authority with effect from the publication of the Fourth Annual Report in May 1989.

Egg donation and sterilization

Although some newspapers and journals picked up on the implications of the Authority's change of name with reports of the VLA 'getting as impatient as the rest of us with the Government's sluggishness in introducing legislation',[11] most of the articles concerned a report which had appeared in that week's Sunday Times entitled, 'Blackmail at fertility clinics'[12] which reported that some centres were offering free sterilization to women who were prepared to donate their eggs to infertile couples. 'The implication was that women awaiting sterilization were being pressured into donating eggs, and that women on a long waiting list could jump the queue and be admitted into a private hospital at no charge, for the procedure, if they agreed to be donors. The media were not prepared to accept 'a wait and see' attitude from the Authority and at a meeting held immediately after the Press Conference a decision was taken on the issue. Members decided that egg donation could not be compared with sperm donation, for which payment was made, since the hyperstimulation regime given to women entailed certain risks. For this reason it was considered that egg donation should remain an altruistic act. The Warnock Report had taken a similar line on payment for human gametes and embryos stating that 'the sale or purchase of human gametes or embryos should be permitted only under licence from, and subject to, conditions prescribed by the licensing body and therefore unauthorised sale or purchase should be made a criminal offence'.[13] A letter was sent to all licensed centres stating that 'The Authority considers that any form of inducement to any woman to give eggs, such as the offer of free sterilization, is equivalent to payment for gametes and is unacceptable. The Interim Licensing Authority is not prepared to license centres adopting this practice and furthermore it is assumed that once established, a Statutory Licensing Authority will make this a criminal offence. The Authority accepts that a number of women may wish to donate their eggs for purely altruistic reasons and this is quite acceptable provided that no inducement of any kind, is offered and the patient receives adequate counselling about the risks of egg collection procedures and ovulation induction techniques. Donors should remain anonymous in line with the Authority's guidelines'.

Following this statement, the Authority received numerous letters from centres giving their views about the propriety of offering sterilization in return for donating eggs; it soon became apparent that the issue was not as clear-cut as originally envisaged. In some centres women were offered free sterilization in return for donation but, if the patient decided to change her mind, the operation was still performed at no charge; was this inducement? Although, from a survey carried out in Scotland[14] it had been shown that altruism alone did prompt the giving of eggs for both research and treatment: the question being raised among centres and in the media, was whether altruism alone could now satisfy an ever-expanding demand amid decreasing availability. The problem of the shortage of egg donors was intensified by the Authority's guideline that donors should remain anonymous, as outlined in previous chapters.   Legally, it could be argued that the same considerations apply as those considered in the Human Organ Transplants Act 1989, which created the offence of making or receiving 'any payment for the supply of, or for an offer to supply, an organ which has been or is to be removed from a dead or a living person and is intended to be transplanted into another person whether in Great Britain or elsewhere .[15] The definition of 'organ' in this Act rules out the possibility of it applying to gametes or embryos but the analogy is clear. Indeed to forbid financial inducement for egg donation would have been consistent with the prohibitions in this Act as well as those in both the Peel Report of 1972[16] and the Polkinghorne Report of 1989[17] covering the sale of fetal tissue; by tradition, blood donation, in Britain, has always been without payment. The Dutch Government, in order to prevent the sale of eggs, had banned the implanting of embryos generated from donated eggs.

In order to give the issue a full hearing and so that all aspects of it could be discussed and debated, the Authority included the question of the propriety of offering free sterilization in return for egg donation, on the agenda for the meeting of centres and ethics committees on 14 February 1989.   Mr Peter Brinsden, the Medical Director of Bourn Hall, presented the case in favour of using this method to recruit donors and Professor Sir Malcolm Macnaughton, a member of the ILA, put forward the opposing view for discussion.   Mr Brinsden set out the advantages of using patients undergoing sterilization: they are on the whole young and parous and therefore healthy eggs could be expected.   They are usually well motivated and would be required to undergo surgery for the sterilization, whereas those donating purely altruistically would undergo surgery for no medical reason.   The main disadvantages were the additional time commitment for injections, consultation and monitoring and the small risk of hyperstimulation of the donor's ovaries.   In Cambridge the question of egg donation was first raised with the patient by the General Practitioner who would explain what was involved and if the patient was interested she would be referred to Bourn Hall for consultation and counselling. The patient was free to change her mind at any time and the sterilization would still be carried out at no charge.   Most of the patients would be receiving sterilization within the National Health Service and therefore the operation would be free of charge regardless; the only possible inducement could be that the procedure would be performed in a private as opposed to an NHS establishment. By far the majority of those at the conference, including the representatives from ethics committees, were in favour of allowing centres to offer sterilization techniques in return for donating eggs and the ILA agreed to reconsider the issue in the light of the points raised. The difficult problem facing the Authority was to weigh up and, if possible, reconcile, the various interests:

1. the interest of the patient seeking sterilization in having the operation (if indicated) skilfully performed with the least avoidable stress or delay;

2. the interest of an infertile woman in receiving donated oocytes, when indicated, in the course of her treatment;

3. the interest of other patients waiting, whether for sterilization or for infertility treatment, further down the list;

4. the interest of medical research dependent upon donated gametes;

5. the interest of the clinic in its own financial stability and, in particular, in being able to fund research and to offer treatment to patients who are unable to afford their needs;

6. the interest of the professions and agencies offering the service in their own integrity, and the interest of the public in being assured of it.

In attempting to do this, the Authority looked to the definition of 'inducement' as being persuasive, morally or materially to action not otherwise contemplated; this would include an appeal to altruism and therefore could not always be seen as improper. There was no doubt among the members that improper inducement, ie a persuasive which takes advantage of a person's needs or vulnerability, or prompts action against the individual's own legitimate interests, was not acceptable. This distinction between 'proper' and 'improper' inducement appeared to give the Authority a way forward; a way of protecting patients who could be vulnerable and at risk of exploitation whilst also easing the shortage of donor eggs available for treatment and research. It was decided that centres should be allowed to offer free sterilization in return for donated eggs, provided that strict guidelines issued by the Authority were met. Each centre wishing to offer free sterilization to women would be required to apply, in writing, to the ILA for permission to do so and each centre's application would be judged independently. In order to ensure that every woman was fully informed of what she was undertaking and knew her rights, the ILA was to provide an information booklet which was to be read by every patient considering donation. The Authority would also provide a consent form to be signed before any procedures were undertaken. The information booklet for patients, 'Egg Donation: Your Questions Answered' (see Appendix 4), was made available with the release of the Fifth Annual Report[18] and contained guidelines for centres wishing to offer egg donation as follows:

'The following general conditions must be taken into account when receiving donated oocytes from both those donating for purely altruistic reasons and those receiving free sterilisation or other operative procedures:

(a)   Skilled and independent counselling, by someone other than the medical practitioner involved in the procedure, must be available to the donor to ensure that sufficient information has been given and understood, particularly in relation to discomfort and risk; and that the donor, if she consents, does so with her judgement unimpaired. The counsellor should look for stability of purpose so that neither consent nor withdrawal during treatment would be lightly undertaken.

(b)   The donor must know that she is free to withdraw consent to the egg donation at any time without threat of financial penalty and, where appropriate, without impairment of her interest in the successful conduct of the primary operation.

(c)   The centre must be prepared to accept, in the event of withdrawal after preparation for egg recovery has begun, the financial loss incurred.

(d)   The donor must be informed of the purpose for which her eggs will be used (ie research or donation to another woman for clinical purposes) and the centre at which the eggs will be used. Eggs must not be sold.

(e)   The donor must be given a copy of the information booklet provided by the ILA. The consent form at the back of the booklet must be signed by the donor and retained in the records of the centre where the donation took place.

(f)   The local Ethics Committee must satisfy itself that the conditions both can and will be met in the centre for which it is responsible.'

The Authority also required the following general conditions to be taken into account when offering free sterilization (or other related surgery) to women in return for donated oocytes.

'(a)   Centres wishing to offer free sterilisation to women in consideration of their donating oocytes must apply in writing to the ILA for permission. Each centre's application will be judged independently.

(b)   The discussion of egg donation must be entirely separate from discussions concerning the management and clinical care of the patient for whom the sterilisation or other operation may be indicated. Only when those decisions have been made may the question of egg donation be raised.

(c)   The fact of egg donation alone should not entitle a patient to transfer to a shorter list or faster lane for sterilisation; such a transfer must have its own clinical justification.'

This can be seen as one of the ways in which the ILA and the centres worked together to provide a mutually satisfactory solution so that the needs of all those involved were met. The centres were happy to abide by the guidelines and, by the time the Authority finished its work in July 1991, eight centres had been given permission to offer free sterilization to patients in return for their donating eggs. The information booklet was well received and more than 3,000 copies were distributed.

Licensed research

Anticipating that legislation would be forthcoming in the near future and that one of the most contentious issues would be that of whether research on human embryos should be allowed to continue or be prohibited, the ILA decided to issue a factual report describing the research licensed by the Authority, the potential benefits of such research and what research was planned for the future.[19] It was intended that this report would have as wide an audience as possible including MPs and Peers. The Authority had discussed at some length, before reaching this decision, how strongly it could be seen to support continued research; although it was not appropriate for the ILA to campaign it was considered appropriate for the Authority to provide facts on the implications of stopping research, in order to counter the opposing arguments being put forward by the so-called 'pro-life' lobby. This document was sent to all MPs and Peers in 1989 and was distributed widely in other areas.

Success rates

As far back as 1979 it had been recognised that there was a need to collect data on the number of attempts at IVF and the outcomes of these attempts. The ILA began to collect these data in 1985 in a very simplistic format. Each centre completed a questionnaire at the end of each year stating how many cycles they had performed, how many egg collection and embryo transfer procedures had been undertaken and how many pregnancies resulted from these attempts. This very basic information was collated and analysed and the cumulative figures were published annually in the Authority's reports. Although the Authority held the data for each individual clinic, these were never released. Other countries in the world, notably Australia, New Zealand and France, were collecting far more detailed information including epidemiological data and these were more beneficial to patients, centres and those planning health care resources. The Authority therefore decided to embark on a more detailed data collection operation. After negotiation with the Office of Population Censuses and Surveys (OPCS) and the Government, it was agreed that the exercise would be set up in collaboration with the Medical Statistics Division of OPCS. Rather than collect data annually, it would be collected prospectively on data sheets designed to form part of the patient's medical records. The forms were discussed at a meeting for centres and attempts were made to include the information required by different groups, to satisfy the Authority's needs for data and to reconcile the views of those who wanted short forms with only basic information and those who were prepared to provide more comprehensive data in order to reap the benefits of the increased availability of information.

In April 1989 all centres were circulated with data collection forms to be backdated to 1 January 1989 and to be completed for all future cyclesof IVF or GIFT. Centres who were offering GIFT only, although not required to complete the forms since they were not licensed centres, did so on a voluntary basis and the response was very positive. The first analyses of these data were published in the Authority's Sixth Annual Report.[20]   In the first year in which the forms were completed, 10,413 IVF and 3,079 GIFT treatment cycle forms were returned. It had been expected that there would be difficulty in collecting the outcome data since some patients return abroad after treatment or do not notify the centre of the outcome. In fact, the response was overwhelming with over 95% of IVF outcome forms and 93% of GIFT outcome forms returned.

The new data collection forms allowed more sophisticated analyses of the data so that the success rates by women's age, indications for treatment, number of previous attempts, primary/secondary infertility and by UK and overseas residency could be calculated. The success rate, in terms of pregnancy rate per embryo transfer, continued to increase and this trend continued when the 1990 data were analysed as can be seen from table 6.1.

Another feature which continued was the variations between the success rates of clinics. For ease of analysis, the centres were divided into large centres (those performing more than 400 cycles of IVF per year), medium centres (performing 100-400 cycles) and small centres (performing less than 100 cycles of IVF). In

1988, the success rates for large centres ranged from 6.1% to 20.4%, for medium centres from 3.7% to 24.0% and for small centres from 0.0% to 15.2%. In the minds of the public, the media and the Authority this variation in success rates raised two questions. Should the Authority continue to license centres whose success rate was very low and should the Authority release the success rates of individual clinics? Both of these issues had been discussed numerous times within the Authority and at the press conference to release the fifth annual report the Chairman announced that any centre which had been operational for at least three years which had a live-birth rate per treatment cycle of consistently less than 6% per treatment cycle would be re-visited and might have its licence withdrawn. Five centres fell into this category and each was visited by a group from the Authority. The most common finding was that those centres tended to treat more difficult cases, such as older women and couples with male factor infertility. In one centre a number of egg collections were performed for women who were about to commence radiotherapy and wanted embryos frozen for their own future use. In such cases there was never any intention to transfer the embryos or to attempt to achieve a pregnancy but the cycles were included in the statistics and were classed as failed attempts. In some centres where the success was very low, it was recommended that for a period of six months, couples were only treated where the woman was less than 36 years old and infertility was caused by a tubal problem. This was to ensure that it was possible for that particular clinic to establish successful pregnancies, given the right circumstances. During this six month period one centre managed to achieve a pregnancy rate per treatment cycle of 11.3%. Once the centre had shown it could successfully establish pregnancies, a licence was issued for a further year. The centre then reverted to its old policy for selecting patients and subsequently to its lower success rate. The director of the clinic, whilst finding this a useful exercise, was determined not to discriminate against older women and those with more difficult cases, who were on the waiting list, for the sake of maintaining a 'respectable' success rate. This highlights one of the difficulties of the second issue raised: that of publishing individual centres' success rates. Had each centre's success rate been published in a 'league-table' format, as had been requested many times, there would be immense pressure on the staff in those clinics, particularly those in the private sector, to maintain high success rates. This would, by the nature of the work, often be at the expense of those who were less likely to be successful in treatment. It would also be very difficult to provide a table which was simple enough to be understood yet sophisticated enough to provide meaningful data. In considering success rates, factors such as age limits, types of infertility treated and whether stimulated or natural cycles are used, must be taken into account if comparable data are to be provided. The difficulty of dividing each centre's data into these groups for analysis is that some of the figures would be so low as to distort the figures, eg, a centre may only treat two women over 45 years old and if one were to get pregnant that particular centre would show a success rate of 50% for patients over 45 years of age. The data also appear to show that there is a learning curve in success rates; if new and smaller centres are publicized as having low success rates, they would be unable to attract clients in order to improve their rate. In time this could lead to smaller clinics closing down with only a small number of large, successful clinics offering treatment which would intensify the limitations on availability of treatment.

The opposing view, however, is also strong. For couples seeking IVF treatment the choice of centre is a crucial determining factor in their chance of success. Without published success rates the couple could be paying large sums of money and going through great emotional trauma with very little chance of achieving the desired outcome. It is argued therefore that couples have a right to know which are the most successful centres. Although this issue was discussed many times within the Authority and in the media, it was one over which the Authority had little control. The data were collected on a confidential basis and the Authority, having given an undertaking that the individual centre's success rates would not be published, had to respect this. The undertaking had been given so that centres would feel confident to send comprehensive and accurate information to the Authority. Since it was not a statutory authority it could not otherwise guarantee co-operation. The Authority decided that accurate and complete cumulative data were of such value as to merit being unable to publish a league table of success rates.

TABLE 6.1

IVF Data 1985-1990

	Patients	Cycles	Transfers	Pregnancies	Live Births	Preg rate/ transfer %	Live birth/ transfer %
1985	3,717	4,308	3,032	481	364	15.9	12.0
1986	4,687	7,043	3,798	754	605	19.9	15.9
1987*	7,488	8,899	5,592	980	760	17.5	13.6
1988	7,515	0,498	6,553	1,354	956	20.7	14.6
1989	8,790	10,413	7,363	1,599	1,157	21.7	15.7
1990	9,964	11,583	8,195	2,004	1,443	24.4	17.6

*Excluding one large centre with incomplete data

Availability of treatment

One of the arguments used by those who wished to see a league table published was that NHS provision for infertility treatment was so limited that couples were forced to pay large sums of money, which frequently involved borrowing money or remortgaging their home, in order to obtain treatment. This had been a concern of the VLA since it was established and had been referred to in all of its annual reports. Access to infertility treatment depended to a very large extent on the couple's geographical location and on their ability to pay. When the ILA finished its work in July 1991 there were only three licensed IVF centres which were wholly funded by the NHS: St Mary's Hospital in Manchester, The Royal Victoria Infirmary in Newcastle and the University Hospital of Wales, Cardiff. As infertility is not a life threatening condition there was a tendency for Health Authorities to give it a low priority for funding. Of the remaining centres, 28 were wholly private and the remainder made use of some NHS facilities such as accommodation, staff or equipment, whilst also charging the patient, or receiving funding from the treatment of private patients, or from charities. Some clinics which had originally treated patients free of charge were, as time went on, forced to levy charges to patients in order to continue their service. Most of these operated on a non-profit making basis so that the actual cost of running the centre was covered by charges for treatment. Many different methods, and combinations of methods, were used to fund infertility clinics. Many used a 'Robin Hood' system of using funds obtained from treating private patients to provide a service to others free of charge, some set up charities and relied upon donations and fundraising activities of staff and patient support groups, some relied upon research funds to pay for the treatment costs. In one centre the director took on an additional part-time job to raise the money to purchase the necessary equipment. The dedication of many of the staff and their determination to provide this service for their patients, in very difficult circumstances, was admirable.

One attempt to overcome the problem of patients' lack of finances, which was immediately condemned by the ILA and the media alike, was to offer IVF on credit, with the money, borrowed from the centre, being paid back over a three year period at interest rates of 13-15%. The Authority and other organizations such, as the British Medical Association and the National Association for the Childless expressed their concerns to the clinic and shortly afterwards the scheme was dropped. Another, less controversial, attempt to provide an IVF service for the local community was the development of a method of treatment known as 'transport IVF'. This technique, which was developed in France, combined treatment between a district general hospital (DGH) and an established IVF unit.

The patient selection, counselling and ovarian stimulation using standard techniques were performed by the staff at the DGH.   Following egg collection the fluid containing the eggs was taken by car to the IVF unit.   The embryologist then assessed and fertilized the eggs and any resulting embryos were transferred 48 hours later. An initial assessment of this technique showed that the average number of oocytes collected and fertilized did not differ significantly from those cycles performed solely at the IVF unit.   Another technique developed around the main theme of IVF was intra vaginal culture (IVC). This technique was also developed in France and involved eggs being collected and placed, together with the partner's sperm, in a small tube containing culture fluid. The tube was then sealed and inserted into the patient's vagina, being held in place by a contraceptive cap. After 24 48 hours the cap and tube were removed and the contents of the tube inspected for evidence of fertilization.   Any embryos resulting from the technique were transferred to the uterus in the usual way. This technique was also used by some centres who were offering a GIFT service with any spare eggs being fertilized in this way; instead of replacing any subsequent embryos into the uterus, the client would attend a licensed IVF centre where the embryos would be assessed and those of a sufficiently high quality would be frozen for the patient's own use in a future cycle, thus dispensing with the need for further stimulation and egg collection procedures.

The Tennessee case

The Authority was often asked to comment on issues which were reported internationally. One of these issues was a divorce case in Tennessee where a custody battle was taking place over seven fertilized eggs which had been stored before the couple's marriage broke down. The wife wished to use the embryos to establish a pregnancy but the husband did not wish her to have his child who would then suffer the pain of a broken home. The wife considered the embryos to be her 'pre-born children' and considered that she was the only person who had a right to them.   The status of the embryo is an issue which has been discussed at length in many countries around the world without agreement. The American Fertility Society issued guidelines stating that a pre-embryo is 'not a legal entity but, because of the potential to become a person, deserves special respect'.[21] The decision which the judge was forced to make was whether the embryos were marital property or children. If they were seen as property he had to consider an equitable division of them between the parties and if they were seen as children he had to decide who would be the better parent and what support the other party should give. The judge was reported as saying, 'I have absolutely no guidance, no direction, not only from the laws in this State, but indeed the world'.[22] In Britain, the Warnock Report had recommended strict limits to the storage of embryos and gave warning of 'legal and ethical complications that might arise over disposal of embryos whose parents have died or divorced or otherwise been separated'; it recommended that 'where there is no agreement between the couple the right to determine the use or disposal of an embryo should pass to the storage authority'.[23]

In view of the delay in preparing legislation on these issues, the fear that a similar case could happen in Britain escalated. Although the ILA's consent form included a statement that no frozen embryos could be removed from storage without the consent of both parties concerned, or the survivor, not all centres used this form and it was not certain that this would stand up in court. Calls were made from all areas for the Government to speed up its legislation; from centres, from patients, from pressure groups, religious groups and, indeed, from the ILA. In the Tennessee case the judge awarded custody to the wife but an appeal was immediately lodged by the husband and the decision was later overturned. This case was interesting because of the principles it raised and because of the increased pressure it brought to bear on the Government to introduce legislation.

The Human Fertilisation and Embryology Bill

Finally, in December 1989, the long-awaited Human Fertilisation and Embryology Bill was introduced to the House of Lords.   In introducing the Bill, The Lord Chancellor noted that it broke new ground in two respects. Firstly, because it was the first attempt to deal in legislation with the full range of problems created by the new reproductive technologies, and, secondly, in dealing with the research issue, it was the first time that a Bill had contained two subsections setting out alternative propositions and a third subsection indicating that only one of them could be in force at any one time. He paid tribute to the work of the Interim Authority stating,

'I should like at this point to pay tribute to the work of the Voluntary Licensing Authority...Although the new authority will in no sense be a direct descendant of the ILA, and will in its membership and functions be a different organisation in that it will have broader powers and function, I am sure it will find it useful to draw on that body's experience when it assumes its full powers...successful though that system (of voluntary regulation) has shown itself to be, it relies on good will and cooperation from the scientists and doctors involved. While I have no reason to think that cooperation and their responsible approach to these matters are in jeopardy, we ought, for everyone's peace of mind, to ensure that sensitive issues of this kind are dealt with in a clear legal framework.' "

As with the responses to the White Paper, the setting up of a statutory authority was almost unanimously accepted as being the right way forward.

Predictably, the issue of research was one of the most contentious issues. The main arguments used in support of continued research were as follows:

1. Up to 14 days after fertilization, the fertilized egg consists of a group of undifferentiated cells which could develop into a fetus but more than likely they will go to form the placenta and membranes which will surround the fetus. Only a very small proportion of the cells, and it is impossible to predict which ones, will go on to develop into a child. It is only after the appearance of the primitive streak, at around 14 days, that the fate of the cells is determined (hence the ILA's preference for the use of the term 'pre-embryo' to refer to this stage in development up to the appearance of the primitive streak).

2. The embryo does not have the potential to develop into a child unless it is implanted into the uterus of a woman; it has no personality of its own and should not therefore be afforded the status of an individual human being.

3. Much of the research using human embryos is species specific and therefore it is not acceptable to use animal models and then extrapolate the information to human beings; this would be putting both the woman and any potential child at serious risk and would be unacceptable.

4. Continuation of research would lead to considerable benefits; - this research has four main aims:

    i)   to improve in vitro fertilization techniques with the aim of improving the success rates;

    ii) to develop techniques for the diagnosis of severe genetic handicap prior to embryo transfer so that those who are carriers of such disorders could begin a pregnancy knowing that their child will not suffer from the disease of which they are carriers;

iii) to understand and prevent miscarriages;

iv) to develop simpler, safer and more reliable methods of contraception.

Set against these were the main arguments against research.

1. Research which leads to the destruction of the embryo is unacceptable because an embryo has the potential to become a child. Research on embryos therefore equates to the destruction of the child in the laboratory.

2. Neither the relief of infertility nor the advance in knowledge can justify the deliberate destruction of human embryos.

3. The 14 day limit proposed for research would be the beginning of a 'slippery slope' and, in subsequent years, there would be calls for this limit to be extended.

4. Relevant research could be done on other species of animal and is therefore not necessary.

5. Techniques for preimplantation diagnosis of genetic disease could be used for sinister purposes allowing sex selection to become the norm and selecting handicapped people out of the population.

6. Therapeutic research could be allowed provided that it is for the benefit of that individual embryo and that there is an intention to replace the embryo in a woman's uterus.

After much debate in the House of Lords, both during the Second Reading debate and the Committee stage of the Bill, on 8 February 1990 the Duke of Norfolk moved an amendment to delete the subsection allowing the new Authority to license research projects using human embryos up to 14 days after fertilisation. Their Lordships divided and the amendment was rejected by 234 to 80. Attempts to limit research by restricting it to embryos created in the course of providing treatment were also defeated by a large majority.

Main areas of debate

A summary of the main provisions of the Human Fertilization and Embryology Act will be covered later in this chapter, but first, some of the main issues of discussion during the passage of the Bill and some of the amendments which were moved will be examined. During the Committee Stage of the Bill, Lady Saltoun of Abernethy moved an amendment which sought to prohibit the provision of treatment to single women, lesbian couples or unmarried couples. Her grounds were that, in the case of single women, the child would be disadvantaged by only having one parent and children born to lesbian couples would lack a suitable male role model. If couples were unwilling to marry, it was usually because one partner wanted to be free to break up the partnership. Again, in such cases, the child may well end up with only one parent. This amendment was defeated by a majority of one.

The section of the Bill which authorized interspecific fertilization 'for the purpose of developing more effective techniques for determining the fertility of human sperm if the resulting embryo is immediately destroyed' caused some concern. The intention of the section was to allow the hamster oocyte penetration test, whereby human sperm is placed with a prepared hamster egg to see if the sperm is able to penetrate the egg and thereby determine the fertilizing capacity of the sperm. An amendment to prevent this test being used was defeated by 61 to 36, although the wording of the section was revised during the Report Stage of the Bill to restrict the practice to the use of the egg of a hamster or any other animal specified in directions.

A controversial amendment was moved by the Earl of Halsbury. This was to include GIFT among treatments requiring a licence from the statutory authority. Although nobody spoke against the amendment Baroness Hooper, the Parliamentary Under-Secretary of State at the Department of Health, informed the House that 'The Government believe that GIFT as such should not be regulated by the Bill but its use should, like other treatments, be a matter for clinical judgement of the doctor concerned as in the case of other kinds of treatment. Therefore we do not feel able to accept the amendment'.[25] The issue of GIFT was raised again during the Report Stage of the Bill where, despite acknowledging the support of the medical and scientific community and the ILA for GIFT to be regulated, the Lord Chancellor again reiterated the Government's resistance and delayed a decision until after the Royal College of Obstetricians and Gynaecologists had reached a collective decision later in that month. Because of the timetable of the Bill, further discussion would take place in the House of Commons. A similar pattern was followed for an amendment moved by Lord Ennals to remove the sections referring to centres paying a licence fee, which again was supported by the ILA. Baroness

Hooper replied to the amendment by stating that 'the Government think it important that those wishing to be licensed should be required to meet a significant proportion of the costs of that system, and indeed of the other costs incurred by the authority'.[26] When the issue was raised again at the Report Stage both parties stuck rigidly to their view and it was agreed that a meeting would be held between those with opposing views in order to reach a suitable compromise before the Third Reading of the Bill.   The Government's view prevailed and, despite strong opposition, the Bill was not amended to remove the offending clauses.

In introducing the Bill into the House of Commons, Kenneth Clarke, the Secretary of State for Health, described it as 'one of the most significant measures to be brought forward by a Government in the last 20 years' dealing with 'matters that are fundamental to the well-being of our society'. He expressed his wish that 'the interim licensing authority sponsored by the Medical Research Council and the Royal College of Obstetricians and Gynaecologists, can continue the work that it began at our request in 1985',[27] this despite the lack of interest from the Department of Health when the Authority was established. Many of the issues which had been discussed in the House of Lords were debated again in the Commons, such as research, GIFT, licence fees and treatment for single women. The Government's views on GIFT and licence fees were expressed very clearly in Mrs Bottomley's closing speech of the Second Reading debate in which it was made clear that the Government would oppose any attempt to include GIFT under the remit of the new Authority or to block the charging of licence fees.

In order to ensure that the ILA was accurately reflecting the views of the GIFT centres it registered, a questionnaire was sent asking their views on the form of regulation required and on 14 June, Dame Mary Donaldson wrote to all MPs giving them the results of the questionnaire. The Authority had written to 74 directors representing the 81 centres registered with the Authority as offering this treatment, 45 of which were offering GIFT in centres not licensed for IVF. Centres were asked to give their preferred option of the four offered:

1.   full licensing and regular inspections by the Statutory Licensing Authority, as with IVF;

2.   monitoring and guidelines by the SLA on a less formal basis;

3.   guidelines issued by the RCOG;

4.   no regulation.

Replies were received from 50 directors representing 57 centres (70%). Of those who replied 54% favoured option 1, 25% favoured option 2, 16% favoured option 3, 3% favoured option 4 and 2% did not support any of the options offered. Overall the ILA found that 98% favoured some form of regulation and 88% favoured regulation by the new Authority.

In the Committee Stage an amendment to include GIFT was tabled by Jo Richardson and, after an unsuccessful attempt by Mr Robert Key to show that, because of the way the Bill was worded, GIFT was a licensable activity, a vote was taken which resulted in 9 votes for the Ayes and 9 votes for the Noes. The Chairman, Mr Michael Shearsby, had the casting vote and voted with the Noes. The issue was raised again during the Report Stage when the Government introduced amendments to the effect that, subject to the affirmative resolution procedures, GIFT, and other similar techniques involving the placing of sperm and eggs into a woman, could be brought within the licensing system should the Government consider it to be necessary in the future. This was accepted, as was an amendment giving the Authority the power to give guidance, in its code of practice, on GIFT. Furthermore, the Government had received an assurance that the Royal College of Obstetricians and Gynaecologists would write to its members reinforcing the advice given by the Authority on matters relating to the practice of GIFT. The Government therefore moved some way towards meeting the concerns without changing its policy on the criteria for licensable activities. There was no compromise on the issue of fees, however, even though the same result was obtained in Committee, with the vote against the amendment depending on the casting vote of the chairman.

When the Bill reached the Commons, as amended in the House of Lords, the clause allowing research was already in place. In order to give MPs the same choice as was given to Peers, the Government tabled amendments to prohibit embryo research. The debate took place on the floor of the House, rather than in committee, and after much heated discussion in which the arguments mentioned above were presented with conviction, the amendment was defeated by 364 votes to 193. Thus ensuring that research involving the use of human embryos would be allowed to continue under licences issued by the new Authority. On the following day the whole House discussed amendments to the Abortion Act of 1967 and agreed to reduce the legal limit for abortion to 24 weeks, and to allow abortions after that time in certain limited circumstances. The issue of treatment for single women and lesbian couples was raised again in the debate in the House of Commons; an amendment to limit treatment to women being treated together with a male partner was moved by Mr David Wilshire in the Standing Committee. After the debate, he sought leave to withdraw the amendment, believing that the floor of the House was the most appropriate place to discuss an issue of such importance. Members of the Committee objected to the amendment being withdrawn and, as a single objection is sufficient to put the matter to a vote, the Committee divided and the amendment was defeated by 13 votes to four. The issue was raised again at the Report stage of the Bill with two amendments being moved, the first ensuring that any child born as a result of licensed treatment will have a father, by virtue of the Act; and the second adding that the requirement on the centre to take into account the welfare of the child includes 'the need of that child for a father'.[28] The first amendment was withdrawn because of a lack of time in the debate but the second was accepted by 226 votes to 174, and thus a partial victory was won by those who would see single women and lesbian couples prevented from receiving treatment. Although the Act does not prohibit this activity, in the minds of many, it makes treating such women harder to justify in terms of the Act.

While the Interim Licensing Authority was, again, thanked for the work it had undertaken in the preceding five years, not all MPs were as supportive; Dame Jill Knight, for example, said, 'The present interim licensing authority is deeply flawed not only because it is biased, one-sided and anxious to stifle all opposition, but because it is dishonest'.[29] These accusations caused much disquiet among the members of the Interim Authority and at a press conference to release the Authority's annual report held shortly afterwards, Dame Mary Donaldson called on Dame Jill Knight to 'come out from behind the skirt of Parliamentary privilege and repeat and explain her statement'; the challenge was not taken up.

The Human Fertilisation and Embryology Act 1990

The Human Fertilisation and Embryology Act received Royal Assent on 7 November 1990. The main provisions of the Act are set out below.

1.   The establishment of the Human Fertilisation and Embryology Authority with the following statutory duties:

i.   to inspect and issue licences to centres undertaking embryo research, gamete donation or the storage of gametes or embryos;

ii.   to publicize the services provided to the public by the Authority and centres providing licensed treatment and to provide information for donors and those seeking treatment;

iii. to keep a register of information about donors and treatments provided for identifiable individuals;

iv. to publish a Code of Practice giving guidance to centres on how they should carry out licensed activities;

v. to keep the whole field under review, whether the activities are licensed or not, and to make recommendations to the Secretary of State for Health, if he wishes the Authority to do so; and

vi. to perform any other functions specified in regulations.

2. The following activities are made a criminal offence:

i. bringing about the creation of an embryo or keeping or using an embryo, without a licence;

ii. placing in a woman a live embryo other than a human embryo or live gametes other than human gametes;

iii. keeping or using an embryo after the appearance of the primitive streak or later than 14 days after fertilization whichever is sooner;

iv. placing a human embryo in an animal;

v.. keeping or using an embryo in circumstances prohibited by regulations;

vi. replacing a nucleus of a cell of an embryo with a nucleus taken from a cell of any person, embryo or fetus;

vii. storing gametes or using for treatment the gametes of a third party without a licence;

viii. mixing the gametes of an animal with human gametes except under a licence which authorises the use of the hamster-oocyte penetration test; and

ix. storing or using gametes in a way prohibited by regulations.

These offences are punishable by up to ten years imprisonment depending on the offence committed.

3. Embryo research may be undertaken under a research licence from the Authority if it is considered that the research is necessary and desirable for one of the following purposes:

i. promoting advances in the treatment of infertility;

ii. increasing knowledge about the causes of congenital disease;

iii. increasing knowledge about the causes of miscarriage;

iv. developing more effective techniques of contraception;

v. developing methods for detecting the presence of gene or chromosome abnormalities in embryos before implantation; or

vi any other purposes as may be specified in regulations.

4. Centres are required, by law, to provide information about those for whom licensed treatment is provided.

5. It is a legal requirement for centres to take account of the welfare of the child (including that child's need for a father) in considering whether to offer treatment.

6. Counselling must be offered to all people considering licensed treatment.

7. The setting of a statutory storage period for gametes of ten years and embryos of five years, unless specified in regulations. Regulations allow for a longer period of storage where the person is under 45 years of age at the date of storage and is about to commence treatment eg. radiotherapy which may render them involuntarily sterile.

8. Centres must pay an initial fee and an additional fee before a licence is issued. The fees will vary over time, but currently 50% of the Authority's running costs are to be met from fees from centres.

9. The legal definition of mother and father are defined. The definition of mother is the carrying mother, ie in surrogacy the surrogate mother is the legal mother unless a Parental Order has been granted. Where donor insemination treatment is used, the woman's partner is the legal father of the child unless he can show that he did not consent to the procedure. If the woman does not have a male partner, the child is legally fatherless; the same is the case if a woman uses the frozen sperm of her husband or partner after his death.

10. The Authority is required to keep a register of information about treatment services provided for identifiable individuals, including information about donors. When a child reaches the age of 18 he/she may ask the authority if information held on the register indicates that he/she was born as a result of licensed treatment services. The Authority is required to give, on request, as much information as is specified in regulations. These regulations have not yet been made but section 31(5) of the Act states that identifiable infomation cannot be provided if, at thetime the gametes were used, the Authority was not required to give identifying information.

11. Surrogacy arrangements are made unenforceable in law by amending the Surrogacy Arrangements Act 1985.

12. The time limit for abortion is reduced to 24 weeks and later abortions are allowed under limited circumstances, by amending the Abortion Act 1967.

13. The legal position of the selective reduction of multiple pregnancy is clarified by amending the Abortion Act to make the miscarriage of any fetus, where the woman is carrying more than one, an offence unless carried out under the terms of the Abortion Act. The Human Fertilisation and Embryology Authority was to take up its full responsibilities on 1 August 1991 and the Interim Licensing Authority agreed to continue its work until that date.

References:

1. *Legislation on Human Infertility Services and Embryo Research. A Consultation Paper* (Cm46), HMSO, London 1986
2. Ibid page I paragraph 4
3. Cunningham, R. L., 'Legislating on Human Fertilization and Embryology in the United Kingdom', in *Statute Law Review,* pp. 214-227
4. *Human Fertilisation and embryology: A Framework for Legislation* (Cm259), HMSO, London 1987
5. Ibid page 3 paragraph 13
6. Anne McLaren (personal communication)
7. *Human Fertilisation and Embryology: A Framework for Legislation* op cit. page 4 paragraph 18
8. Hansard, House of Commons, 4 February 1988, column 1204
9. Animals (Scientific Procedures) Act 1986, HMSO, London
10. Hansard, House of Commons, 16 December 1988
11. *The Lancet,* 20 May 1989
12. *Sunday Times,* 14 May 1989 pp. 1 and 3
13. *Report of the Committee of inquiry into Human Fertilisation and embryology* (Cm9314), HMSO, London 1984, p. 79
14. Alder E.M., Baird D.T., et al (1986), 'Attitudes of women of reproductive age to in vitro fertilisation and embryo research', *J. Biosoc. Sci,* **18,** pp. 155-167
15. Human Organ Transplant Act 1989, HMSO, London
16. *The Use of fetuses and Fetal Material for Research* (The Peel Report), HMSO, London 1972
17. *Review of the Guidance on the Research Use of fetuses and Fetal Material,* Report of a Committee chaired by Dr John Polkinghorne (Cm762), HMSO 1989
18. Interim Licensing Authority for Human Fertilisation and Embryology (1989), *The Fifth Report*
19. Interim Licensing Authority for Human Fertilisation and Embryology (1989), *IVF Research in the UK: A Report on research licensed by the Interim Licensing Authority (ILA) for Human Fertilisation and Embryology 1985 1989*
20. Interim Licensing Authority for Human Fertilisation and Embryology (1990), *The Sixth Report*
21. American Fertility Society (1986), Ethical Considerations of the new reproductive technologies, *Fertility and Sterility,* **46 no 3,** Supplement I

22.   *Daily Telegraph*, 11 August 1989

23.   *Report of the Committee of Inquiry into Human Fertilisation and Embryology*, op cit.

24.   Hansard, House of Lords, 7 December 1989, columns 1009 and 1011

25.   Hansard, House of Lords, 6 February 1990, column 815

26.   Hansard, House of Lords, 13 February 1990, column 1288

27.   Hansard, House of Commons, 2 April 1990, columns 912 and 922

28.   Hansard, House of Commons, 20 June 1990, column 1019

29.   Hansard, House of Commons, Standing Committee B. Fourth Sitting 15 May 1990 (morning) column 13

7 From Voluntary to Statutory Regulation

The setting up of the HFEA

The membership of the Human Fertilisation and Embryology Authority was announced before the Act received Royal Assent. Its Chairman was to be Professor Colin Campbell, Vice-Chancellor of Nottingham University and its Deputy Chairman, Lady Brittan, magistrate and member of the Equal Opportunities Commission. Six members of the Interim Authority were to move over to the new Authority: two clinicians, two scientists and two 'lay' members (for the full membership of the HFEA see Appendix 6). Some members of the Interim Licensing Authority would have preferred the new Authority to be set up in a comparable way to the Animals Inspectorate set up under the Animals (Scientific Procedures) Act. In that case, the non-statutory body took on a statutory role and gradually members were replaced until a completely new membership was formed, thus gaining maximum benefit from the existing experience. Although there are advantages to such a system, it was not surprising that the Government decided against this option. The so called 'pro-life' lobby had been very critical of the Interim Authority and the Government was keen to ensure that those on all sides of the debate had confidence in the new Authority. One member of the new Authority expressed a personal view, at a public meeting, that the HFEA should

111

have nothing to do with the Interim Authority and should be a totally new organization with its own views and methods of working. What actually happened fell somewhere between these two extremes; the HFEA and the ILA had some cross membership and there was some contact between the two organizations.

Shortly before the Bill had begun its passage through Parliament the Department of Health had found new accommodation for the Interim Licensing Authority and seconded a member of its staff to assist the Authority's secretariat with the deluge of enquiries from the press and the public who wanted more information. The secretariat of the HFEA, all of whom were seconded from the Department of Health, later moved into adjoining rooms in the same building. This made for easier relations between the staff of the two organizations although both were very busy and had only limited time available to discuss issues of mutual interest. Two members of the HFEA's secretariat and the Chairman and Deputy Chairman attended ILA inspection visits to get an idea of how the ILA worked in practice and how the inspection procedure had been set up.

The HFEA took up its full responsibilities on 1 August 1991 which meant that for nine months both Authorities were in existence. This was a matter of concern for the Interim Authority on two counts. Firstly, it was worried that once centres knew that the HFEA was in existence they would no longer wish to be licensed by the ILA which would become something of a 'lame duck' and lose the respect it had earned over the years. This concern proved to be unfounded. The second concern was its inability, because of the lack of information available to its members and secretariat, to provide the answers and reassurance being sought by the centres who were worried about their future. The ILA felt that the HFEA might have been more forthcoming with information about its plans and was disappointed that it was not given the privileged position or advance information it felt it deserved. Members of the Interim Authority, who had worked for many years to set up a system which would, to a greater or lesser extent, be taken over by the statutory body, considered that despite its work in drawing up sensible guidelines and the international reputation it had developed, it was being pushed to one side by those involved in the new Authority. It appeared to some members that the HFEA was effectively reinventing the wheel going back over the fundamental issues the ILA had discussed, in detail, many times during its lifetime. The HFEA, however, as a new body with a different, although similar, role and a different membership, had to operate within a statutory framework and felt the need to discuss all issues in order to determine its own policy. Many of the members were new to the field and therefore had to quickly develop an understanding of the medical issues and the fundamental principles involved before being able to debate the more difficult ethical problems in detail. The HFEA was able to draw upon the experience of those who were members of both Authorities and were thus able to obtain clarification of the ILAs views where necessary. However, ultimately, the HFEA had to ensure that its policy represented the views of its own members. Consultation with the ILA took place, on both a formal and informal basis, where it was felt appropriate, but because of the potential for confusion it was not considered sensible for anyone outside the HFEA itself to be given information until the policy had been determined. Both bodies considered that it was important that any questions from centres about HFEA matters should be referred directly to HFEA staff and ILA matters should be dealt with by ILA staff.

In order to give the centres some information about what was planned Professor Campbell, the HFEA Chairman, addressed the ILA's meeting for centres and ethics committees on 14 February 1991. To the relief of many of those present he commented that 1 August 1991, when the HFEA took up its full licensing role, was not intended to mark a major change and it was hoped that many centres would hardly notice the transfer of responsibilities. Although the HFEA was a new body with certain statutory duties, it would continue to build on the work of the ILA.

Continued demand for ILA approval

A transitional period had been provided by the legislation so that, although all applications had to be submitted by 31 July 1991, any services being offered on or before that date could be continued until the outcome of the licence application to the HFEA was known or until 31 July 1992 whichever was sooner. Any research projects involving the use of human embryos which had been licensed by the ILA and started on or before 31 July 1991 could continue on the same basis as above. Rather than the amount of work and influence of the Interim Authority declining, as had been feared, it actually increased as centres rushed to get ILA approval for their centres and research projects before the HFEA took over. This was particularly true for research projects because, under the transitional arrangements, any research project which did not have ILA approval could not be started until a full inspection had been carried out by the HFEA. This would inevitably lead to delays in getting the projects off the ground. At the last meeting of the Authority, 14 research applications were considered, bringing the total number of research projects licensed by the ILA to 93 as shown in the table below:

TABLE 7.1

	New projects licensed	Cumulative total
1985	14	14
1986	9	23
1987	16	39
1988	12	51
1989	9	60
1990	15	75
1991(Jan-July)	18	93

Similarly, the number of centres licensed by the Authority increased over the six years it was in existence as shown in Table 7.2.

TABLE 7.2

	Number of centres licensed
1985	26
1986	33
1987	34
1988	38
1989	45
1990	53
1991	59

In the nine months between the HFEA being set up and the ILA finishing its work 16 new centres were inspected of which seven were refused a licence; two of these centres dealt with the problems highlighted by the Authority and licences were subsequently issued. At the same time a small number of centres were forced to close because of lack of funding. At the Authority's meeting in July five centres were given permission to use the SUZI technique (microinjection of sperm) in clinical practice and were therefore able to continue to offer this treatment under the transitional arrangements. One experienced team of workers in a centre which had recently been set up and had therefore not been inspected by the ILA, began to offer microinjection without a licence from the ILA for the last few days in July so that they could continue to offer it under the transitional arrangements. The centre was advised of the Authority's concerns but, as it was not acting illegally under the terms of the legislation governing the transitional period, no further action was taken.

Comparison between the ILA and HFEA

Although the ILA and the HFEA were set both set up to supervise assisted reproduction techniques, there are inevitably fundamental differences between the two Authorities. The HFEA has a statutory basis and centres wishing to undertake licensable activities are required by law to apply for a licence to do so and to pay a licence fee; operating without a licence is a criminal offence. The ILA, on the other hand, was set up on a voluntary basis and centres agreed to be licensed and comply with the guidelines out of choice. This may, in some cases, have been to avoid adverse publicity and peer pressure rather than because of the benefits to the centre or society as a whole. Each of these systems of regulation has advantages and disadvantages. It could be argued that the role of the HFEA is made easier because it has sharper 'teeth' in the form of statutory powers and centres have no choice but to be licensed. But this basis in statute also has disadvantages in that the Authority is not a free agent and must work within the terms of an Act which largely dictates what it may and may not do. The ILA had to persuade centres that it was in their own interest to be licensed and had limited sanctions against those who failed to follow its guidelines but once this voluntary regulation was in place it could, within reason, make up the rules as it went along and change them as it saw fit. The debate as to the value of statutory intervention continues but, regardless of the success or otherwise of the voluntary system of regulation, after the Warnock Report was published, it was inevitable that a statutory body would be established.

The remit of the HFEA is considerably wider than that of the ILA, involving the licensing of over twice as many clinics. In addition to regulating the IVF centres and embryo research projects previously licensed, it also regulates any treatment involving the use of donated gametes (donor insemination and egg donation) and the storage of gametes and embryos. As discussed in the previous chapter, the HFEA does not license those centres offering GIFT unless donated gametes are used. The HFEA's statutory responsibility for the collection of data is also more comprehensive than the requirements of the ILA. Although the ILA set up a prospective data collection system for IVF and GIFT, the system itself was operated by the Office of Populations Censuses and Surveys. Because of the problems of confidentiality of patient information, the HFEA was required to set up and run its own system. The IVF form was based on that devised by the ILA and new forms were devised for the donor insemination treatment, of which there are in the region of 20,000 cycles per annum, and for the collection of information about donors.

Under the Human Fertilisation and Embryology Act the Authority is required to inspect each centre on an annual basis unless for any centre in a particular year 'the licence committee considers an inspection in that year unnecessary'.[1] The inspection process, arrangements, papers and format are essentially the same as the ILA system, although because of specific provisions in the Act the HFEA is required, in addition, to formally assess issues such as the welfare of the child and the availability of suitable counselling, which were previously considered on a less formal basis. Because of the number of inspections this entailed, itwould not be possible for the HFEA members alone to undertake this task and therefore a pool of around 80 inspectors has been drawn up from a range of clinical, scientific, nursing, counselling and lay backgrounds; all previous ILA members were invited to join this pool and many accepted. As with the ILA, inspection teams are, generally, made up of a clinician, a scientist, a lay inspector (or nursing or counselling) and a member of the Executive. Inspections are usually chaired by a member of the HFEA. The inspection team takes the role of fact-finder and makes recommendations about the application being considered to a Licence Committee which is made up of between three and five members of the Authority; it is this committee which decides whether a licence should be granted, taking into account the recommendations of the inspection team. If, when notified of the committee's intention, for example, to refuse a licence, the centre disagrees with the decision, it may make representations to the committee. If, after representations have been made, the committee decides to uphold its decision the applicant has the right to an appeal hearing. This is made up of members of the HFEA who did not take part in either the inspection visit or the Licence Committee. At this hearing both the appellant and the Authority may call witnesses and the application is considered again. If the appeal is unsuccessful and the applicant considers that he has grounds, on a point of law, he may appeal to the High Court. With the ILA, the inspection team made recommendations to the whole Authority and there was no automatic right of appeal.

ILA Guidelines and HFEA Code of Practice[2]

The ILA's Guidelines for Centres, replaced by the HFEA's Code of Practice is the 'rule book' for infertility clinics. The Code of Practice is a 40 page document compared with the four pages of the ILA Guidelines. It covers many of the same issues, and a lot about the provisions of the Act itself and matters about which assurances were given by Ministers during its passage through Parliament. The Code is divided into 11 sections. Each of these sections is briefly examined, highlighting areas of similarity and major differences from the ILAs Guidelines.

1. Staff

   The Code of Practice gives details of the relevant qualifications each group of staff should have; these are very similar to the standards applied by the ILA although these were not written in detail in the guidelines. The 'Person Responsible' required by the HFEA has the role of the Medical Director in the ILA's time; the main difference being that the Person Responsible does not need to be, and frequently is not, medically qualified.

2. Facilities

   As with the guidance on staff, the Code of Practice and the Guidelines are basically the same but the Code of Practice gives far more detail. Both insist on access to back-up emergency facilities for people being treated and that laboratory and clinical facilities should be of an appropriately high standard.

3. Assessing Clients, Donors and the Welfare of the Child

   The introduction of the Human Fertilisation and Embryology Act made it a legal requirement for centres to take account of the welfare of the child, including that child's need for a father and the needs of any other child who may be affected by the birth. The Code of Practice gives detailed advice on how this can be assessed whilst balancing the need for all potential clients to have a fair and unprejudiced hearing. It does not, therefore, automatically prevent any group, eg single women and lesbian couples, from having treatment. The ILA always insisted that the welfare of the child was paramount (although this was not written into the guidelines) whereas the HFEA places neither the needs of the child nor the needs of the people seeking treatment as paramount over the other.

   One major difference between the HFEA and the ILA concerns the anonymity of donors. The ILA believed that donors should remain anonymous and that donation from close relatives should be avoided. Issues such as the potential problems arising from the donor having a continuing relationship with the child and the possible pressure on close relatives to donate were all taken into account in reaching this decision. This issue is covered in more detail in Chapter 5. The HFEA allows donation between known donors provided the centre has considered 'the implications for the welfare of the child if the donor is personally known within the child's family and social circle'.[3] The HFEA sets an age limit for donors of 35 years for women and 55 years for men. The ILA left this to the discretion of the clinical staff involved but would have been concerned had these ages been regularly exceeded by more than a few years. The ILA's guideline on screening for HIV where donated gametes were used was that both the donor and the recipient should be tested, so that if the woman were HIV positive before the treatment, the centre could not be blamed for infecting her. The HFEA only insists that donors are tested although many IVF centres continue to screen both donor and recipient for their own protection.

4.   Information

Both the ILA and the HFEA emphasize the need for detailed information to be available for potential patients to enable them to understand the implications, side effects, chances of success, cost, etc and, therefore, to make an informed decision about whether to go ahead with treatment. To this end the HFEA has issued a series of written information leaflets.

This section of the Code of Practice lists among the points about which information should be given to clients 'a child's potential need to know about his or her origins'. This contributes to the wider debate about whether a child born as a result of treatment using donated gametes has a right to be told about the donation and, if so, how much information should be given about his or her genetic origins. It is probably true to say that views in this area have begun to change with more openness being advocated. This change is reflected in the information provided by the RCOG for patients undergoing donor insemination. The 1987 leaflet stated 'unless you reveal this to your child, there is no reason for him or her ever to know that he or she was conceived by Donor Insemination'.[4] The 1992 version of the leaflet stated that 'You will be encouraged to consider telling your child about his or her origin by donor insemination'.[5] The debate about what information should be provided to the child when he or she reaches the age of 18 continues. The HFEA Register of Information contains information about the donor's physical characteristics, occupation and interests as well as the name. Donors are also given the opportunity to provide a pen-picture of themselves which could, at some time in the future, be passed to any child born as a result of the donation. How much of this information will be given to the child is a matter for regulations which have still to be made. However, the law does not allow the children to know the identity of present or past donors.

5. Consent
    All patients or donors must consent in writing before beginning any licensed treatment; this is another area of similar practice between the ILA and the HFEA. The main difference under the HFEA is that the Act requires that anyone signing a consent form indicates what is to happen to their gametes or embryos in the event of their death or their being unable to revoke or vary the consent. The ILA had insisted that any stored embryos could not be released from storage without the written consent of both partners (or the survivor). This, it was hoped, would prevent a situation such as the Tennessee Case (see Chapter 6) happening in this country. This is now covered by the Act.

6. Counselling
    The Act states that counselling must be offered to all potential and existing patients; this is formalizing what was already the case in IVF units. The ILA insisted that an independent counsellor should be available in all centres. The Code of Practice says that counselling should be available from someone other than the clinician responsible for the person's treatment and explains what is meant by counselling. It makes the same distinction as the Kings Fund Report on Counselling[6] between implications counselling, support counselling and therapeutic counselling. Counselling must also be made available to potential and existing donors and to children seeking information about their genetic background.

7. Use of gametes and embryos
    The ILA Guidelines allowed for three embryos to be transferred in a single cycle unless there were exceptional circumstances when four could be transferred. The HFEA Code of Practice removes the exceptional circumstances from the ILA guideline. The ILA, had it continued, would almost certainly have taken the same step. Another issue on which the ILA would have taken action, had it continued, was that of the export of embryos. Concern had been expressed about this after embryos were exported to America and used in a commercial surrogacy arrangement (see Chapter 5) and centres were informed that express permission from the ILA was required before the export took place; this is the same system set up by the HFEA under directions made by the Authority.
    Both the ILA and the HFEA followed the recommendations of the Warnock Report[7] in deciding that the maximum number of children to be born from a single donor should be 10. The HFEA's decision was based on the concern

among the public about the idea of one person producing very large numbers of offspring and the need to prevent the overuse of donors with particular characteristics. The ILA's view of this changed towards the end of its life-time and, in its response to the HFEAs consultation on its Code of Practice, suggested that the number should be linked to the size of the population covered. In some small centres, only providing gametes to people in the locality, the number could be lower than 10, whereas in some of the larger centres which are supplying donated sperm to centres all around the country, the number could safely be raised to 20.

A ruling introduced by the HFEA is that a woman may not be treated with the gametes of more than one man or woman during any treatment cycle. This is to prevent the practice, which had been used in a few clinics, of mixing the sperm of the woman's partner and that of a donor, or of fertilizing some eggs with the sperm of the partner and some with the donor sperm and replacing embryos resulting from each in the same cycle. In both of these cases the true genetic father could not be positively identified. An allowance was made for embryos, in storage on 1 August 1991 created in this way, provided they were recorded as the child of the donor and, should any information be sought by the child, at a later date, the information given would be that of the donor.

8. Storage and handling of gametes and embryos
    As with the ILA, the HFEA puts a very strong emphasis upon high security for records and genetic material and on accurate and efficient labelling systems. The HFEA suggests annual reviews of stored gametes and embryos as opposed to the two yearly reviews suggested by the ILA.

9. Research
    The basic guidelines on research are almost identical between the two organizations, including the reasons for which research may be undertaken, that embryos used for research must not be used in clinical practice and, that each research application must first be approved by an ethics committee. The ILA insisted that, because of the nature of the work, each centre should have an ethics committee to oversee its clinical protocol and to advise on difficult ethical issues. The reasons for, and background to, this decision are set out in more detail in Chapter 4. The HFEA insists only on the use of ethics committees for research since it considered it premature to impose the system on all centres. This would include the newly regulated donor insemination clinics, which did not have ethics committees on which they could call. However, where centres find it helpful to use ethics committees they are

encouraged to do so. The HFEA has announced that it will keep this matter under review.

10. Records
    Both the ILA and the HFEA specify what records centres needed to keep and how they should be stored.

11. Complaints
    The HFEA insists that each centre should have its own procedure for acknowledging and investigating complaints. This should be available to all patients and centres should have a senior member of staff designated as the complaints officer. This was not a requirement under the ILA guidelines.

It is clear that the Code of Practice and the ILA guidelines are very similar and, despite some minor differences there are only two areas where they differ significantly. These are related to the anonymity of donors and the need for centres to have an ethics committee, both of which were controversial when introduced by the ILA. Despite the HFEA's more relaxed attitude to both of these issues, many IVF centres still use ethics committees out of choice and a few still refuse to consider known donors.

Problems with registering donors

The ILA held its last meeting on 24 July 1991. One of the things it had to consider was a large number of letters received from centres expressing concern about what was to happen to embryos in storage on 1 August. The HFEA had issued directions instructing centres that any embryo resulting from donated sperm or eggs which was in storage before 31 July could not be used unless the donor had given permission for his or her name to be released to the HFEA for its register of information. The newspapers had picked up this issue with headlines such as 'Embryos will be allowed to die because of the new Act'.[8] The Chairman immediately contacted Mrs Bottomley, then the Minister for Health, and the Chairman of the HFEA to add their weight to the calls for some action to be taken to allow these embryos to be used for the purpose for which they had been created. The HFEA had already been addressing this problem and a statement was issued stating that: 'The Human Fertilisation and Embryology Authority recognizes that the question of what happens to embryos in storage on 1 August is a very serious and important matter. It is taking further legal advice to see what can be done, and will be issuing clear directions to centres shortly'. On 29 July 1991 the Chairman of the HFEA wrote to all centres stating that embryos in storage before 1 August 1991 using donated gametes, where the centre had been unable to obtain the donor's consent to being registered with the HFEA, could be used without giving the name to the HFEA for its register, provided that the donor had given consent for the use of his/her gametes for that purpose. This letter was followed up by a formal direction issued on 9 October. In such cases the donor information form needed to be completed with all information except the donor's name, so that some information could be given, on request, to any child born as a result of the treatment.

The availability of donors and the need to supply identifying information for treatment after 1 August continued to cause problems. Because of the requirement for donors to have their name recorded by the HFEA, many men decided to stop donating and, being unable to supply the donor's name, centres could not use the sperm already in storage. This led to a shortage of sperm available for donation and a small number of centres suspended their treatment service completely whilst they tried to recruit new donors. This was compounded by an increase in the quarantine period for sperm from three to six months. The HFEA received representations from both centres and patients and on 1 October 1991 a direction came into force allowing centres to use and supply sperm which was already in store on 1 August without recording the name of the donor provided the sperm was used in treatment on or before 31 March 1992. This was intended to give centres six months in which to recruit new donors and for those donors recruited after 1 August to complete their quarantine period. After this six month transitional period, the Authority was receiving conflicting anecdotal evidence about the availability of donors. Some centres claimed that men were still reluctant to donate and therefore called for the number of children allowed to be born from a single donor to be increased. Other centres reported that, after an initial dip in recruitment, the numbers had increased as it had become clear that anonymity would be preserved. In order to clarify the situation the HFEA commissioned a survey of donor insemination and storage centres and also of actual, potential and non-donors; the results of this survey will enable the Authority to base its policy on accurate, up-to-date information.,

A transitional arrangement was also allowed for patients wishing to have a full sibling for a child already born using a particular donor. Many centres had expressed their concerns to the HFEA that, in cases where the donor did not agree to having his/her name released to the HFEA, the gametes could not be used. On 1 October, a direction came into force stating that up until 31 March 1992 a couple could register their intention to use an unregistered donor to produce a full sibling, by providing the following information:

1. a copy of the woman's request, in writing, to the centre requesting further treatment with the sperm from a particular donor;
2. evidence that the woman was originally treated before 1 August 1991;
3. evidence to show which particular donor was used;
4. evidence that the treatment resulted in a live birth.

Once this information had been provided the treatment could take place at any time in the future. As with the embryos already in storage on 1 August and the use- of unregistered sperm donors, a donor information form needed to be completed which could omit the name of the donor. These transitional arrangements to cover activities which had occurred before 1 August 1991 smoothed the way towards statutory regulation.

A model Authority?

On 31 July 1991, after six years as the regulatory body, the ILA handed over its responsibilities to the HFEA. So how effective had the voluntary regulation of IVF and embryo research been? In order to establish the views of those connected, either directly or indirectly, with the work of the Voluntary Licensing Authority we have sought comments from members of the VLA, the centres licensed by the Authority and related organizations both in the UK and overseas. The opinions of each of these groups will be analysed in turn.

Views of licensed centres

All 59 centres which were licensed by the Authority received a questionnaire asking about their centre and the VLA/ILA. Replies were received from 35 centres, a response rate of 60%. These centres were representative in terms of the length of time their service had been operating and the size of the centre. The earliest centre to open, of those from whom replies were received, was 1982 and the most recent opened in 1991. The remainder were spread evenly over the years in between. For purposes of analysis, the Authority divided centres into small, medium and large centres, depending on the number of IVF treatment cycles performed in a year. Large centres performed 400 or more cycles, medium centres, 100-400 and small centres performed less than 100 cycles per annum. Of the replies received, six were small centres (17%), 15 were medium (43%), seven were large centres (20%), three carried out research only (9%) and the remaining four centres did not complete this question on the form. Almost half of the centres replying to the questionnaire were undertaking embryo research projects licensed by the Authority; three of these centres were only licensed for embryo research and the remaining 13 were undertaking research alongside a clinical IVF programme.

Centres were asked whether they welcomed the setting up of the VLA in 1985 or whether they considered that the regulation of IVF should have been left to professional self-regulation or until the establishment of a statutory authority. 'The establishment of the VLA was welcomed by 94% of those who replied, one centre (3%) replied yes and no, but gave no further details and one stated that in the circumstances, where government legislation was inevitable, the VLA was a good compromise but that regulation could have been left to professional self-regulation. Another, whilst welcoming the VLA, expressed the view that the medical profession had managed to self-regulate in other areas of medicine and the same could have been true in this field. One centre welcomed the establishment of the VLA as a necessary requisite to contesting the notion of clinical freedom. Others commented on the need to gain the confidence of the general public, and society as a whole, who were concerned about science fiction and cloning and hence the need for a visible, independent regulatory body with lay representatives. The majority of those replying (77%) found the composition of the Authority acceptable although two would have preferred more clinicians, three more scientists, two more women, two more 'lay' and one less 'lay' members. One centre would have preferred to see more counsellors and one, more patient representatives.

When asked whether they agreed with the VLA guidelines, 80% said yes, 14% said no, 3% agreed with all but one of the guidelines and 3% did not comment. Three centres criticized the lack of flexibility about the number of embryos to be replaced in a single cycle, two were unhappy about the Authority's guidelines, on egg donation, one was unhappy with the 14 day limit for research which, they commented, 'greatly restricts the acquisition of knowledge which could be of great benefit'. One of those who did not agree with the guidelines made the following comment: 'Several guidelines reflected the necessary care over public concern, etc. There was inadequate rigor over ethical decisions and many guidelines were more a sop to public opinion than sound pointers'. One of the roles of the VLA was to give advice to centres, 30 centres felt that the Authority was helpful in providing advice, one thought the Authority was unhelpful and three did not have specific views on this. One centre felt that the Authority was well-equipped for giving advice on the legal or regulatory aspects but was poor on the provision of scientific advice.

All centres received and read the annual reports and most (28 centres representing 80% of the total) found the statistical analysis of IVF and GIFT data the most interesting part of the reports. Four centres found the list of research projects most interesting, two the ethical discussions, one the recommendations, one the publication list, one the new technologies, and one could not define one part as more interesting than any other.

When asked whether the VLA influenced the centres approach to practice, 15 (43%) said yes, 18 (51%) said no and two did not know. Of the 15 who said the VLA did influence their practice, seven commented on the limit to the number of embryos to be transferred, three said they were influenced by the ILA's views in setting up or amending their programme, one centre remained within the 14 day limit for research because of the Authority's guideline and one centre stated that: 'the VLA made us feel guilty over entirely ethical procedures', no detail was given about the procedures in question. Another centre stressed that the guidelines reinforced the centres own views'. Every licensed centre was inspected at least once and some centres were inspected on two or three occasions. Twenty six centres (74%) found the inspections helpful, eight (23%) did not find them helpful and one centre did not comment. Of those who found them helpful seven commented on the internal audit and review of procedures which took place prior to a visit, 12 mentioned the role of inspection visits in providing advice and comments on the service in a constructive way, three expressed the value of reassurance to themselves and their patients of knowing that their practice was being monitored. The value of questioning by a third party and the general discussion on ethical and therapeutic issues was also expressed. Two of those who did not find the visits helpful also commented. One considered that the visits were 'too short, too inquisitorial, looking for fault and did not provide constructive or helpful advice. There was also no opportunity to discuss, amplify and exchange views'. The other centre, although not finding the visits helpful, pointed out that they were in no way unwelcome or a waste of time.

Centres were asked whether, in their opinion, the VLA/ILA played a significant role in the development of IVF in the UK; 80% of the respondents felt that it had played a significant role and 20% considered that it had not. Most of the comments received focused on three areas in which the Authority's work had been influential:

1. in setting and maintaining standards whilst still retaining flexibility to respond to changes;
2. by disseminating information and reassuring the public and Parliament in a way that contributed to the passing of sensible legislation;

3.   in leading the way for the establishment of the statutory body and the HFEA's Code of Practice.

The final question on the questionnaire to centres was whether the VLA/ILA had been effective in regulating IVF and embryo research and, if so, what factors had contributed to its success. In response to this 77% of centres considered that it had been effective, 14% thought it had not been effective, and 9% either were not certain or were not prepared to comment. The main reasons given for its success are as follows:

1.   by providing universal guidelines and maintaining standards, it gained the confidence of both the centres and the public;
2.   the professional standing of and respect for members of the Authority and, in particular, the Chairman;
3.   the moral obligation and peer pressure to adhere to the guidelines;
4.   the threat of withdrawal of licence;
5.   the knowledge that a statutory body was to follow and the fear of tight restrictions on the work;
6.   the Authority's flexibility, ie it was not constrained by statute.

Views of related organizations in the UK

Views were sought from a total of 61 organizations in the UK, who were selected either because they had a direct interest in the Authority's work, such as professional associations related to IVF, medical organizations and IVF patients' groups, or they were on the VLA mailing list or they had been involved in the debate on IVF and embryo research during the passage of the Human Fertilization and Embryology Act. Only 21 replies were received, representing a 34% response rate, furthermore eight of the respondents had not completed the questionnaire. In most cases this was because the person who had been dealing with this issue had left and the new staff or members did not have any detailed recollection of the work of the Authority. The 13 completed questionnaires were received from medical organizations (4), patient organizations (4), interest/pressure groups (3) and professional societies (2). Most of these organizations had first learnt about the Authority's work through contact with members, other organizations or through others working in the field, two organizations first heard about the Authority through the media, two at meetings and two through IVF clinics.

The majority of respondents (69%) received the Authority's reports and, again, the statistics were found to be one of the most interesting parts although one of the patient organizations was very critical of the Authority's policy of not publishing individual centres' success rates. Three of the organizations found all of the report interesting and did not consider one part to be of more value than any other; the list of centres and research projects were found particularly useful by some. The Authority's guidelines were accepted by nine of the organizations (69%), one (8%) disagreed and two organizations did not express a view. One organization agreed at the time they were in force but in retrospect would have preferred the maximum number of embryos to be limited to a maximum of two, except in exceptional circumstances. The organization which disagreed was a patient group who considered that insufficient notice had been taken of the views of infertile couples and that clinical matters should have been left entirely to the discretion of the clinicians and patients. Ten of the organizations (77%) concluded that the VLA/ILA had played a significant role in the development of IVF, the main examples given were in the setting and maintaining standards, in paving the way for the HFEA and in allaying public fears. One patient group was critical of the Authority for generating 'a lot of negative publicity for the whole idea of IVF by conducting a low level newspaper debate based on exceptional cases'; no further details were given. In response to a question about the effectiveness of the VLA/ILA the same group considered that the Authority had been ineffective because it could not decide who it was representing and was too weak to regulate clinics effectively. This was a minority view with 69% (nine organizations) replying that the Authority had been effective in regulating IVF and embryo research, one medical organization considered that the Authority had been effective to the extent that it had moral weight but it did not have the required sanctions to regulate the field on a permanent basis and the remaining 15% did not comment on this question. The main reasons given for its effectiveness are as follows:

1. its establishment of reasonable guidelines which were seen as such by the majority of those in the field therefore it was able to exert pressure on those who did not agree to conform;
2. the willingness of professionals to be regulated;
3. the diplomatic, sensitive and authoritative manner in which it conducted its business;
4. the broad membership which commanded respect and acceptance by professionals.

The final question was about the reputation of the VLA; 88% considered it had a good reputation with the following comments being made:

1. Good;
2. Very good/excellent;
3. Competent;
4. Highly regarded/respected;
5. Highly regarded by those who know of its work but not widely known among other disciplines.

The one organization which did not think it had a high reputation was a patient group who stated that the Authority had been hampered by the voluntary nature of its work and that it did not take enough notice of the wishes of infertile couples and was therefore regarded by them with 'fear and mistrust'. One medical organization did not comment on this question.

Views of organizations overseas

We wrote to a total of 31 organizations overseas and replies were received from 18, a response rate of 58%. The countries represented by these 18 respondents were as follows: America, Australia, Canada, Japan, Israel, Zimbabwe, Belgium, Denmark, France, Holland, Italy and Norway. One of the three organizations from the United States had not heard of the Authority and was therefore unable to complete the questionnaire. Six of the remaining 17 respondents had learnt of the Authority's existence in 1985, the rest became aware of the Authority between 1986 and 1990. Most had heard about the work either from meetings, journals or throughcontact with the members or the secretariat of the Authority. Reports were sent to 75% of the respondents and all of those who received them found them interesting. Through reading the reports and through correspondence with the Authority, 94% were aware of the Authority's guidelines.

In reply to a question about whether the VLA/ILA influenced either their personal or their organization's views the positive and negative answers were equal. Those organizations who answered positively came from America, Australia, Canada, Japan, Zimbabwe, France and Norway. One organization stated 'being in Zimbabwe with no laws or guidance on IVF we adhered rigidly to the VLA guidelines and relied heavily on help from friends and colleagues...in the UK'. The other comments from the organizations who had been influenced by the VLA focused on the help and advice the Authority had given and the fact that the

Authority's guidelines were taken into account in reaching their own decisions. One individual commented, on a personal note, that the VLA showed him that voluntary regulation could be successful. Representatives from organizations in Sydney Australia, Virginia USA, France and Zimbabwe felt that the regulatory system in the UK had influenced their own form of regulation. Two organizations from Japan and Canada commented that, although the VLA had not influenced regulation in their country, it had influenced clinical practice in that the VLA guidelines were taken into account when drawing up guidelines. In total 31% of those replying said that clinical practice in their country had been influenced by the VLA, 56% said it had not been influenced and 13% did not know.

Finally, the organizations were asked to comment on the international reputation of the VLA. The comments received fell into the following categories:

1. Good;
2. Very good/excellent;
3. Very highly regarded ('the conscience of the profession');
4. A worthwhile interim body;
5. A model for other countries with modification depending on the ethical and social background of the country.

Views of members of the Authority

Views were received from all of those who had, at some stage, been members of the Authority; some comments were received by letter, others by speaking to the individuals concerned. The members were asked about their time with the Authority, the relationships with centres and their perception of the work carried out. Regardless of the length of membership, all members had found the work enjoyable although a couple of members were more cynical about the value of their work than the others. One member was uncertain that the setting up of 'Authorities' was the right way to tackle the ethical implications of medical innovations and was concerned about the effect that such action has upon the development of work in the area. This is based, the member stated, on the belief that 'scientists and even doctors are as trustworthy as the generality of mankind'. How far should such bodies be extended? Should they be set up for every new innovative set of techniques? These philosophical questions cannot be addressed in detail here, but are certainly of great interest and relevance. The other member who was more cynical expressed more specific concerns, whilst also questioning the overall value of the work of the Authority in practical terms. One of the specific concerns was about the role of the lay member of the Authority whose role, it was stated, 'became more and more token'. Other members contradicted this by stating, in the words of one member, that the role of the lay member was in 'jumping on the scientists' and clinicians' feet and bringing them down to earth and aware of what real people's feelings involved'; the view, expressed by many members from all disciplines, was that this role was accepted and respected by all of those involved. Another specific criticism was that the social implications of IVF and associated techniques were never discussed in any detail and the implications for children born as a result of these techniques were not fully explored. It was stated that 'the Authority worked with the assumption that (these) techniques were a proper part of patient care, but nevertheless failed to use its influence to get them included in the NHS'. Other members described their time with the Authority as 'challenging', 'exciting', 'stimulating', and 'interesting'. One of the clinical members commented 'I thought that the work was very interesting indeed, seeing the different centres and assessing the people working there was fascinating ... the difference in ethical values was also interesting. What people thought was ethical and unethical varied considerably. ... I thought the whole exercise was very well worthwhile and I am sure that the ILA laid the foundation for the HFEA'. A scientific member said 'my time with the ILA was exciting and challenging. Both socially and intellectually it was stimulating. Above all it provided a sense of social relevance of the scientific sphere ... it was a privilege that I enjoyed immensely'. Both scientific and clinical members mentioned their role in providing specialist knowledge and interpreting new developments for the benefit of the other members and the need to justify the work to the lay members who were prepared to challenge their pre-conceived notions and make sure they considered the wider implications of the work. The lay members mentioned the difficulty of grasping the ideas and techniques involved as well as evaluating the importance of the work. This was described by one member as follows: 'I found my first few months puzzling/difficult. It was when I got involved in visits that I began to see what I could usefully contribute'.

When asked why centres agreed to be licensed, the replies closely reflected those given by the centres themselves. The main reasons given were as follows:

1. peer and media pressure;
2. the authority of the MRC and RCOG;
3. the moral weight of the Authority;
4. the respectability licensing implied;
5. the knowledge that a statutory authority would be established and the fear of restrictions;
6. the fairness and flexibility of the Authority.

Most members commented on the welcome they received whilst undertaking inspection visits and the great respect with which Authority members were treated. Initially, there was a degree of uncertainty on both sides, but as time went on this subsided and centres came to value the advice and assistance the Authority was able to give. The inspections themselves changed in that, as the Authority gained experience, they became tougher and the questioning more intense.

It is easy, with hindsight, to look back and criticize actions which seemed, at the time, to be reasonable. However, on the whole, members of the Authority had few regrets about the way things had been handled. One member expressed the view that the Authority had been perhaps too keen to intervene in clinical matters. However, a number of other members commented that, with hindsight, the Authority could have intervened to a greater extent and been more forceful in withdrawing licences, particularly in relation to those centres who were replacing more than three embryos in cases which could not be described as 'exceptional'. One member also expressed regret that the Authority had not been more keen to speak out against individual entrepreneurs setting up IVF clinics as a way of making money, rather than for the benefit of patients, and also about the take-over of two large centres by a drug company manufacturing drugs used in ovarian stimulation. A concern expressed by a few members was that the Authority had not always been consistent in its policy on licensing.

Some members expressed personal views on individual issues such as, that: more attention could have been given to sperm donation, rather than focusing solely on egg donation; the situation regarding the clinical application of microinjection (see Chapter 5) could have been handled differently to prevent the researchers continuing the work abroad where ethical standards were not so high; the guidelines on egg donation were perhaps too tough; the insistence on research ethics committees overseeing clinical practice rather than insisting that clinical ethics committees were established was a mistake; the Authority should have published individual centre's success rates to help patients choose a clinic (although another member commented that the decision not to publish success rates was one of the reasons why the Authority received cooperation from centres).

Finally, members were asked whether, in their opinion, the VLA/ILA had been successful and, if so, what had contributed to its success. One member considered that the Authority had been successful in keeping the public happy and preparing for legal regulation but that it had not succeeded in opening up the debate to the lay public or in ensuring that decisions about the future of medical specialities were 'determined by the ethics of the nation rather than the ethics of the profession'. The rest of the members considered that the Authority had been a great success and had more than achieved what it had set out to do. Its major successes were seen as allaying public fear, making IVF acceptable at a time when it could have been rejected as 'unsavoury' practice and in persuading centres to abide by its guidelines. The members' views of why the Authority was successful can be summarized as follows:

1.   the establishment of a good working relationship, communication and mutual trust between the Authority and centres;
2.   the flexibility, willingness to listen and the 'human face' portrayed by the Authority;
3.   the lack of bureaucracy and willingness to accept that it may not always get things right first time;
4.   the establishment of reasoned, reasonable and acceptedguidelines;
5.   the support of the MRC and RCOG
6.   the team spirit engendered within the Authority;
7.   the quality and professional standing of the members;
8.   the excellent Chairmanship of Dame Mary Donaldson.

As one of the members pointed out, the success of the Authority was reflected by the fact that, despite initially being set up for two years, the Authority's work continued for over six years. Had there been real concern about its ability to regulate the clinics, the establishment of a statutory body would have been given a much higher priority.

References

1.   *Human Fertilization & Embryology Act 1990*, HMSO, London
2.   Human Fertilization and Embryology Authority (1991), *Code of Practice*, HFEA, London
3.   Ibid para 3.15 (c)
4.   Royal College of Obstetricians and Gynaecologists (1987), *Donor Insemination. Patient Information Booklet.* RCOG, London
5.   Royal College of Obstetricians and Gynaecologists (1992), *Donor Insemination. Patient Information Booklet.* RCOG, London
6.   Counselling for Regulated Infertility Treatments, *The Report of the King's Fund Centre Counselling Committee*, January 1991.
7.   *Report of the Committee of Inquiry into Human Fertilization and Embryology* (1984), Cmnd 9314, HMSO, London
8.   *The Independent*, 24 July 1991.

8 The Human Fertilisation & Embryology Authority

This chapter looks at some of the main issues the HFEA has addressed since taking up its full responsibilities on 1 August 1991.

Problems of confidentiality

Of all the teething problems experienced by the HFEA, probably the one which caused the most difficulty and concern for centres, patients and the HFEA was the confidentiality provisions in the HF& E Act. Section 33(5) of the Act stated that:

> 'No person who is or has been a person to whom a licence applies and no person to whom directions have been given shall disclose any information falling within section 31(2) of this Act which he holds or has held as such a person.'[1]

The intention of this section was to continue the trend in other areas of medicine and allow the patient to have control over the dissemination of information about her treatment. In practice it meant that the patient could not consent to information being given to anyone, even to other health professionals, not directly involved in the treatment. This was far more restrictive than had been intended, to the possible detriment of the well-being of the patient. Breach of these provisions was a criminal offence punishable by up to two years imprisonment or a fine or both. The HFEA received a constant stream of enquiries, concerns and complaints about this provision and it soon became apparent that they did not stem from a dislike of change but that there were very serious problems with this part of the legislation. Initially this was a difficult time for relations between the centres and the HFEA, but once the centres realized that this was a section of the Act and not something the Authority itself had decided upon, the centres and the Authority worked together to find a solution.

Listed below are some of the main problems caused by this section of the Act.

1. Should a patient undergoing treatment require urgent medical attention by a consultant not covered by a licence, the unit staff could not provide the consultant with details of the drugs or treatment the patient had received. This fear of breach of confidentiality could have very serious consequences for the well-being of the patients and could put lives at risk.

2. Centres could not send details of the treatment being undertaken to the patient's General Practitioner, even with the patient's consent to such disclosure. In the event of an emergency the GP would have no information about the treatment or drugs provided. Another problem was that GPs were often asked to prescribe drugs for the patient and many GPs felt unable to take full responsibility for the patient without having all the facts about treatment and were therefore refusing to prescribe the drugs. A letter sent to the patient which she could give to the GP could solve this problem but was seen as discourteous, upsetting many GPs, and also put extra pressure on the patient, since any slight change to her treatment protocol would need to be relayed by her to her GP.

3. A centre being sued could not give its lawyer information about treatment services provided for an identifiable individual. The centre could give anonymous information but it would not be possible for a lawyer to prepare a proper defence case on this basis. This left clinicians unable to defend themselves against any claims made against them and unable to sue for unpaid fees.

4. A centre storing sperm for young men undergoing medical treatment which could affect their fertility would, prior to 1 August, consult the

patient's GP annually to check whether the patient was still alive, thus saving the family from further distress if the patient had died. This information would not be provided by the GP without knowing the reason why it was being requested.

5. In many large hospitals parts of the licensed treatment, eg egg collection, were performed in a general gynaecology theatre and ward. This meant that theatre staff, porters, general gynaecology ward staff etc needed access to information about the provision of treatment services for an identifiable individual.

6. Invoicing for treatment became a problem where services were being purchased by health authorities, who needed to know the name of the people being treated to ensure they were being charged the right amount. Similarly some centres had arrangements with foreign embassies to provide treatment for patients from that country with the invoice being sent to the government for payment. The foreign governments were not happy for information about the cost of treatment to be sent to the patient and some threatened to withdraw their contracts.

7. Medical and financial audit needed to see receipts and information about treatment. Although in some cases anonymous information would suffice this was not true for all cases and the work involved in anonymizing all records would be quite phenomenal.

Whilst solutions to some of these problems were found they invariably caused a dramatic increase in the administrative burden and bureaucracy for centres and patients. Many private centres could cope with this by recruiting additional administrative staff and the costs were passed on to the patients. In the case of NHS and other units based in NHS hospitals, the resources could not be made available to cope with the increased workload without a knock-on effect elsewhere. In real terms this would have meant that fewer patients could be treated or that centres could not comply with the law. Some of the problems could not be overcome even with additional resources, one of these being the risk to patients brought about by the restrictions on communications between centres and GPs and other health professionals. Legal advice confirmed that the clause was watertight and there could be no form of indemnity from prosecution in the sort of situation outlined above. The Authority could not operate a policy of not fully implementing the Act since this would prejudice its reputation as a regulatory body and its integrity in giving guidance on the implementation of the rest of the Act. The Authority was concerned that many centres, though not unwilling, might be unable to comply with the confidentiality provisions of the Act and this raised questions as to whether they could be granted a licence. In the light of these problems it was concluded that this section of the Act was unworkable and the only option available was to seek an amendment to the Act which, whilst retaining the principle that the patient has control over the information would allow her to give consent to the disclosure of specific information to particular people. The Chairman immediately wrote to Mrs Bottomley, then the Minister for Health, setting out the position and seeking her support for urgent action to remedy the situation. In the meantime the HFEA Executive continued to give guidance on the basis of the following tenets:

1.   that the law is complied with;
2.   that it is generally in the patient's interest that treatment relevant to her medical care is passed on to those involved in that care;
3.   that the patient must be involved in the decisions about who receives relevant information about her treatment.

There had also been some confusion about the treatments to which the confidentiality provisions applied. The definition of 'treatment services' in the Act is, 'medical, surgical or obstetric services provided to the public or a section of the public for the purpose of assisting women to carry children'.[2] However, legal advice the Authority had received was that information restricted by section 33(5) related only to information about patients undergoing licensed treatment. This was a relief for many gynaecologists for, if this were not the case, communication with GPs would be restricted for any treatment for the 'purpose of assisting women to carry children' which would, no doubt, cover most of the gynaecologist's work.

Human Fertilisation and Embryology (Disclosure of Information) Act[3]

There had been concern in some quarters that, should an amendment to the Act be required, opening up the legislation would lead to amendments to restrict or prohibit embryo research or to reduce the time limit for abortion, etc. However, this was avoided by a short Bill drawn sufficiently tightly to prevent any repetition of the long and controversial debates on those issues which had dominated the consideration of the original Bill. On 20 May 1992, the Human Fertilization and Embryology (Disclosure of Information) Bill was introduced into the House of Lords; this passed through both Houses unamended and received Royal Assent on

16 July 1992. The Act allowed for identifying information about the provision of treatment services to be disclosed under the following circumstances.

1. With the patient's consent:
    i.   to someone specified by the patient;
    ii.   to unspecified persons who need to know in connection with providing medical, surgical or obstetric services for that patient, or for medical or financial audits.
          Before consent is requested reasonable steps must be taken to explain tothe patient the implications of compliance with the request.

2. Without the patient's consent:
    i.   in an emergency where disclosure is necessary to avert an imminent danger to the health of the patient and it is not reasonable to expect the patient's consent to be obtained. If consent could be obtained but is refused, the information must not be disclosed;
    ii.   if it is necessary for any purpose preliminary to, or in connection with, legal proceedings or formal complaints procedures;
    iii. for the purpose of establishing the genetic parenthood of a child who is subject to an application for a parental order in a surrogacy case;
    iv   in accordance with section 3 of the Access to Health Records Act 1990.

3. If disclosing the identity of any child resulting from treatment cannot be avoided as a result of disclosing the client's name in one of the situations described in 1 and 2 above, this is not an offence.

The first year of licensing

A transitional period allowed centres to carry on treatments they were performing on or before 31 July 1991 until the outcome of their application to the HFEA was known, or until 31 July 1992 whichever was sooner. This meant that all centres had to be inspected and applications determined by 31 July 1992. The inspection process was fully established and ready to begin at the end of November leaving eight months to do a full year of licensing. The Authority had received 116 treatment applications, 51 research applications and eight applications for storage only centres. During this eight month period [122] centres were inspected of which [69] were IVF clinics. The inspection visits covered all aspects of the Code of Practice and many focused particularly on those areas which were explicitly stated in the Act such as issues of counselling, confidentiality, welfare of the child and information for patients. The aim of the HFEA, as had been that of the ILA, was to improve standards and to bring all clinics to the level of the best. Its intention was not to close down clinics, but rather to advise on how the service in a clinic could be improved to a level whereby it would reach the required standards. In many cases therefore conditions were attached to licenses where a breach of the Act or theCode of Practice had been identified. Where there were numerous conditions or they were of a particularly serious nature, a licence was issued for a short period of time such as three or six months with a review visit after that period. Most licenses were issued for a period of one year, and later, in a few cases, licences were issued for fifteen months.

Two IVF treatment applications were refused. These were cases where the centres had failed in significant ways to meet the standards required and it seemed unlikely that they would be able to reach the required standard within a reasonable period of time. One of these was a centre which had also been refused a licence by the Interim Authority and the other had not been inspected by the ILA because the amount of work it was doing, at that time, was minimal and the centre did not intend to replace any embryos. This centre was using IVF, in a GIFT centre, as a diagnostic means of establishing the likelihood of fertilization in vivo. However, it was considered that the quality of embryological support was not high enough to provide worthwhile information and as the centre was unable to provide the level of embryological cover required for IVF, the licence was refused. An appeal was lodged and heard by other members of the Authority and the original decision was upheld.

Policy matters

In most cases, the information required to approve an application was contained within the Code of Practice but on some occasions, where new issues arose, advice was sought from the whole Authority and a policy decision made. In order to obtain the views of interested parties about these and other policy issues, a proposed revision of the Code of Practice was distributed for consultation. These revisions addressed the following issues.

1. Diagnostic IVF
   The case mentioned above concerning 'diagnostic IVF' was one such example of an area of new policy which was put out for consultation.

The new guideline only allows 'diagnostic IVF' to be undertaken in centres licensed for IVF and then only if it is to be used for treatment, storage or a licensed research project or is likely to provide worthwhile information about the treatment of that particular couple. Diagnostic IVF should not be used in a centre only offering GIFT.

2.   Production of sperm at home

Another practice, which came to light during inspection visits, was that some centres were allowing donors to produce their sperm at home. While it was recognized that allowing this practice to continue might prevent a further reduction in the number of donors, there was a real concern that the sperm may be substituted with that from another man, who had not received the counselling and screening or that the sperm may be interfered with in some way. It was finally decided that the benefits outweighed the problems and the practice should be allowed in exceptional cases but the responsibility was placed on the licensed centre to satisfy itself that the sperm belonged to the donor who had received counselling and screening, and that the sample had been produced not more than two hours before it was brought to the centre.

3.   Surrogacy arrangements

A concern expressed by some interested parties was that, with the increased success rates for IVF and the more frequent use of surrogacy arrangements, these techniques might be adopted for social or convenience reasons on the part of the commissioning woman. The Authority decided that surrogacy for social reasons was not 'necessary or desirable for the purpose of providing treatment services'[4] and therefore could not be licensed under the Act. Furthermore it was considered that the risks associated with pregnancy were being passed on to the surrogate without adequate reason. There were also concerns relating to the welfare of the child; since surrogacy arrangements are unenforceable in law and the carrying mother, ie the surrogate, would be the legal mother. Unless a parental order was sought either the commissioning mother or the surrogate mother could become the child's legal parent. Additional paragraphs were therefore inserted into the Code of Practice stating that surrogacy should only be initiated where it was physically impossible or highly undesirable for medical reasons for the commissioning mother to carry the child.

4.   Transport IVF

An unforeseen difficulty which arose during this first year related to 'transport IVF' which is described in Chapter 6. Attention was drawn to a satellite centre undertaking the egg collection for IVF, which was not licensed by the Authority since it was not, itself, undertaking any licensable activities. Consequently, the Authority could not legally impose upon it the high standards that were applied to licensed centres relating to, for example, appropriate information being given to patients, the offer of counselling and ensuring that account had been taken of the welfare of the child. The Authority was determined to ensure that those receiving treatment by transport IVF should receive the same standard of care as those where all parts of the treatment are carried out in a licensed centre. The new guidelines therefore made it clear that the responsibility for ensuring that these issues were covered rested with the licensed centre which was undertaking the embryo replacement.

5.   Matters relating to donor insemination

The HFEA also revised some of its guidelines relating to donor insemination clinics. For example, to allow the practice to continue whereby clinicians supply screened donor sperm to patients to inseminate themselves in their own home. Initially this caused some legal problems because the Act specifically forbids the supply of frozen sperm to anyone other than a licensed centre. By providing sperm 'in the process of thawing' this difficulty can be avoided. The new guidelines state that this treatment should only be used where there are exceptional circumstances making it impractical and undesirable for the woman to be inseminated at the centre. In such cases the standard procedures for the giving of information, counselling and determining the welfare of the child must be followed and the same information must be provided to the HFEA as if the procedure took place on licensed premises. The centre must also take all reasonable steps to satisfy itself that the sperm will only be used for the treatment of the woman to whom it is supplied.

These suggested amendments, together with those relating to the Disclosure of Information Act have been incorporated into the revised Code of Practice which was published in March 1993.

It was never intended that the Code would contain fixed guidelines but that it would be amended as developments were made and more information came to light. The Code of Practice will continue to be reviewed on a regular basis.

Public consultation

As well as consulting on proposed revisions of the Code of Practice, the Authority also consults on difficult ethical issues in order to gauge the weight of public opinion before reaching any conclusions or taking action. In January 1993, a consultation document on sex selection was published. Although this coincided with the opening of Britain's first clinic offering couples the opportunity to choose the sex of their child for social reasons, the matter had been under discussion within the HFEA for a number of months. Sex selection for medical reasons to avoid a life-threatening genetic disease affecting only one sex has been available, using pre-implantation diagnosis, on a very limited basis for a couple of years in this country and selective abortion for the 'wrong' sex, is performed in some circumstances. The new clinic used a technique, readily available in America, whereby the sperm containing X- and Y-chromosomes are separated by swimming them through albumen. The woman is then artificially inseminated with X or Y bearing sperm in accordance with her choice. As this does not involve the creation of an embryo outside the body or the use of donated gametes, nor is the centre storing sperm, a licence is not required under the Human Fertilisation and Embryology Act. However, the general principles involved were of interest to the Authority because the techniques could be applied in licensed treatment. The consultation document described the ways in which the sex of the child can be determined, either by pre-implantation diagnosis or by the separation of sperm, the reasons why a couple might wish to select the sex of their child, either for medical or social reasons and the arguments for and against this practice. The document was distributed to interested organizations including licensed centres, religious groups and professional organizations. Members of the public were also encouraged to submit their views. In this way the Authority hoped to stimulate wide public debate on issues which affect society as a whole.

Another issue on which the Authority wishes to stimulate wide debate is the use of fetal ovarian tissue or ovarian tissue from cadavers for the treatment of infertility. Work has been under way in animals for some time to mature oocytes in vitro. In the future it may be possible to remove oocytes or ovaries from female aborted fetuses or cadavers, to mature the oocytes in vitro and to use them in the treatment of infertile patients or, alternatively, to transplant the ovarian tissue to infertile women; a novel way of overcoming the shortage of donor eggs. This raises profound ethical problems, not least the fact that, in the case of an aborted fetus, the genetic mother of the child will never have been born and the maternal grandmother will be the woman having the termination. The problem is also raised of who has the right to consent on behalf of the aborted fetus. These techniques are unlikely to be available for treatment purposes in the short term but the stage will soon be reached when the fertilizability of fetal eggs matured in vitro will need to be tested and permission for such work sought. In anticipation of this, the Authority is seeking to gauge public opinion, so that this can be taken into account in determining its policy on this issue. Do the ends justify the means? Do the benefits of a more assured supply of donor eggs outweigh the difficult ethical issues involved? These are some of the fundamental questions which need to be resolved.

In a field such as infertility where new developments regularly occur, the regulatory body will constantly need to look ahead at the possibilities and give consideration to how far science should be allowed to go. Things which today seem like science-fiction are tomorrow's practical possibilities; it is difficult to imagine anywhere that this has been demonstrated more vividly than in the development of in vitro fertilization. The question which remains is, can a regulatory body, with a basis in statute, keep abreast of such a rapidly-developing field or will the constraints of the law render it ineffective? Only time will tell.

References

1. *Human Fertilisation & Embryology Act 1990*, HMSO, London
2. Ibid. section 2 (1)
3. *Human Fertilisation & Embryology (Disclosure of Information) Act 1992*, HMSO, London
4. *Human Fertilisation & Embryology Act 1990* op. cit., Schedule 2 para 1(3)

9 International Overview of IVF Regulations

Internationally the ethics of human in vitro fertilization and embryo research is still very much a subject under discussion. In those countries which have legislated or set up some sort of regulation a variety of approaches have been adopted but generally the statutory instruments enacted fall into two categories which reflect different views on the status of the embryo. In the first category all non-therapeutic research on embryos is prohibited; therapeutic research may be allowed where the intention is to replace the embryo. The second category allows regulated non-therapeutic research but some forms of research, such as cloning or the creation of interspecific hybrids, remain prohibited. The polarity of view is epitomized by the fact that the first category allows embryos which have been the subject of therapeutic research to be replaced to give them the opportunity of life. But in the second category, although research is seen as necessary it is also considered to be potentially damaging and embryos which have been the subject of research may not be replaced. In those countries where discussion still continues and there is no formal statutory regulation some form of professional self regulation may exist, promulgated by professional bodies. It is in these countries that ethical boundaries are most likely to be breached.

What follows is a relatively comprehensive, but by no means exhaustive, account of the regulatory approaches to human in vitro fertilization and embryo research taken by a number of countries around the world.

143

Australia

Pioneering work on in vitro fertilization was undertaken in Australia and it was the first country to produce guidelines on IVF and embryo research. In Supplementary Note 4 to its 1982 Statement on Human Experimentation[1] the National Health and Medical Research Council (NH&MRC) offered guidelines for clinical IVF and embryo research. These are set out in Chapter 3. In 1985 the NH & MRC undertook a review of the 12 centres then undertaking IVF to establish whether their guidelines were being observed and the relevant report was published in 1986.[2] No significant departures from the guidelines were found and further recommendations were made regarding the composition and conduct of Institutional Ethics Committees, on trials involving the modification of culture media and on policies on embryo storage. The Fertility Society of Australia (FSA) was asked to oversee consent procedures.

Having established early guidelines the NH & MRC no longer concerned itself with the clinical provision of IVF and, in order to ensure consistent standards across the Commonwealth, the FSA in 1986 established a Reproductive Technology Accreditation Committee and promulgated a code of practice relating to IVF and related technologies. A National Bioethics Consultative Committee (NBCC) was set up in 1989 to review, among other things, the new reproductive technologies and in 1991 this was merged with the Medical Research Ethics Committee of the NH & MRC to form the Australian Health Ethics Committee (AHEC). While both its forerunners undertook work on reproductive technologies and embryo research, these areas are not currently on the agenda of the AHEC.

There is no Commonwealth legislation although, in 1985, Senator Harradine (Tasmania) introduced a *Human Embryo Protection from Experimentation Bill* which led to a Senate Select Committee enquiry. The States of Victoria, South Australia and Western Australia have, however, introduced legislation specifically addressing infertility and reproductive technology.

The first Australian IVF birth occurred in the State of Victoria in 1979 and as a result the Victorian Government set up a Committee of Enquiry. Following the final report of this Committee the *Infertility (Medical Procedures) Act* was published in 1984. This set out the provisions under which IVF and embryo research would be allowed and provided for the establishment of a Standing Review and Advisory Committee (see also Chapter 3). The Act permits the fertilization of ova outside a woman's body only for implantation and only married couples are allowed to enter an IVF programme. Research on human embryos is prohibited unless approved by the Standing Review and Advisory Committee - that is, research on embryos surplus to clinical requirements may be permissible - but research involving cloning or the fertilization of human by animal gametes is entirely forbidden. Counselling is mandatory and couples may only enter an IVF programme provided that twelve months have elapsed since investigation by another medical practitioner indicated IVF to be the appropriate treatment. Gamete donation is allowed, subject to consent, but surrogacy contracts are to be considered void. The Act requires that IVF may only be carried out in hospitals approved by the Minister (in effect tertiary referral hospitals) and IVF programmes to be subject to statutory regulations prescribing matters relating to records and counselling.

The Standing Review and Advisory Committee was set up in 1985 under the chairmanship of Professor Louis Waller, Chairman of the Victoria Law Reform Commission. On the recommendation of the Committee the Act was amended in 1987 to include GIFT and related procedures and to allow research on the process of fertilization before syngamy on eggs not destined to be replaced. Syngamy is defined in the Act to mean 'the alignment on the mitotic spindle of the chromosomes derived from the pronuclei.' The *Infertility (Medical Procedures) Regulations 1988* finally brought into force the statutory rules which had been announced in 1984.

Although the 1984 Act remains virtually unchanged with regard to research, since the publication of the *Infertility (Medical Procedures) Amendments Act 1987* there has been confusion in the Victorian Parliament as to when research is allowed, some Members interpreting the Amendment relating to syngamy as setting this time limit for all research. This led to a moratorium on an embryo biopsy project and all embryo research in Victoria came to a standstill. The issue was taken up by the Standing Review and Advisory Committee which, in three parts published between May 1990 and October 1991, issued a report entitled *Review of 'post syngamy' embryo experimentation.*[3] Part III of the report contains recommendations for the further amendment of the *Infertility (Medical Procedures) Act 1984* in order to clarify the legislation. Particularly to this end, the Committee drafted a plain English version of the legislation and stated that in doing so it had two major aims:

'to make this pioneering Victorian legislation as accessible as possible to the community in general, people directly affected by the Act and research, medical, health services and counselling professional persons in the area, as well as to those government officers concerned with its effective application and administration;'

'to establish a statutory system of licensing institutions and persons and of approving counsellors.'

In suggesting modifications to the legislation the report also addresses the need for appropriate definitions (the Act fails to define an embryo); the need for information and education programmes; the import and export of gametes and embryos; the role of day procedures centres in IVF programmes; the distinction between a clinical procedure, a clinical trial, research and experimentation, and an experimental procedure; mandatory counselling; membership of the Standing Committee; record keeping; and the penal provisions of the Act. On a number of these issues the Standing Committee was unable to reach agreement and, as yet, the Act has not been amended.

The next State to legislate in the Commonwealth of Australia was South Australia where the Reproductive Technology Act 1988 makes provision for the establishment of the South Australian Council on *Reproductive Technology*, to formulate a code of ethical practice for artificial fertilization procedures and research and for the licensing of centres and research by the South Australian Health Commission. Artificial fertilization procedures are allowed only for 'married couples', defined as a couple having cohabited continuously for at least five years. Only research that is not detrimental to an embryo may be permitted and embryo flushing is prohibited. A human embryo may not be cultured outside the body beyond the implantation stage. Human embryos may be stored for a period not exceeding ten years with persons on whose behalf embryos are stored having a right to review their decision at intervals of no more than 12 months.

Subsequent to the Act, the South Australia Council on Reproductive Technology was set up with 11 members, together with proxies for each member, appointed by the Governor General of South Australia. The membership was selected to ensure that the Council contained expertise in the various facets of reproductive technology as well as experience from other disciplines and backgrounds such as religion and law, that it was representative of the community in general and that, as far as it was practicable, to contain equal numbers of men and women.

In Western Australia legislation was enacted in 1991. The Human Reproductive Technology Act received assent on 8 October 1991 and establishes the Western Australian Reproductive Technology Council to compile a code of practice relating to the procedures used in, and the ethics governing, human reproductive technology and to make provision regarding the use of that technology in relation to artificially assisted conception and for the regulation of research and related purposes. The aim of the legislation is to make assisted conception available to infertile couples and those whose children are likely to be affected by genetic disease. It is considered that the primary purpose and only justification for the creation of a 'human egg in the process of fertilization or an embryo in vitro' is to assist these couples to have children. All such eggs and embryos are therefore required to be given all reasonable opportunities for implanting. Although it is recognized in the preamble that research enabled the development of current procedures, and it is accepted that certain non harmful research and diagnostic procedures may be licit, the Act does not allow the fertilization of eggs or the creation of embryos other than for implantation in the body of a woman. 'The freezing and storage of embryos is accepted only as a step in the process of implanting and would be allowed only in extraordinary circumstances once the freezing of eggs can be carried out successfully. In addition to in vitro fertilization the Act also covers artificial insemination procedures.

In Australia there are over 20 clinics offering IVF and a high proportion of these (nine in 1989) are in New South Wales. Some aspects of clinical procedures, for instance pathology and ultrasound, are available under Medicare and for married IVF patients with not more than two IVF children Commonwealth funds are available for the cost of certain drugs. Comprehensive statistics are collected by the National Perinatal Statistics Unit (NPSU) in Sydney. The NPSU also monitors the incidence of abnormalities among IVF children. These would appear to be within the range found among children conceived normally and although, among these, an excess of neural tube defects and cardiac abnormalities has been reported the number of births recorded so far is still too small to provide data with any statistical significance.

Austria

In 1986 the Ministry of Sciences and Research published a report on the fundamental aspects of genetics and reproductive biology.[4] This was intended to form the foundation for legislation. But the 1992 Act No. 275 regulating medically assisted procreation is in fact much less liberal. The Act covers the techniques of artificial insemination, in vitro fertilization, GIFT and embryo transfer. The Act requires medically assisted procreation to be used as a treatment to alleviate infertility only when other treatments have failed. The procedures may only be offered to couples who are married or in a stable relationship and who are deemed to be able to provide a satisfactory home for the child. No more eggs should be fertilized than are intended to be returned to the womb but if there are surplus embryos they may be frozen for up to one year. This limit also applies to stored gametes. Frozen embryos may only be used by the couple from whom the gametes originated. Donor sperm may be used in the context of IVF but egg and embryo donation are not permitted nor is the mixing of sperm from different men. Embryo research is not allowed though examination and treatment may be allowed if such action is necessary to achieve a pregnancy.

The Act contains conscience clauses allowing physicians and nursing staff to refuse to participate in medically assisted procreation. Counselling is mandatory, with referral for psychological counselling or psychotherapy to be offered to the husband or partner, and where a couple is unmarried or donor sperm are to be used counselling before a notary regarding the legal consequences of consent is required before treatment may proceed. The Act amends the Civil Code with regard to legitimacy and the Marriage Law to the effect that refusal of a partner to take part in assisted procreation does not form grounds for divorce.

There are 22 assisted reproduction clinics in Austria - the highest number per capita of any country other than Israel.

Belgium

There is no formal regulation of IVF and embryo research in Belgium and no legislation. In 1985 the Ethics Committee for the Belgian Fund for Medical Research decided to follow the recommendations of the Warnock Report. Following the Vatican Instruction of 1987,[5] the Catholic Universities in the Low Countries undertaking IVF (Nijmegen, Leuven, Louvain, and Lille) discussed the issue and decided to continue. They will not, however, undertake research or use donor gametes. At Leuven there is a cryopreservation programme for embryos surplus to clinical treatment. Donor insemination is provided without IVF.

At the Free Universities, which are secular, treatment is less restricted. Gamete donation and selective reduction in conjunction with IVF are undertaken. Only one or two centres undertake embryo research, as opposed to altering procedures to improve clinical IVF. Altogether there are 14 IVF centres in Belgium, seven at university hospitals and seven at private clinics and patients seeking treatment may have some of their costs covered by social security. However, the lack of an official regulatory body means that no IVF statistics or records of research are kept. There is no control over human experimentation in general and no obligation for ethical review although a number of faculty or hospital ethics committees do exist. Medical practice in Belgium is therefore relatively free when it comes to clinical research. The Belgian College of Physicians from 1984 has required ethical approval for research projects and doctors can be disciplined if they are found conducting experiments without ethical approval.

Canada

There has been considerable debate in Canada over a number of years on the new reproductive technologies but there is, as yet, no provincial or federal legislation to regulate IVF or embryo research. The Society of Obstetricians and Gynaecologists of Canada (SOGC) and the Canadian Fertility and Andrology Society have issued guidelines along the lines of those published by the American Fertility Society.[6] Although the SOGC has stated that there should be a strong research component in any IVF programme it is not clear that any embryo research is currently being undertaken in Canada. The Medical Research Council of Canada (MRC) included in its Guidelines on Research Involving Human Subjects[7] ethical guidelines for embryo research but these were designed to apply only to those seeking research funding through the MRC. These guidelines find human embryo research acceptable if the research is scientifically valid and would allow research up to 14-17 days of development; the creation of embryos specifically for research is not considered acceptable. Research should be limited to that directed towards the improvement of infertility management.

In 1985 the Law Reform Commission of Ontario published a report on human artificial reproduction.[8] The Commission acknowledged the need for human embryo research and recommended regulatory control but remained silent on substantive and other ethical guidelines that ought to be followed, not considering that this was within the Commission's expertise. It did, however, suggest that research only be carried out up to 14 days of development and that embryos might be stored frozen for up to ten years and thereafter destroyed.

More recently, the Law Reform Commission of Canada has published a working paper on medically assisted procreation.[9] This comprehensively addresses the medical and legal aspects of assisted reproduction, makes 22 recommendations and sets out the proposed contents of a Medically Assisted Procreation Act. This would provide that access to treatment should be denied to no one unless cost or scarcity of resources required that there should be a selection procedure. The use of gametes and embryos would be restricted to fertilization, experimentation and destruction. The selection of gametes or embryos with specific qualities would be forbidden unless undertaken with the objective of preventing the transmission of serious genetic disease. Control over gametes or embryos would be vested in the persons from whom they derived and the donation of gametes and embryos would be permitted with the written consent of the donors with such consent withdrawable, also in writing. All commercialization of gamete or embryo donation would be prohibited. The proposed Act would restrict clinical and storage services to certified clinics and gamete or embryo banks. Clinics would be obliged to keep records and to file written annual reports to a central registry. Every clinic would be required to provide counselling services for patients. Finally, a national regulatory agency is proposed which would certify clinics and banks and ensure compliance with the Act and regulations.

In 1989 the Canadian Government established a Royal Commission on New Reproductive Technologies under the chairmanship of Dr Patricia Baird, a medical geneticist from the University of British Columbia. The Commission's mandate was to:

> 'inquire into and report on current and potential medical and scientific developments related to new reproductive technologies, considering in particular their social, ethical, health, research, legal and economic implications and the public interest, recommending what policies and safeguards should be applied.'

Since then the Commission has undertaken a vast exercise of public consultation and research, inviting written and telephone submissions from the general public, holding public hearings and funding over 130 studies and analyses of the legal, sociological and medical aspects of the new reproductive technologies. The Commission was due to report back to the Government in 1992 but this was delayed partly because of the Commission's decision to extend the consultation period and partly to hostilities between members of the Commission itself resulting in the sacking of four members.

There are 13 IVF clinics in Canada, 12 of these (four of which are private) are situated in the eastern and most populous part of the country. Public health funding is on a provincial basis and Ontario is now the only province which covers the costs of IVF. There is no formal regulation of IVF, though provincially funded programmes do get checked, and no formal collection of statistics.

Denmark

In 1987 the Danish Parliament passed an Act setting up a National Ethics Council. The Council's principal remit is to make recommendations on embryo research, pre-implantation diagnosis and gene therapy although it is also to make recommendations on other general ethical questions. The Council has a direct link to Parliament through a Parliamentary Committee and the Minister of Health who are jointly responsible for its membership. The Ethics Council started its work in

January 1988 and, following two years of public consultation and education, presented its report *Protection of Human Gametes, Fertilized Ova, Embryos and Fetuses* in 1990.[10,11] The consultation and education exercise involved public hearings, the commissioning of a film and an anthology of opinions and poems. Opinions were canvassed from schoolchildren upwards. The Act of 1987 also decreed that until the Council had reported there should be a moratorium on embryo research and the uses of assisted reproduction limited.

The Report of the Ethics Council was debated in Parliament and a Bill drafted and subsequently amended in 1991. The resulting Act No. 503 of 24 June 1992 came into force in October 1992 with a statutory obligation for its review and revision if necessary by 1995-96. The Act accepts that IVF is a recognized treatment and that research is necessary to its further development; to prohibit all research would be consciously to offer less than optimal treatment. The legislation therefore provides that any biomedical research project involving human individuals, human gametes intended for use in fertilization, fertilized human eggs and pre-embryos or embryos should be reported to regional ethics committees. Denmark has seven of these committees, established according to local boundaries. They have nine or 11 members, three of whom are nominated by the state authorized scientific committee.

These ethics committees are required to oversee and to approve research within the terms of the Act. Fertilized eggs may only be kept in vitro for up to 14 days, excluding any period of cryopreservation. Fertilized human eggs which have been subject to research may not be returned to the uterus unless this can be done without risk of transmitting hereditary disease, defects, abnormalities or similar deformities. The purpose of this provision is to allow the preimplantation diagnosis of genetic disease. In addition the Act prohibits cloning, the production of individuals by fusion of genetically different embryos or parts of embryos prior to implantation and experiments whose objective involves cross species fertilization in order to produce human/animal hybrids.

The donation of fertilized eggs is prohibited although the Act is worded to allow the Minister of Health to make further rules with regard to the cryopreservation and donation of human eggs, together with further regulations to secure donor anonymity. A further order under the Act (Order No. 650 of 22 July 1992) stipulates that frozen oocytes, fertilized or unfertilized, may be stored for a maximum of one year. It is specified that the donation of unfertilized eggs must be anonymous and, while the Act does not address sperm donation, this is in line with existing donor insemination procedures.

Civil law questions of family rights are deemed to lie within the domain of the Ministry of Justice and are not covered by this legislation. These issues are to be dealt with by a new Commission.

A treatment service is now available in Denmark in seven clinics, four of which are in public hospitals. Following the introduction of legislation a further six private clinics have started to offer assisted reproduction and provide treatment for patients who do not meet the selection criteria imposed by the public hospitals. Treatment is available free in the public hospitals.

France

The ethical debate on embryo research goes back to 1983 when the National Ethics Committee was established by decree. Its remit is to provide advice on ethical issues raised by medical and biological research and to promote public debate. The chairman is appointed by the President (recently Professor Jean Pierre Changeux has succeeded the long standing Chairman Professor Jean Bernard) and the Committee reports to the Prime Minister. The Committee has 37 members, each serving a four year term with half turning over every 2 years. Five members are nominated by the President to represent various religious and philosophical groups; 16 are chosen because of their competence in ethical matters and a final 16 because of their experience in medicine or science.

The Committee made recommendations on embryo research in 1986[12] stating that research would be permissable up to seven days after fertilization but introducing a three year moratorium for research on developing pre-implantation diagnosis. However the result is that little research is being undertaken in France other than methodological research related to the technique itself. There appears to be general agreement that the creation of embryos specifically for research should not be allowed.

Subsequently the Conseil d'Etat - a permanent advisory body to the government on matters of legislation - was asked to look at assistedreproduction, taking as its basis the recommendations of the National Ethics Committee. It recommended in its proposals for legislation[13] that the creation of embryos for research should be prohibited but that strictly limited research on embryos surplus to clinical requirements should be allowed. Such research should have the free and informed consent of both progenitors and should be authorized by the National Ethics Committee. Research leading to the artificial modification of the genome, to complete gestation in vitro, and to parthenogenesis, cloning or the production of chimeras, should be forbidden. An embryo should not be kept in vitro beyond 14 days and all research should be followed by local ethical committees which should report on progress to the National Ethics Committee.

Following on from the recommendations of the Conseil d'Etat a draft bill (avant-projet de loi) was prepared in April 1989.[14] This more or less followed the Conseil's recommendations but the time limit for in vitro research was reduced again to 7 days with extension to 14 days to be permissible only under exceptional circumstances. Subsequently a further report was commissioned by the Prime Minister from Mme Noelle Lenoir to provide an in depth study of recent developments in biology, genetics and assisted conception. The aim was to provide an international overview of the technology available together with a summary of the bioethical approaches adopted. The report was published in November 1991[15] and, concerning research on human embryos, stated that embryos should not be created specifically for research, that embryos which had been the subject of experiment should not be replaced and that consent should be obtained from donors before using surplus embryos for research. A bill introduced into the French Parliament in March 1992[16] addresses the clinical provision of assisted reproduction in terms of the licensing of clinics and laboratories and the establishment of a National Council for the Biology and Medicine of Reproduction. Research projects on human embryos are to be submitted to the Council for authorization under conditions to be defined by regulation and the Council will be required to report annually on centres carrying out research and on the purposes of research. The Bill was passed by the Assemblée Nationale at its first reading and is now before the Sénat.

Over 100 clinics offer IVF in France but 90% of all treatments are carried out in 80 of these. The organization which collects IVF data, FIVNAT, recorded 19,000 treatment cycles in 1988. In France IVF is reimbursed 100% by Social Security unless the clinic charges exceptionally high fees. Patients sometimes have to pay laboratory charges (about F 2,500). In April 1988 a National Commission to regulate reproductive medicine was established by decree.[17] This reviewed the provision of IVF in France and set a geographical limit of one clinic for every 125,000 women between the ages of 20 and 40. This allowed 74 clinics to cover the whole of France and the excess were given 6 months notice to close. Clinicians have objected to being assessed on geographical grounds and have continued to practise IVF in protest. The Conseil d'Etat, the appeal body in this case, will not change the regulations and it is likely that women attending unapproved clinics will not be able to claim reimbursement. The current Bill seeks to regularize the situation.

German Federal Republic

In Germany the official debate on embryo research started in 1984 with the Benda Commission which was established to review the ethical implications of IVF. Later, in 1986 the Deutsche Juristentag (a private assembly of jurists meeting every 3 years) formally debated assisted reproduction and constitutional law. A form of consultation document was produced in 1986 and in 1988 this was followed by a 'white paper' setting out proposed legislation.

In 1989 a bill was presented to the German Parliament and in January 1991 the Embryo Protection Act came into force.[18] Although the Act centres almost entirely on penal provisions it does not form part of the Criminal Law.

The Act is entirely restrictive and prohibits:

a) fertilization other than for the purposes of pregnancy;

b) the fertilization of a human egg cell for any purpose other than to start a pregnancy in the woman who produced the egg;

c) the fertilization of more eggs than may be necessary for transfer in one cycle;

d) the transfer of more than three eggs or embryos in one treatment cycle;

e) lavage other than in order to maintain the embryo for reimplantation;

f) to allow sperm to penetrate an egg other than for the purposesof producing a pregnancy.

It defines an embryo as a fertilized developing human egg from the time of karyogamy (fusion of the two pronuclei), also any totipotential cell which is able to divide and develop into an individual. Within the first 24 hours after karyogamy the embryo is considered to be capable of development unless it can be proved to the contrary.

Ectogenesis (gestation outside the womb) is forbidden other than for achieving a pregnancy. Other punishable offences include cloning, germline manipulation, and the formation of human/animal hybrids or chimaeras. In all cases it is the practitioner who is punishable under the Act, not those seeking treatment.

There is no comment as to whether, in the event of more than three eggs being fertilized, all embryos have to be transferred or on the destruction of surplus embryos nor is mention made of freezing. It would, presumably, be allowable to freeze surplus embryos with a view to later transfer.

There are 51 centres undertaking IVF in Germany but despite the number of centres there is no regulatory body and no central collection of statistics. In 1987 a total of 14,400 treatment cycles reached the stage of egg collection in 36 clinics.

Greece

Currently there is no legislation regulating assisted reproduction, however, a law on the modernization and organization of the health system introduced in July 1992 paves the way. This makes provision for a presidential decree which will regulate the conditions for the establishment and functioning of units for artificial fertilization. The same decree will regulate ethical, deontological, legal and economic aspects of the issue of artificial fertilization. Assisted reproduction units will be allowed to function only in the context of specifically organized hospitals, public or private, or specifically organized private clinics. Provision is also made for the establishment of a national ethics committee. The Central Committee on Health is going to comment on the presidential decree and legislation is likely to follow the Council of Europe Recommendation No. 1100. Under the Civil Code a husband who has given consent to assisted reproduction cannot refuse paternity.

At present assisted reproduction services are provided predominantly in the private sector. The first sperm bank was set up in 1973, the first IVF clinic established in 1984 and the first IVF births occurred in 1986. The Orthodox Church has not expressed an opinion on the issue.

Italy

There is no legislation or formal regulation of IVF or embryo research in Italy, neither is there any central collection of IVF statistics and it is therefore not possible to obtain reliable information about the number of treatments carried out and their outcome. However, the Istituto Superiore di Sanità, on behalf of the Minister of Health, is setting up a register of all groups working on the new reproductive technologies with the purpose, eventually, of regulating and controlling this activity. A more or less common code of practice has been agreed by the university hospitals and in 1984 a group of gynaecologists and researchers made the following recommendations for the practice of IVF:

IVF is only justified when other therapeutic techniques have been unsuccessful, have no possibility of succeeding or when alternative therapeutic techniques are too risky.

The couple must be married and be adequately informed about the technique and related risks.

Embryos should be reimplanted whenever possible.

Donation of eggs or sperm is acceptable but IVF embryos should not be donated from one couple to another.

No research for commercial purposes should be allowed.

Manipulation of the genotype of germ cells should not be allowed.

IVF must be carried out under the direction of a physician in a facility authorized by the Ministry of Public Health.

A National Ethics Committee should be established to formulate guidelines.

In July 1989 the outgoing Health Minister, Donat Cattin, called together a Committee of Experts to discuss genetic engineering and biotechnology. The composition of the Committee was heavily biased towards the Catholic sphere. As a result the 'lay' front, in the following September, announced the establishment of an alternative Council on Bioethics composed of 64 members representing a wide range of disciplines. Finally, in March 1990, the Italian Government established a National Ethics Committee under the chairmanship of Senator Adriano Bompiani. It has a membership of 39 composed of lawyers, philosophers, scientists and physicians and has so far produced reports on biotechnology, gene therapy, the collection and testing of human semen and on the determination of death. No recommendations have emerged so far on assisted reproduction or human embryo research.

Although the issue of reproductive technology has been discussed in Parliament on a number of occasions regular changes of government have meant that no Bill has succeeded in being passed. The Christian Democrats form the largest coalition party and have a close relationship with the Catholic Church. In 1984 the Christian Democrat Minister of Health, Donat Cattin, established a Commission to study reproductive technologies. The Commission published a report in November 1985 (the Santosuosso Report)[19] which, while accepting IVF for married couples, recommends that only sufficient eggs should be fertilized to achieve a successful implantation and that all embryos should be transferred to the uterus. The report also recommends that all embryo research should be forbidden, whether on embryos surplus to clinical requirements or on those created specifically for research, and made a criminal offence. Cattin was succeeded by a Liberal Minister of Health, De Lorenzo, who was himself a doctor and who disbanded the

Commission set up by his predecessor. Legislation in this area seems unlikely in the near future.

Most IVF in Italy is carried out in ten university hospitals and is also available in a number of private clinics. It is estimated that there are some 70 assisted reproduction centres in total. Catholic hospitals are subject to the Vatican Instruction, which condemns the procedure, and do not practise IVF although some will undertake GIFT. The costs of homologous IVF are reimbursable by the state and in Sicily, which has a pronatalist policy, heterologous IVF undertaken at Palermo, the biggest IVF centre in Italy, is also reimbursable. A certain amount of research is carried out, mainly clinical and methodological. The micro-injection of sperm and zona drilling are performed routinely in a number of centres to overcome problems of male sub fertility. Pre-implantation diagnosis of genetic disorders is performed in a number of centres. The Italians have been among the first to treat women who have passed the age of natural menopause.

Japan

Assisted reproduction procedures are carried out in Japan under the guidance of the Japanese Society of Obstetrics and Gynaecology which has issued regular statements as the technology has advanced. The Society's first statement on in vitro fertilization and embryo transfer was issued in 1983. It states that these techniques are to be used only after evaluation of their effectiveness and safety, fully taking into account their ethical and legal implications and the social circumstances in Japan. The procedure should be performed only on patients who have no prospects of achieving pregnancy by any other medical means and should be offered to married couples. The procedures should be fully explained to the patients who should provide written consent and the physician is obliged to respect their and their child's privacy. Only practitioners with advanced training in reproductive medicine are allowed to undertake IVF; fertilized ova must be handled with the care and respect due to all forms of life and genetic engineering shall not be practised.

A statement issued in 1985 addresses in more detail the handling of gametes and fertilized ova, particularly in relation to research. Research is considered permissible only in the context of basic research intended to advance the state of reproductive medicine or of research intended to contribute to the diagnosis and treatment of infertility. Human gametes and fertilized ova may only be used for research with the consent of the donors and with the protection of their privacy. Fertilized ova may not be used for research more than two weeks after fertilization and the same time limit applies to embryos which are to be stored. All research involving the handling of human gametes or embryos is to be reported to the Society.

In 1987 the Society issued a statement on sex selection. In Japan a method had been devised of separating X and Y chromosome-bearing sperm by centrifugation. The Society suggests that many points regarding the method's reliability, safety and effectiveness require further investigation and the method may not be used clinically except to prevent the conception of children with severe sex linked recessive disorders. If the method is used, it is only to be practised by physicians with advanced training in reproductive medicine who are registered to do so with the Society. They are obliged to report to the Society on their findings with regard to reliability and safety of the procedure and to explain the nature of the method fully to their subjects. Society members planning researchon or the clinical application of similar methods are requested to seek the advice of an ethics committee.

Cryopreservation was the subject of the next statement in 1988. This requires written consent from patients before the procedure is undertaken. A time limit is placed on the period of cryopreservation. This must not exceed the marital life of the patients nor should it be longer than the wife's reproductive age. Freeze thawed embryos or ova are to be replaced in the woman from whom they were collected, each time with the written consent of both husband and wife. The equipment used must enable all frozen embryos to be properly identified. Society members undertaking cryopreservation are required to register and report to the Society.

Finally, a statement on microinsemination was issued in 1992. It is to be performed only after evaluation of its effectiveness and safety, taking full account of its ethical, legal and social implications. It is indicated only for patients who are diagnosed to be infertile due to severe fertilization failure. Similar requirements with regard to training and consent are made in line with the Society's previous statements.

In 1990 there were in Japan 116 centres offering IVF and embryo transfer, 44 offering GIFT and ten elsewhere having cryopreservation facilities. A total of 6,597 cycles of treatment were carried out on 5,277 IVF patients and 726 cycles on 617 GIFT patients.

Netherlands

The first Parliamentary debate on IVF began in 1982 and, following a request from the Minister of Health, the Health Council in 1983 established a commission to look into IVF and embryo research. The Commission published an interim report in 1984 suggesting that IVF be made available only in cases of poor tubal pathology and that these services should be developed primarily in the eight academic hospitals. The final report,[20] published in 1986, was extended to cover donor insemination, oocyte donation and surrogacy but did not differ much in its conclusions on IVF. In its latest report *Heredity: Science and Society*[21] the Health Council once again considers the issue of research on human embryos and draws up a number of procedural stipulations which represent the majority view. These are that an embryo should not be grown in vitro beyond 14 days of development; that the information gained from the experiments must not be obtainable by other means; that embryos which have been the subject of research must not be implanted; that ethical approval should be sought and, finally, that there should be a moratorium on human germ line gene therapy.

In 1989 the Minister of Health established the Kern Commissie Ethiek Medisch Onderzoek (KEMO) an independent national multidisciplinary committee whose task is to analyse complex moral, legal and societal issues and to provide support for local ethics committees. Its recommendations are not binding. The KEMO has been consulted on embryo research and has accepted the stipulations of the Health Council. It has also discussed the morality of the creation of embryos for research and has concluded moral justification for the creation of embryos for research cannot be excluded as a possibility.

The regulation of IVF and embryo research seems to remain haphazard. Following the advice of the Hospital Facilities Council that the number of hospitals offering IVF could be controlled under Article 18 of the Hospital Facilities Act the Minister, in 1985, published a temporary Order under the Act. The Order stated that for a period of two years no hospital should offer IVF without a licence from the Ministry and that only clinics established by the time of the Order would be considered for licence; clinics performing only IVF would not be considered. There were 13 IVF clinics in operation in 1985. In 1986 the Hospital Facilities Council advised the Secretary of State that two general hospitals should be licensed and two others provided with a temporary licence. However, a report by the Public Health Inspectorate in 1988 stated that 33 hospitals were undertaking IVF implying that some 21 clinics were evading the Order of 1985.

In August 1988 the Ministers of Health and of Justice published a decree on artificial reproduction and surrogacy.[22] This announced that the Government intended to bring IVF fully under the Hospital Facilities Act and to maintain the licensing system proposed in 1985. The Government would be prepared to approve of embryo research in exceptional cases and took the position that surrogacy was allowable for medical reasons but that no commercial mediation would be approved.

An enquiry undertaken by a commission of the Second Chamber of Parliament found that there is currently no embryo research being undertaken in Holland. There is a moratorium on the creation of embryos for research and written consent has to be obtained for research on those embryos surplus to clinical requirements. The Government has stated its intention to draft a bill on artificial procreation techniques.

The first IVF work in Holland started in 1977, the first baby was born as a result of this technique in 1983 and by 1988 there were over 30 clinics offering IVF treatment. The situation is much as in the UK with a small number of hospitals undertaking the majority of the treatments and a number of small peripheral clinics undertaking very few treatments. A system of 'transport IVF' has also developed whereby peripheral IVF clinics perform the first three steps of IVF treatment, namely patient selection, ovulation induction and oocyte aspiration. The oocytes are then transported to a central laboratory within one hour and the central IVF clinic undertakes embryo culture and transfer. It is estimated that more than half of all Dutch IVF treatments may be carried out in this way.

About two thirds of the clinics agreed to collaborate in a study of IVF in Holland and in 1988 these 21 clinics undertook 2,377 treatments. It is estimated that the remainder probably undertook a further 600 treatments bringing the total to about 3,000. There are no formal statistics available.

Whether or not the cost of IVF treatment should be reimbursable through Sick Funds has been the subject of debate since 1982. In 1986 the Sick Funds Council, having previously refused to allow reimbursement for IVF, decided to subsidize 1,600 IVF treatments in five hospitals over a period of two years to evaluate the procedure in order to take a well-founded decision on future Sick Funds coverage. In March 1989 the Sick Funds Council advised the Minister of Health to continue the subsidy scheme until 1991 but decided not to bring IVF under coverage of the Sick Funds Law until further notice. Private insurance will pay for IVF costs in Holland.

Norway

The Norwegian Act of 1987[23] limits IVF to married couples and prohibits research. While artificial insemination with donor sperm is allowed in cases of male infertility donor gametes are not allowed in conjunction with IVF. Embryos surplus to a treatment may be stored for 12 months. Patients over 37 years old may not be treated.

Clinics comply strictly with the Act and couples are asked to sign a declaration that they are married. Clinicians do, however, have criticisms of the law, namely, the 12 months' storage period is too short and they would like to see it extended to 3 years; IVF currently is only obtainable for female indications and needs to be extended to male; the restriction to homologous IVF is illogical when donor insemination is permitted.

Seven clinics offer IVF in Norway, only one is a private hospital. The State pays 90% of the cost at public hospitals. There is no limit on the number of treatments a patient may have but there is an agreement between all seven clinics that there should be an upper age limit for the woman of 38. Each clinic undertakes 400-500 treatment cycles each year.

The Act forbids research on fertilized ova but, since the term 'research' is not defined clearly, it is uncertain that this is intended to apply to methodological evaluation or non-invasive therapeutic research intended to be of direct benefit to the embryo.

In 1990 the National Committee for Research Ethics of the Norwegian Council for Medical Research published a report on the ethical questions on research related to human fetuses.[24] The report was intended primarily for the research community, politicians, the government administration and those with a special interest in the subject and was based on a series of three seminars which had been held on the subject. For the purposes of the report the term 'fetus' was applied to all stages of gestation from fertilization to birth. It makes the following recommendations.

1. For research on fetuses, the guidelines of research ethics which apply to research on *born* persons should be adopted.

2. Fetuses as subjects of research should receive the same protection as other groups of research subjects who are not themselves capable of giving their *informed consent.*

3. *Destructive research* on fetuses - ie, research which causes the death or irreversible injury to the subject of the experiment, and procedures which involve the production of fetuses for research purposes - are ethically unacceptable.

4. *Non-therapeutic research* on fetuses which involves risk or discomfort to the fetus or the mother in the short or the longer term is ethically unacceptable.

5. *Non-therapeutic research* on fetuses which is free from risk and cannot be performed in other ways can be ethically acceptable, for instance systematic registration of cardiac rhythms.

6. *Therapeutic research* on fetuses can be ethically acceptable, provided the given research is of direct or indirect benefit to the fetus in question (innovative treatment), possible side effects are known, and the experiment does not involve short or long term risks of irreversible injury to the fetus or the mother.

7. Therapeutic research on fetuses in cases where possible side effects are not known is ethically unacceptable; this includes gene therapy on germ cells and somatic cells from fetuses.

8. All genetic research on fetuses, the aim of which is to *change* normal characteristics, is ethically unacceptable.

9. All research on fetuses which is intended to make it possible to *clone* human beings, form *hybrids* between humans and other species, or create human beings on the basis of the fusion of genetically distinct fetuses, is ethically unacceptable.

10. The guidelines which apply to the use of organs from born donors should be adopted in the event of the use of fetuses as donors of tissue or organs.

11. Research involving the purchase or sale of fetuses or of cells, tissue or organs from fetuses is ethically unacceptable.

12. Separate legislation ought to be considered covering the legal position of pregnant women and fetuses in medical research and antenatal care.

Portugal

Provision for the establishment of a National Council of Ethics for the Life Sciences was made under Law No. 14/90 of 9 June 1990[25] and the Council was formed under the chairmanship of Dr Mario Raposo, the Purveyor of Justice (ombudsman), in 1991. Among the issues it is to address is the subject of medically assisted procreation and embryo research. In doing so it is likely to consider a project of law, or white paper, on medically assisted fertilization which has been drawn up by the Centro de Estudos de Direito Medico at the University of Coimbra School of Law. On the question of embryo research, the paper would allow research on spare embryos only up to 14 days of development and would prohibit the creation of embryos in vitro specifically for research.

Donor insemination is currently available at two centres, in Lisbon andOporto, where there are sperm banks. Three university hospital centres offer assisted conception; two in Lisbon offering IVF and GIFT and one in Coimbra offering GIFT only.

Spain

The Spanish Law 35 *Health: Assisted Reproduction Techniques* received the Royal Assent on 22 November 1988. This followed, and was largely based upon, the Report of the Special Commission set up by the Cortez to study human in vitro fertilization and donor insemination. The President of the Commission was Marcel Palacios (who was also rapporteur to the Science and Technology Committee of the Parliamentary Assembly of the Council of Europe on the same issue) and the report was presented to the Cortez in April 1986.

The Spanish law is comprehensive and extends to cover GIFT, and related techniques, and donor insemination as well as IVF. The law is also remarkably liberal in that it makes these services available to any woman, whether married or not, and allows research on surplus embryos though the creation of embryos for research is forbidden. The law uses the term pre-embryo to describe the embryo up to 14 days of development.

Other prohibited procedures are uterine lavage, the freezing of oocytes and any research involving cloning, parthenogenesis or genetic manipulation. The law also makes void any surrogacy contract.

Donation of both gametes and embryos is authorized, not more than six children being allowed to be born from one donor. All clinics are expected to have cryopreservation facilities in order to store surplus embryos.

Research is permitted only on non-viable embryos from a therapeutic programme. It is left to the scientists to decide the criteria for non-viability - generally failure to cleave or excess pronuclei. No research is allowed beyond 14 days development.

The law decrees that regulation of infertility services shall be by a National Commission for Assisted Reproduction. The Spanish Fertility Society established an IVF register to collect statistics, starting in 1989. There are some 24 centres offering IVF, ten of which are private clinics, and a further 45 centres offer donor insemination. Women attending private clinics may recover the cost through private insurance but treatment is free at public hospitals. The largest centre, in Barcelona, undertakes about 600 treatment cycles a year.

Law No. 35 was challenged, by the Popular Party, immediately following its enactment in 1989. It was contested that the law was unconstitutional because although it addressed matters of human rights it had not been made an organic law but had been enacted as an ordinary law. The issue was referred to the Constitutional Court from which a decision is still awaited.

Sweden

The Swedish Law on in vitro fertilization came into force on 1 January 1989.[26] The Act sets out the conditions under which IVF is permitted and embryo research undertaken. These are as follows:

> Couples must be married or living together in a permanent relationship (more than 2 years) to be eligible for IVF.

> The use of donated gametes in the context of IVF or the donation of surplus embryos to another couple is forbidden. The reasoning is that donor insemination in itself constitutes a deviation from the natural biological process; a combination of sperm donation and external fertilization represents an even greater departure from that process. Where the donation of ova is concerned it is considered that use of eggs from a third party woman is contrary to the human biological process. Surrogate motherhood is also prohibited.

> Freezing of surplus embryos is allowed for up to one year and only with the couple's consent. Couples may also consent to the use of spare embryos for research. Research is permitted for up to two weeks following fertilization but only for research related to the improvement of IVF techniques and all projects must be approved by an ethics committee. Manipulation of ova, genetic or otherwise, is not permitted.

Seven university departments and three private centres in Sweden offer IVF and between them undertake 2,000-2,500 treatment cycles each year. Patients bear the cost of treatment which is partially subsidized in university departments.

In 1984 the Swedish government passed a law on artificial insemination[27] following the publication of a report by a Government Committee set up in 1981 to look at issues related to assisted reproduction. This law restricted donor insemination to married couples, or those in a long standing relationship. Treatment requires written consent from the husband or cohabitant who will be regarded as the legal father of the child. The most radical aspect of this law is the section relating to information about the donor. It is decreed that the child should have the right to obtain identifying information about the donor. It has been the tradition in the past for non identifying information only to be held.

The net effect of this change in the law was, firstly, to reduce and change the type of donors available - older married rather than younger single men offered themselves as donors - and, secondly, a reduction in the demand for donor insemination. In fact, many Swedish couples seeking donor insemination seek treatment in other countries where donor anonymity is still guaranteed.

Switzerland

In Switzerland there is a cultural division with respect to attitudes on assisted reproduction and on in vitro fertilization in particular. Of the Cantons which have introduced legislation, the French and Italian speaking Cantons allow homologous IVF (Geneva, Neuchatel, Vaud and Ticino) but the German speaking Cantons are more inclined not to.[28] Of the latter, only the Canton of Aargau has legislated in favour of homologous IVF for married couples. In St Gallen the clause in the legislation prohibiting the use of IVF was declared unconstitutional, thus technically allowing use of this treatment. The Cantons of Glarus and Basel allow only the use of artificial insemination by husband and prohibit the use of all other methods of assisted reproduction. The Basel Law of October 1990[29] came into force in March 1991 and effectively replaced a previous Directive of 1987.

All these Cantons specifically, or by implication, prohibit research and surrogacy. Those which allow in vitro fertilization do so strictly in accordance with the guidelines of the Swiss Academy of Medical Sciences.[30] These state that assisted methods of procreation should only be allowed for married couples or unmarried couples who live in similar conditions and third party gamete donation is allowed provided that they are not used from both sexes simultaneously. Gamete donation must be free of charge and the number of offspring from one donor is limited to ten. Gametes and embryos may be preserved for a period of up to five years but generally they should be kept alive only for the treatment in progress. Research is prohibited as is insemination with a husband's sperm after his death, embryo donation or the establishment of surrogacy arrangements. Treatment is subject to

In May 1992 the Federal Constitution of Switzerland was amended to address issues related to procreation and genetic engineering.[31] Section 24 novies states that:

'(1) Man and the environment shall be protected against abuses in the field of procreation and genetic engineering techniques.

(2) The Confederation shall issue provisions concerning the use of the germ cell and human genetic heritage. It shall thereby endeavour to ensure the protection of human dignity, personality and family'.

It then proceeds to prohibit interventions which would affect the genetic heritage of human gametes and embryos and human germline manipulation. Access to assisted procreation is allowed only where infertility or the risk of transmission of serious disease cannot be avoided in any other manner and in vitro fertilization is authorized only under conditions laid down by law. Only as many eggs may be fertilized and developed to the embryo stage as may be immediately implanted. Embryo donation and surrogacy are prohibited as is any form of commerce in human germ cell heritage and products derived from embryos. The amendment guarantees a person access to data relating to his parentage but a person's genetic heritage may only be analysed, recorded and disclosed on the basis of that person's consent or on the basis of legal provision.

United States of America

There is no Federal law relating to embryo research or IVF and in such situations rules tend to be established on a case by case basis.
A small number of States have laws specifically mentioning IVF:

Kentucky: An adoption statute states that nothing in the statute prohibits IVF.[32]

Illinois: Prohibits non-therapeutic experimentation on a 'fetus produced by the fertilization of a human ovum with a human sperm' but states that the statute is not intended to prohibit the performance of in vitro fertilization.[33] Furthermore, all embryos produced outside the womb must be afforded the 'care and custody of a child'.[34]

Furthermore, all embryos produced outside the womb must be afforded the 'care and custody of a child'.[34]

Louisiana: A law, passed in 1986, concerning in vitro fertilized ova[35] forbids the purposeful creation of an in vitro embryo solely for the purpose of research or sale. The sale of human ova is also prohibited. The law also grants juridical status (entitlement to sue or be sued) to the fertilized ovum until implanted. Its status is then governed by the State law applying to the products of conception in utero. These do not have juridical status. No person may intentionally destroy an IVF embryo that appears capable of normal development. Further legislation in 1990[36] requires couples who wish to discard embryos surplus to treatment to donate them to another couple for implantation and development.

New Mexico: A 1979 law[37] appears to allow research involving human IVF, provided that it is performed in the treatment of infertility and that each fertilized ovum is implanted in a human female recipient.

Pennsylvania: Requires that all persons conducting or experimenting in IVF 'file quarterly reports with the department which shall be available for public inspection and copying'. Failure to file a report is subject to a fine of $50 per day. Reports must include names of persons conducting or experimenting in IVF, location, sponsor of research, number of eggs fertilized, destroyed or discarded and number implanted.[38] However, programmes do not appear to be monitored.

There has been an effective moratorium on Federal funding for embryo research since 1975 when the Department of Health Education and Welfare (now Department of Health and Human Services, DHHS) published regulations for the protection of human subjects of research (45CFR46.204(d)) which decreed that no embryo research project should be funded without ethical approval from the Ethical Advisory Board. Such a board was appointed in 1978 and reported to the Secretary for Health both on a specific application and on embryo research in general, both of which it found acceptable. No time limit was set on a decision from the Secretary, no action was taken on the report and the Board's charter expired in 1980. As there was now no EAB researchers were discouraged from seeking NIH funds and no fundable applications were forthcoming. The situation changed in 1988 when an application for funding was highly recommended by NIH and the

US Office of Technology Assessment report *Infertility: Social and Medical Choices* criticized DHHS for its posture.[39] In June 1988 the Assistant Secretary for Health, Dr Robert Windom, announced that the EAB would be re-established and in September a proposed charter for the new EAB was issued for comment.

Since that time the US Administration has taken no action to re-establish the EAB. In the meantime, the applicant seeking NIH support obtained funds from a private foundation and completed his research without Federal funds. With the recent election of President Clinton the situation may now change.

A survey by a Congress Subcommittee (Regulation, Business Opportunities and Energy) estimated that there are some 200 clinics undertaking IVF in the United States. Of these, 146 provided data for the years 1987 and 1988; 14,619 treatment cycles were undertaken at these clinics in 1988 and the overall success rate, in terms of live births, was 9%.

Subsequently a bill was introduced into Congress in April 1992 by Representatives Ron Wyden (Oregon) and Norman Lent (New York) to provide for reporting of pregnancy success rates of assisted reproductive technology programs and for the certification of embryo laboratories. After discussion and amendment by the Congress Committee on Energy and Commerce the bill (House Report 102-624) passed to the Senate Labour Committee. The Senate Report (102-452) was passed on 8 October and Public Law 102-493 was signed by President Bush on 24 October 1992. The principal provisions of the law address assisted reproductive technology programs and the evaluation of their services and success rates; the certification of embryo laboratories; the accreditation of organisations; certification revocation and suspension; the publication of success rates. With effect from two years after the enactment of the law each assisted reproduction programme will be required to submit an annual report (through the Centers for Disease Control) to the Secretary of Health and Human Services on pregnancy success rates, the identity of each embryo laboratory used by the programme and whether the laboratory is certified. Assisted reproductive technology is defined as 'all treatments or procedures which include the handling of human oocytes or embryos including in vitro fertilization, gamete intra fallopian transfer, zygote intra fallopian transfer, and such other specific technologies as the Secretary may include in this definition, after making public any proposed definition in such manner as to facilitate comment from any person (including any Federal or other public agency)'. An embryology laboratory is defined as 'a facility in which human oocytes are subject to assisted reproductive technology treatment or procedures based on the manipulation of oocytes or embryos which are subject to implantation.'

There is no regulatory body for clinical IVF though guidelines, setting out minimal standards and making recommendations for certain procedures, have been issued by the Ethics Committee of the American Fertility Society[6] (the Society uses the term pre-embryo to describe the fertilized egg up to the appearance of the primitive streak). As a result the provision of IVF is very diverse with facilities ranging from large university medical complexes to single doctor offices and the professional qualifications of those offering the procedure are equally disparate.

The costs of IVF are largely met out of insurance and 6 States -Delaware, Maryland, Hawaii, Texas, Arkansas and Massachusetts - have mandated that IVF be covered by insurance. Coverage for IVF under State Medicaid programs varies; many will pay for drugs, counselling and surgical procedures related to infertility treatment, but the Office for Technology Assessment, in its recent report, was unable to identify any State Medicaid payments for IVF. However, it is likely that IVF component procedures are inadvertently paid by most Medicaid plans. At present no Federal Government programmes cover IVF procedures.

Council of Europe

The role of the Council of Europe is changing with the growth of influence of the EC and the Single European Act. Before the establishment of the EC there was no will for integration amongst the countries of Europe and the Council of Europe functioned as a forum for obtaining consensus on a number of issues particularly human rights. It is in this latter field where the Council will continue to be of importance, particularly on social rights issues.

The issue of IVF and embryo research has received attention in the Parliamentary Assembly of the Council of Europe although insufficient agreement has been achieved in the Committee of Ministers for a legal instrument to be drafted. Recommendation 1100 of the Parliamentary Assembly[40] on the use of human embryos and fetuses in scientific research which would have allowed some limited research was not adopted when it reached the Committee of Ministers and was published as an information document. The ad hoc Committee on Bioethics which advises the Committee of Ministers recommended that no act or procedure should be permitted on any embryo in vitro other than for the benefit of the embryo in question but, where the State allows, pre-implantation diagnosis may be permitted and other investigative and experimental procedures. In December 1989 the Council of Europe held a symposium on bioethics which addressed the field more generally.[41] Subsequently the Secretary General of the Council, Mme Catherine Lalumière, has established a secretariat to draft a European Convention on Bioethics which would, *inter alia*, address human in vitro fertilization. The object and purpose of the Convention is to protect the dignity, identity and integrity of human beings and guarantee all individuals, whatever their nationality or residence, the respect of their rights and fundamental freedoms with regard to the application of biology and medicine.

European Community

Currently there is no European directive on human in vitro fertilization or embryo research. Until recently activity on these areas had taken place primarily in the European Parliament which in 1989 adopted two resolutions, one on artificial procreation and one on genetic engineering, which called for limitations on the use of human in vitro fertilization, for example, that it should only be used for therapeutic purposes and that only homologous IVF should be allowed. In 1991 the new biomedical technologies, including IVF, were further discussed at a meeting, in Milan, of the Parliament's Scientific and Technology Options Assessment. This resulted in 1992 in the publication of a report, *Bioethics in Europe*,[42] which addressed the ethical implications of a wide range of medical and non-medical technologies.

In March 1990 Ministers of the Member States of the EC met at Kronberg to discuss ethical issues in human embryology and genome research. Subsequently the Council of Ministers and the European Commission agreed to monitor developments in legislation and in current practice, in the field of human embryo research, and a Working Group was established by the Commission with this remit and with the requirement to report back annually to the Council and to the Commission. The Group met for the first time in March 1991 and is currently undertaking a survey of relevant legislation in all Member States. The European Commission has additionally set up a high level advisory group on the ethical implications of biotechnology which will look more broadly than the Working Group on Human Embryos.

The following table summarizes the information in this chapter.

SUMMARY TABLE: International comparisons of IVF regulation

Nation	Legislation	Embryo research allowed	Regulatory Body
United Kingdom	Human Fertilisation and Embryology Act 1990	Up to 14 days	Human Fertilisation and Embryology Authority
Australia	Victoria: Infertility (Medical Procedures) Act 1984, amended 1987, Regulations 1988	On fertilization up to syngamy or on surplus embryos up to 14 days	Standing Review and Advisory Committee reviews research hospitals approved by Ministry
	S. Australia Reproductive Technology Act 1989	Non-detrimental research to implantation stage	S. Australian Council on Reproductive Technology
	W. Australia Human Reproductive Technology Act 1991	No	Western Australian ReproductiveTechnology Council
Austria	Act No. 275 1992	No. Examination and treatment of embryos may be allowed in order to achieve a pregnancy	

Nation	Legislation	Embryo research allowed	Regulatory Body
Belgium	No	Yes - no legal restriction	No
Canada	No - awaiting report of Royal Commission	Yes - no legal restriction	No - Profession uses guidelines of SOGC
Denmark	Act No. 503 24 June 1992	Yes up to 14 days	Regional Ethics Committees
France	Not yet - Projet de loi presented to Assemblée Nationale March 1992	Accepted up to 7 days on surplus embryos	National Commission licenses clinics
Greece	Act No. 123 15 July 1992 makes provision for presidential decree	Yes - no legal restriction	No
Germany	Embryo Protection Act 1990	No	No
Italy	No	Yes - no legal restriction	No
Japan	No	Yes - no legal restriction	No - Japanese Society of Obstetrics & Gynaecology issues guidelines
Netherlands	No	No legal restriction but research undertaken	No but Ministry of Health inspects clinics

Country	Legislation		
Norway	Act No. 628 1987 relating to artificial procreation	No	No - clinics reach mutual agreement
Portugal	No - legislation under consideration	Likely to be allowed on spare embryos up to 14 days	No
Spain	Law 35/1988 - Health: Assisted Reproduction	Yes on non-viable spare embryos up to 14 days	National Commission for Assisted Reproduction
Sweden	In vitro Fertilization Act 1988	Up to 14 days	No
Switzerland	Aargau: Law on Health of 10 November 1987 Art.50	No	Swiss Academy of Medical Sciences provides professional regulation
	Basel: Law on Human Reproductive Medicine of 18 October 1990	No	
	Geneva: Regulations Concerning the Conditions Governing the Practice of In Vitro Fertilization	No	

Nation	Legislation	Embryo research allowed	Regulatory Body
Switzerland (contd)	and Embryo Transfer in Private Medical Establishments of 28 May 1986		
	Glarus: Resolution concerning Art. 33 of the Law on Health of 1 May 1988	No	
	Neuchatel: Directives Concerning the Artificial Insemination by Donor and In Vitro Fertilization of 16 October 1986	No	
	St Gallen: Decree Concerning Interventions in Human Reproduction of 24 February 1988	No	
	Ticino: Law on Health of 18 April 1989, Art.13	No	

Switzerland (contd)	Vaud: Law on Public Health of 29 May 1986 Art.72 and Art. 13/4	No	
	Amendment to Federal Constitution inserting Section 24 novies, 13 August 1992	No	
USA	Public Law 102-493 provides for reporting success rates and certification of embryo laboratories	No Federal funding for research	No - American Fertility Society has issued guidelines
	Ky. Rev. Stat. Sec 436.026 (1985) Kentucky		
	Ill. Ann. Stat. ch. 38 paras 88-26,32 (1987)	No	
	Ill. Ann. Stat. ch 38 para 9-1.2 (3) (b) (1989) Illinois		

Nation	Legislation	Embryo research allowed	Regulatory body
USA (contd)	La. Rev. Stat. Ann. Secs. 14:87, 121-133 (1987) Louisiana	Forbids creation of embryos for research	
	La. Rev. Stat. Ann. Sec. 9:126 (1990) Louisiana		
	N.M. Stat. Ann. Secs 24-9A-1to 6 (1979) New Mexico	Yes	
	Pa. Stat. Ann tit. 18, Secs. 3203,3216 (1983) Pennsylvania	Yes	

References

1. National Health and Medical Research Council (1982), NH & MRC *Statement on Human Experimentation and Supplementary Notes*, Australian Government Publishing Service, Canberra, Australia

2. National Health and Medical Research Council (1985), *In Vitro Fertilization: Centres in Australia*, Australian Government Publishing Service, Canberra, Australia

3. Standing Review & Advisory Committee on Infertility (1991), *Report to the Minister for Health on matters related to the Review of 'post- syngamy' Embryo Experimentation Part III: Recommendations for amendment of the Infertility (Medical Procedures) Act 1984*, SRACI, Melbourne

4. Ministry of Sciences and Research (1986), *The Fundamental Aspects of Genetics and Reproductive Biology*, Vienna, Austria

5. Congregation for the Doctrine of the Faith (1987), *Instruction on Respect for Human Life in its Origin and on the Dignity of Procreation*, Vatican City

6. The American Fertility Society (1986), Ethical considerations of the new reproductive technologies, *Fertility and Sterility*, **46 no 3**, supplement 1

7. Medical Research Council of Canada (1987), *Guidelines on Research Involving Human Subjects*, Ottawa, Canada

8. Ontario Law Reform Commission (1985), *Report on Human Artificial Reproduction and Related Matters*, vols 1 and 2, Toronto, Canada

9. Law Reform Commission of Canada (1992), *Medically Assisted Procreation (Working Paper; 65)*, Canada Communication Group Publishing, Ottawa, Canada

10. The Danish Council of Ethics (1989), Protection of Human Gametes, Fertilized Ova, Embryos and Fetuses, *Second Annual Report*, Copenhagen, Denmark

11. The Danish Council of Ethics (1989), *Recommendations for Regulations for Protection of Fertilized Human Ova, Living Embryos and Fetuses*, Copenhagen, Denmark

12. Comité Consultatif National d'Ethique pour les Sciences de la Vie et de la Santé (1986), *Journées annuelles d'éthique*, La Documentation Francaise, Paris, France

13. Conseil d'Etat (1988), *Sciences de la Vie; De l'Ethique au Droit.* 2nd ed, La Documentation Française, Paris, France

14. Conseil d'Etat (1989), *Avant-projet de Loi sur les Sciences de la Vie et les Droits de l'Homme*, The Council, Paris, France (unpublished)

15. Lenoir N. (1991), *Aux frontières de la vie: une éthique biomédicale à la francaise*, La Documentation Française, Paris.

16. Assemblée Nationale (1992), *Projet de Loi Relatif au don et à l' Utilisation des Eléments et Produits du Corps Humain et à la Procréation Médicalement Assistée, et Modifiant le Code de la Santé publique*, No.2600, Paris, France

17. *Décret No 88-327 du 8 Avril 1988*, D.S. 1988. 242, France

18. Law of 13 December 1990 for the Protection of Embryos, Bundesgesetzblatt, Part 1 at 2746-48, Germany

19. Commissione Ministeriale per una Specifica Normativa in Tema di Fecondazione Artificiale Umana (1985), *Prima Proposta: Norme sui Procedimenti non Naturali per la Fecondazione con Seme del Marito. Seconda Preposta: Norme della Fecondazione Artificiale Umana e sui Tratamento di Gameti ed Embrioni*

20. Gezondheidsraad (1986), *Artificial Procreation*, The Health Council, The Hague, Netherlands

21. Gezondheidsraad (1989), *Heredity: Health and Society*, The Health Council, The Hague, Netherlands

22. Tweede Kamer der Staten Generaal, *Kunstmatige Bevruchting en Draagmoederscap*, 1987-1988, 20 706, nr.2.

23. *Act No. 68 of 12 June 1987 Relating to Artificial Procreation*, Norway

24. The National Committee for Medical Research Ethics, The Norwegian Research Council for Science and the Humanities (1990), *Research on Fetuses*, Oslo, Norway

25. *Diario da Republica*, Series I, 9 June 1990, no. 133, pp. 2516-2517

26. *Law No. 711 of 14 June 1988 on Fertilization Outside the Human Body*, Sweden

27. *Law No. 1140 of 20 December 1984 on Insemination*, Sweden

28. Stepan J. (1990), *International Survey of Laws on Assisted Procreation*, Publications of the Swiss Institute of Comparative Law, Schulthess Polygraphischer Verlag, Zurich, Switzerland.

29. Canton of Basel Stadt, *Gesetz betreffend die Reproduktionsmedizin beim Menschen Vom 18 Oktober 1990*

30. Swiss Academy of Medical Sciences (1990), *Medico-ethical Guidelines on Medically Assisted Procreation.*

31. *Recueil Officiel des Lois Fédérales*, 25 August 1992, **no. 32**, pp. 1579-1580

32. Ky. Rev. Stat. Sec. 436.026 (1985) Kentucky

33. Ill. Ann. Stat. ch. 38 paras 88-26,32 (1987) Illinois

34. Ill. Ann. Stat. ch. 38 para 9-1.2 (3) (b) (1989) Illinois

35. La. Rev. Stat. Ann. Secs 14:87, 121-133 (1987) Louisiana

36. La. Rev. Stat. Ann. Sec. 9:126 (1990) Louisiana

37. N.M. Stat. Ann. Secs 24-9A-1 to 6 (1979) New Mexico

38. Pa. Stat. Ann tit. 18, Secs 3203, 3216 (1983) Pennsylvania

39. US Congress, Office of Technology Assessment (1988), *Infertility: Medical and Social Choices*, OTA-BA-358, US Government Printing Office, Washington D.C., USA

40. Parliamentary Assembly of the Council of Europe (1986), *Recommendation 1100 on the Use of Human Embryos and Foetuses for Diagnostic, Therapeutic, Scientific, Industrial and Commercial Purposes*, Council of Europe, Strasbourg, France

41. Council of Europe (1990), *Europe and Bioethics: Proceedings of the 1st Symposium of the Council of Europe on Bioethics - Strasbourg 5-7 December 1989*, Council of Europe, Strasbourg, France

42. European Parliament STOA Programme (1992), *Bioethics in Europe*, Gruppo di Attenzione sulle Biotecnologie, Milan, Italy

Appendix 1: Membership of the Voluntary Licensing Authority

Chairman: Dame Mary Donaldson, GBE

MRC Nominees:

Sir Douglas Black, MD FRCP

Formerly Professor of Medicine, Manchester University. Formerly Chief Scientist, Department of Health and Social Security. Past President of the Royal College of Physicians. 1985-1991

Professor G S Dawes, CBE, DM, FRCP, FRCOG, FRS

Formerly Director of Nuffield Institute for Medical Research, Oxford. 1985-1991

*Anne McLaren, DPhil, FRS

Director, MRC Mammalian Development Unit. 1985-1991

Dame Cicely Saunders DBE, FRCP

Founder and Medical Director of St. Christopher's Hospice. 1985

RCOG Nominees

*Professor I D Cooke, MB,
BS(Sydney), DGO, FRCOG

Professor of Obstetrics and
Gynaecology, Jessop Hospital,
Sheffield. Chairman, RCOG Fertility
Sub-Committee. 1989-1991

J D O Loudon, MB, ChB, FRCSE,
FRCOG

Consultant Obstetrician and
Gynaecologist, Edinburgh. Chairman,
RCOG Ethics Committee. 1985-1991

Professor M C Macnaughton MD
FRCP(Glas), FRCOG, FRSE.

President of the Royal College of
Obstetricians and Gynaecologists.
Professor of Obstetrics and
Gynaecology, Glasgow University.
1985-1991.

Professor R W Shaw, MD, FRCS
MRCOG

Professor of Obstetrics and
Gynaecology, Royal Free Hospital
School of Medicine, London. 1985-1991

Professor W Thompson MD,
FRCOG

Professor of Midwifery and
Gynaecology, Queens University,
Belfast. Chairman, RCOG Fertility
Committee. 1985-1991

Joint MRC/RCOG Nominees:

*Miss Margaret Auld, MPhil,

Fellow of Royal College of Nursing of
the DSc(Hon).
UK. Vice-President of the Royal
College of Midwives. Member of the
Committee on the Ethics of Gene
Therapy. 1989-1991

John Clarke, BSc (W.Aust),
MA, DPhil (Oxford)

1990-1991 Retired. Formerly at the
Department of Zoology, Oxford

Sir Cecil Clothier, KCB, QC

Chairman of the Police Complaints Authority. Formerly Parliamentary Commissioner for Administration. Formerly Health Service Commissioner for England, Scotland and Wales. 1985-1989

Mrs Alwyne Cox

Magistrate. Member of National Council for the Probation Service. 1986-1991

Professor the Revd Canon G R Dunstan

Emeritus Professor of Moral and Social Theology, in the University of London. 1985-1991

Miss Susan Hampshire

Actress. Author. Executive Committee of Population Concern. Director of Conservation Foundation. 1985-1991

Miss Patricia Lamburn, CBE

Editorial Director, IPC Magazines. Chairman, General Advisory Council to IBA (1982-85). 1986-1991

Penelope Leach, PhD, DipSocSci

Research Psychologist. Author. Vice-President, Health Visitors' Association. Research Consultant International Centre for Child Studies. 1985-1989

Miss Mary-Lou Legg, MA

Historian. Author. Governor of Birkbeck College, London. Lay member of the Research Ethics Committee at the Royal Postgraduate Medical School, London. 1989-1991

Professor R D G Milner, ScD, MD, FRCP

Professor and Head of Department, Department of Paediatrics, Sheffield University. 1987-1989

*Rabbi Julia Neuberger, MA

Rabbi, South London Liberal Synagogue. Member of the Committee of Ethics of the Royal College of Nursing. Member of Council of St. George's Hospital Medical School. 1987-1991

Professor I C S Normand, DM FRCP

Professor of Child Health, University of Southampton. Chairman, British Paediatric Association Ethics Advisory Committee. 1989-1991

Sir John Osborn

Formerly Conservative MP for Hallam. Formerly Member of the Parliamentary Assembly of the Council of Europe. 1987-1991

* later member of the Human Fertilisation and Embryology Authority

Appendix 2: Guidelines for both Clinical and Research Applications of Human In Vitro Fertilization

Introduction

The purpose of these Guidelines is to set out the principles which the Joint Medical Research Council/Royal College of Obstetricians and Gynaecologists Interim Licensing Authority believes should guide those whose clinic practice or research involves the use of in vitro fertilization with human gametes. They have been based on the recommendations of the 'Committee of Inquiry into Human Fertilisation and Embryology' under the Chairmanship of Dame Mary Warnock (the Warnock Committee), the Medical Research Council Statement on 'Research Related to Human Fertilisation and Embryology' (MRC Statement) and the 'Report of the RCOG Ethics Committee on In Vitro Fertilisation and Embryo Replacement or Transfer' (The RCOG Ethics Committee Report).

During their discussions the ILA considered it was important to define the term 'pre-embryo' used in these Guidelines. The term 'embryo' has traditionally been used to describe the stage reached in development where organogenesis has started, as shown by the appearance of the primitive streak and the certainty that thereafter one or more individuals are developing rather than a hydatidiform mole, for example. To the collection of dividing cells up to the determination of the primitive streak we use the term 'pre-embryo'.

Background

After many years of medical research the birth of the first child resulting from the technique of in vitro fertilization took place in July 1978.

The Government established in 1982 the Warnock Committee and its Report was published in July 1984.

One of the recommendations made by the Warnock Committee was that urgent action be taken to control work involved in vitro fertilization. Recognising that appropriate legislation would not be enacted immediately the Medical Research Council and the Royal College of Obstetricians and Gynaecologists agreed to set up a Voluntary Licensing Authority for Human In Vitro Fertilisation and Embryology (VLA). To emphasise that the Authority was an interim measure until the Government introduced a statutory licensing scheme, the Authority changed its name, in 1989, to the Interim Licensing Authority (ILA).

As its first task the Authority prepared Guidelines which are consistent with the recommendations made by the Warnock Committee together with the MRC Statement and the RCOG Ethics Committee Report.

When preparing these Guidelines the Authority, in addition to referring to reports from various expert committees, was aware of the deep public concern that has been expressed about some aspects of in vitro fertilization and the ethical and moral issues that the application of the technique has raised.

The Authority has agreed that soundly based clinical practice involving in vitro fertilization should proceed and it should be regarded as developing therapeutic procedure covered by the normal ethics of the doctor/patient relationship.

It has also been agreed that scientifically sound research involving in vitro fertilization - where there is no intent to transfer the pre-embryo to the uterus - should be allowed to proceed if its aims are clearly defined and acceptable.

The Authority will consider research projects on a case by case basis but certain types will not be approved, eg modification of the genetic constitution of a pre-embryo: the placing of a human pre-embryo in the uterus of another species for gestation: cloning of pre-embryos by nuclear substitution.

Guidelines

(1) Scientifically sound research involving experiments on the processes and products of in vitro fertilization between gametes is ethically acceptable, subject to certain provisions detailed in sections 2-10 below.

(2) Any application made to the Authority must give reasons why information cannot be obtained from studies of species other than the human.

(3) The aim of the research must be clearly defined and relevant to clinical problems such as the diagnosis and treatment of infertility or of genetic disorders, or for the development of safe and more effective contraceptive measures.

(4) Pre-embryos resulting from or used in research should not be transferred to the uterus, except in the course of clinical research studies designed to enhance the possibility of establishing a successful pregnancy in a particular individual.

(5) Suitable signed consent to research involving human ova and sperm should be obtained in every case from the donors; sperm from sperm banks should not be used unless permission for its use in research has been obtained from the donor. Approval for each project must be obtained from the local ethical committee prior to seeking approval from the ILA.

(6) When human ova have been obtained and fertilized in vitro for a therapeutic purpose and are no longer required for that purpose it would be ethical to use them for soundly based research provided that the signed consent of both donors was obtained, subject to the same approval as the preceding section.

(7) Human ova fertilized with human sperm should not be cultured in vitro for more than 14 days excluding any period of storage at low temperature (see Guideline 8) and should not be stored for use in research other than that for which local ethical committee and ILA approval has been obtained.

(8) Where a pre-embryo has been preserved at low temperature, whether donated for research purposes at the time of preservation or subsequently, it may continue to be grown to the equivalent of 14 days' normal development provided that approval has first been obtained from the local ethical committee and the ILA. Storage of individual pre-embryos at low temperature should be reviewed after two years and the maximum storage time should be ten years.

(9) The means of disposal of the pre-embryo must be carefully considered before the start of each project. At the end of a study steps must be taken to stop development of the pre-embryo and the appropriate disposal must be

considered in discussion with the local ethical committee and details given to the ILA. The means of disposal will depend on the nature of the particular study that the pre-embryo has been used for. In view of the scarcity of the material, it would be inappropriate to discard any pre-embryo without thorough examination.

(10) Studies on the penetration of animal eggs by human sperm are valuable in providing information on the penetration ability and chromosomal complement of sperm from subfertile men and are considered ethically acceptable provided that development does not proceed beyond the early cleavage stage.

(11) The clinical use of ova stored at low temperatures, involving subsequent in vitro fertilization should not proceed to transfer to the uterus until such time as scientific evidence is available as to the safety of the procedure.

(12) Consideration must be given to ensuring that whilst a woman has the best chance of achieving a pregnancy the risks of a large multiple pregnancy occurring are minimized. For this reason whether IVF or GIFT procedures are used either jointly or separately no more than three eggs or pre-embryos should be transferred in any one cycle, unless there are exceptional clinical reasons when up to four may be replaced per cycle.

(13) The following general considerations must be taken into account when establishing clinical facilities where in vitro fertilization or GIFT is carried out:

    (a) each centre must have access to an ethical committee*, and no procedure should be undertaken without the knowledge and consent of the ethical committee,

    (b) detailed records must be kept along the lines recommended in the Warnock Committee Report, and should include details of the children born as a result of in vitro fertilization; the records should be readily available for examination by duty authorized staff and for collation on a national basis for a follow-up study,

    (c) where the director either does not have accredited consultant status, or the equivalent, or is a non-clinician, full clinical responsibility must be assumed by a Consultant Adviser who takes an active role in overseeing the centre's treatment protocols and emergency procedures; all other medical, nursing and technical staff must have appropriate experience and training,

    (d) specialist medical, surgical and nursing facilities appropriate for the specific techniques used for the treatment must be available,

(e) arrangements for emergency treatment must be made,

(f) there must be adequate arrangements, where appropriate, for the transfer of gametes and pre-embryos between clinical facilities and the laboratory,

(g) centres should have appropriate counselling facilities with access to properly trained independent counselling staff,

(h) whenever donor gametes are to be used both donors and recipients should be tested for hepatitis B and HIV antibodies,

(i) donor sperm should be obtained only from a bank where all appropriate screening tests are undertaken including those recommended by the DHSS AIDS Booklet 4 *AIDS and Artificial Insemination - Guidance for Doctors and AI Clinics* (CMO(86)12),

(j) egg donors should remain anonymous and for this reason donation for clinical purposes from any known person including close relatives should be avoided,

(k) the use of close relatives for IVF surrogacy should be avoided.

* Refer to the Authority's Guidelines for ethics committees for centres offering assisted reproduction. These may be obtained from the Secretariat.

Appendix 3: Consent Form for In Vitro Fertilization

Consent Form for In Vitro Fertilization
(For use of pre-embryos for research a separate consent form must be used)

Name and address of Centre

We ....(full name of woman)

and ....(full name of man)

of ....

....

being unlikely to have a child by other means, have requested the
.... Centre, through its medical and scientific staff,
to assist the woman to give birth to a child by the man.

1. We had a full discussion with .... on .... and we understand that the methods to be used may include:

   (i)   preparation of the woman by the administration of hormones and other drugs described in the attached schedule;

   (ii) egg retrieval by means of..;

   (iii) fertilization with the man's semen of any eggs from the woman;

   (iv) maintenance of pre-embryos resulting from such fertilization until such time as, in the view of the medical and scientific staff, they are ready for replacement in the woman;

   (v) selection by the medical and scientific staff of the most suitable pre-embryos for such replacement;

   (vi) transfer of selected pre-embryos to the woman.

2. We consent to these procedures and to the administration of such drugs and anaesthetics to the woman as may be necessary. We also consent to any further operative measures which may be found to be necessary in the course of treatment.

3. We understand and accept that there is no certainty that a pregnancy will result from these procedures, since the success rate is uncertain even where an egg is recovered and replacement carried out. We further understand and accept that the medical and scientific staff can give no assurance that pregnancy will result in the delivery of a normal living child.

4. * delete as required

   (a) *We request that any pre-embryos which are not replaced should, at the discretion of the medical staff, be preserved by freezing or other methods and stored for a period of not more than two years from the date of fertilization.

   (b) *We understand that if before the period of two years has expired we wish any pre-embryos to be preserved for a further period, the Centre will be prepared, at our request, to consider such further period of preservation on terms to be negotiated.

   (c) *We understand that, if we so wish, any suitable pre-embryos so stored may be used for replacement (but only on the above-named woman) and at the discretion of the medical and scientific staff. We further understand that no assurance can be given that any such pre-embryos will survive or be suitable for replacement.

(d) *We agree that no stored pre-embryo shall be removed from the custody of the medical and scientific staff of the Centre without the written consent of both of us (or the survivor), such consent to be given within twenty-eight days before replacement or removal. In the event of both our deaths we request that any stored pre-embryos should be disposed of at the discretion of the Centre, as at section (e).

(e) *We agree that after the period of two years (or such extension as may be agreed) has expired the Hospital or Centre (subject to the general terms of this agreement) may dispose of the stored pre-embryos at its discretion by:
*(i)   donation to another individual determined by the clinician in charge,
*(ii) destroying by approved methods.

5. We accept that decisions as to the suitability and number of pre-embryos for replacement, at any time and whether frozen or not, will be at the discretion of the medical and scientific staff at the Centre, subject to the Guidelines of the ILA.

6. We do not consent to the transfer of any pre-embryos so produced into a woman other than the above named woman.

7. We have read the information booklet relating to IVF and have understood what is involved in this procedure.

8. We have been given time to consider the contents of this document and we have been given the opportunity to make such further enquiries as we wish before signing.

DATED   the ....day
              of....................199..............

SIGNED   .... woman
              .... man
              .... for the Centre

WITNESS ....
              ....

Agreement for the use of pre-embryos for research

We understand that pre-embryos not used for replacement or storage and any pre-embryos remaining after the agreed period of storage may be used for the advance of medical and scientific knowledge and we consent to such use.

We realise that the development of such pre-embryos cannot proceed for long outside the body and the period of survival will be brief.

We have been given at least 24 hours to consider the use of spare pre-embryos for use in an approved research programme and to make such further enquiries as we wish before signing.

DATED   the..day of 199

SIGNED   ....woman
              ....man
              ....for the Centre

WITNESS   ....
                ....
                ....

Appendix 4: Guidelines for Ethics Committees for Centres Offering Assisted Reproduction 1989

An Ethics Committee has as its duty the protection of both patients and public. By being seen to ensure that a Centre maintains appropriate ethical standards it also protects the Centre from unjustified criticism. Usually the existing hospital Ethics Committee will be judged competent to oversee an Assisted Reproduction Centre. If none exists a committee must be set up for this purpose.

The objectives of an Ethics Committee are:
(i) to protect the interests of patients and of any children resulting from the use of assisted conception in particular; and those of society in general; and to provide reassurance to the public that this is being done;
(ii) to consider and, where appropriate, approve medical research and the development of new clinical procedures in the fields of embryology and infertility.

Research

When considering research projects an Ethics Committee should follow the Guidelines proposed by the World Health Organisation and Council for International

Organisations of Medical Sciences as set out by the Royal College of Physicians (1984). Before commending a project to the Interim Licensing Authority (ILA) the Committee members should satisfy themselves that the project is within the current Guidelines of the ILA and, in particular, that:

(i)   the required information cannot be obtained from animal models or that the appropriate animal work has already been undertaken;

(ii) there is no intention to replace any pre-embryo resulting from or used for research procedures unrelated to its own preparation for replacement.

Clinical procedures

An Ethics Committee will also be expected to approve the Centre's proposed clinical programme with regard to ethical issues and to discuss any changes later introduced into that programme.

Centres are expected to follow the current ILA Guidelines and any proposed departure from these Guidelines must be approved by the Ethics Committee and reported to the ILA.

In approving such a proposed departure the Committee members should assure themselves that:

(i)   no alternative procedure exists for the case in question - the fact that a clinic may have difficulty in meeting the requirements of the ILA is not a basis for circumventing its Guidelines;

(ii)   the prospective patients have been fully counselled with regard to the possible consequences of the proposed procedure;

(iii) the interests of the potential offspring as well as those of the parents are taken into account when assessing the risks and benefits of the procedure;

(iv)   the interests of any third party are taken into account (eg donor);

(v)   the effects of the procedure on the wider interests of society in terms of its norms and obligations, and of the adequacy of its provision for consequent after-care, have been given consideration.

Membership

(i)   It is not necessary that those who become members of the Committee are experts in moral philosophy or in particular disciplines; they need to be reflective people of good will, with a high regard for the human personality, for truthfulness and for the continued advance of reproductive medicine and medical science. Those who are totally opposed to work involving the human pre-embryo should be left to attack the system from outside; but neither should individuals be included who are acquiescent and likely to give automatic approval. Of the medical and scientific members there should be a majority who are employed in providing clinical care. It is also important that there will be individuals who will look at applications critically from the patient's point of view.

The membership should comprise the following interests:
- (a) medical and scientific - these members should include a general practitioner and someone with experience related to infertility who may, if necessary, be co-opted for relevant items;
- (b) nursing - a nurse who is in active practice with patients;
- (c) lay - there should be not less than two lay members and they should provide effective representation of community rather than sectional interests. A lay member with legal training can be of value but his or her role should not be restricted to answering questions of law.
  The Committee should include women amongst its members.
- (ii) The Committee may elect its own Chairman and should also have a Secretary who will keep a record of business. It is suggested that either the Chairman of the Vice-Chairman be chosen from amongst the lay members to emphasize lay involvement.
- (iii) The Chairman of an Ethics Committee should have no financial interest in the Centre for which that Committee is responsible. Any Committee members who have such an interest should declare it.

Frequency of meeting

- (i) An Ethics Committee should meet at least twice per year or more frequently if matters arise.
- (ii) The Chairman and some members should visit regularly the centre for which they are responsible. This should be at least once a year.

Mode of working

- (i) Business should be conducted at meetings of the Committee and not only by post or telephone.
- (ii) It is useful to circulate to the Committee publications relevant to the

ethical conduct of assisted reproduction or pre-embryo research which may appear from time to time such as publications from the Government the Royal Colleges or the ILA.

(iii) If the Committee finds a project unacceptable, reasons for the decision should be given to the Director of the Centre in writing. It may be possible for projects to be modified in discussion with the Director. Where the Committee finds itself uncertain about the ethics of a particular project or procedure, referral may be made to the ILA.

(iv) While it is impracticable for an Ethics Committee to monitor approved projects or procedures in detail, some follow-up is desirable to ascertain progress. Committees may consider requesting reports of work completed, or an annual report from clinical Centres.

(v) In the event of an Ethics Committee discovering that its advice is unheeded or that projects or procedures are being carried out which infringe the Guidelines of the ILA, these facts should be reported to the Authority as well as to the Committee's parent body.

(vi) Confidentiality should be preserved, not only for the protection of individuals but also because the issues considered are often complicated and delicate, and uninformed or unbalanced publicity could raise emotions that are damaging to all concerned, especially the patients.

(vii) It is undesirable to take important decisions in the absence of, for instance, a lay member and the Committee should define the composition of a Quorum as well as its number.

Business

(i) As well as keeping a watch on the practice of its own Centre one of the main duties of an IVF centre's Ethics Committee is to see that the Guidelines of the ILA are observed.

(ii) Not all Centres undertake research projects: Ethics Committee should also provide guidance for Centres on their clinical programme. In the current field of IVF it is often difficult to distinguish between experimental and therapeutic clinical treatment, which is where the role of the Ethics Committee becomes critical.

(iii) IVF and other techniques for assisted reproduction are areas of practice in which there is rapid development both in terms of clinical and of scientific advance. Their impact on society requires constant assessment. Legislation is in prospect which would affect both clinical services and research. Local Ethics Committees should keep themselves informed of all advances and taken the opportunity to discuss together their implications whenever necessary. It may be advisable to delegate members with a particular knowledge or interest to report on such items at meetings of the Committee.

(iv) The record of relevant business should be made available to the ILA upon request.

Appendix 5: Egg Donation: Your Questions Answered

Introduction

It has been suggested that you might like to consider donating eggs, either to help another woman establish a pregnancy or for research purposes. This booklet has been written in order to explain why egg donation is needed and to answer some of the questions you may want to ask.

Why is egg donation needed?

Some couples are infertile because the woman is unable to produce eggs. This may occur because the ovaries have never developed properly (eg, Turner's Syndrome), because of ovarian failure (premature menopause) or because surgery or chemotherapy has caused sterility. For these couples in vitro fertilization (IVF) - often referred to as the 'test-tube baby technique' - using donated eggs offers their only chance of achieving a pregnancy.

Some women are carriers of sex-linked diseases such as Duchenne muscular dystrophy or haemophilia; these diseases are passed on by females but only boys are affected. Rather than risk giving birth to a child who may suffer greatly and die at an early age, the woman may request egg donation. The donated egg would be fertilized by her husband's sperm and the couple would be given the chance of having a healthy child. Techniques are now being developed which will enable the woman's own eggs to be fertilized in the laboratory and tested to find out whether they are affected by the disease in question; only those which are free of the disease will be transferred. However, this is still in the very early stages and it will be some time before the test is readily available.

In vitro fertilization was developed following many years of research; more research is required to improve the success rate of this and other treatments for infertility. Some pre-embryos (fertilized eggs up to 14 days after fertilization) which are 'spare' from IVF treatment are available for research but their number is limited. This research has five main aims:

   (i)   to promote advances in the treatment of infertility;
  (ii) to increase knowledge about the cause of congenital abnormalities (defects present at birth);
 (iii) to increase knowledge about the cause of miscarriage;
 (iv) to develop more effective methods of contraception;
  (v) to develop methods for detecting the presence of gene or chromosome abnormalities in pre-embryos before implantation.

There are some types of research which cannot be carried out on 'spare' pre-embryos but only on donated eggs (also called oocytes) fertilized in vitro for research purposes. These are projects that involve fertilization itself and include the freezing of eggs, the development of a contraceptive vaccine and the development of techniques to inject sperm directly into the egg for use in case of male infertility where sperm cannot penetrate eggs in the normal way.

Who will benefit from it?

Egg donation for clinical purposes would benefit those women who are unable to produce their own eggs and those who are carriers of sex-linked diseases.

Egg donation for research purposes could potentially help many thousands of people by improving treatment of infertility and methods of contraception, increasing knowledge of miscarriage and congenital abnormalities and developing techniques for the pre-implantation diagnosis of genetic diseases.

Who are potential donors? (Why me)

Patients undergoing IVF or GIFT (Gamete Intrafallopian Transfer - another form of infertility treatment) who have more eggs than they need themselves.
Volunteer donors.
Women undergoing sterilization or other related surgery.
Relatives or friends of recipients whose eggs are given to a women unknown to the donor.

Will the donation be anonymous?

Yes, except for very rare cases; in these cases your approval and that of the recipient must be obtained before any information is divulged. In normal circumstances your identify will not be disclosed to any person other than the staff of the centre at which the operation is performed. If your eggs are used to enable another woman to become pregnant, the choice of recipient will be entirely at the discretion of the medical staff; you will not be told her identity and neither will she be told yours.

Will I have a continuing responsibility to any child born following the donation?

No. At the time of the donation you relinquish all legal rights and claims over any offspring that may result from the donated eggs and all duties towards it.

What tests will be done before I am accepted?

This will vary between centres but all donors will be tested for hepatitis B and HIV antibodies (AIDS). You should discuss with the counsellor what information you wish to be given following these tests.

What does egg donation involve?

In your normal menstrual cycle several follicles (little sacs of fluid each containing one egg) begin to grow but only one grows enough to release an egg. Although it is possible to donate this one ripe egg, most centres would prefer to collect more and give you medication to stimulate the ovaries so that more eggs can be obtained.

Egg development will usually be monitored by ultrasound scanning, a safe, simple and painless procedure which enables a picture to appear on the screen, showing the ovaries containing the follicles. Hormone levels in the blood may also be measured to monitor egg development.

The eggs will be collected either using ultrasound guidance or by laparoscopy (see below). If eggs are to be collected using ultrasound, you may be given a general anaesthetic but more probably a mild sedative. A fine needle will be passed either through the bladder, urethra or vagina and into each follicle in turn. The fluid containing the egg is sucked out of the follicle through the hollow needle. This can be done as an outpatient procedure.

Laparoscopy requires a general anaesthetic. A small cut is made just below the navel for the laparoscope (an instrument for looking into the abdomen) to be inserted and a needle is inserted separately to remove the eggs.

Laparoscopy is frequently used to perform sterilization. If you are donating eggs at the same time as undergoing sterilization, no additional operative procedures will be required.

What medication will I be given?

This will vary between centres but some of those most commonly used include clomiphene, pergonal, metrodin and buserelin. These are used to stimulate your ovaries to produce more than one egg.

What are the risks and possible side-effects?

(i) **Medication**

On rare occasions there can be side-effects which last while taking the medication. They are uncommon but may consist of hot flushes, weight gain due to salt and water retention similar to period discomfort and restlessness at night.

The medication is carefully monitored but very occasionally a woman reacts abnormally and cysts can develop on the ovaries. These may be painful but usually subside with bedrest; if they do not subside, admission to hospital may be required.

(ii) **Egg collection**

Women undergoing ultrasound-directed egg recovery may notice a small amount of blood in their urine or from their vagina for a day afterwards. This is quite common and should not cause concern. Laparoscopy carries the usual minor risks and side-effects of any procedure requiring a general anaesthetic. Most women have very little discomfort and no pain after laparoscopy. Some women experience soreness in the stomach, chest or shoulders, or vaginal bleeding for a few days after the operation.

Will any part of the procedure be painful?

Following laparoscopy there may be some abdominal pain which is similar to that of a painful period. The pain usually disappears in a short time. The operation to remove eggs under ultrasound should not be painful because pain killing drugs can be given before the procedure. It is uncommon to experience any pain after the operation is over.

Will I be given any counselling?

Yes. The guidelines issued by the ILA state that skilled and independent counselling, by somebody other than the medical practitioner involved in the procedure, must be available to the donor. You should ensure that you are given and have understood sufficient information to make an informed decision. If you are in doubt about any of the procedures or the ethical aspects involved, ask!

What will happen if I change my mind?

You are free to withdraw consent to the egg donation at any time before the operation without threat of financial penalty or fear of recrimination. If you are undergoing sterilization or other related surgery, that operation will still be performed on the terms already agreed.

Guidelines

The Interim Licensing Authority (ILA)) was established in 1985 to oversee centres offering in vitro fertilization (IVF)) and carrying out research involving the use of human pre-embryos. The ILA produces guidelines which licensed centres must agree to abide by; the guidelines relevant to egg donation are as follows:

A   The following general conditions must be taken into account when receiving donated oocytes from both those donating for purely altruistic reasons and those receiving free sterilization or other operative procedures:

(a) Skilled and independent counselling, by somebody other than the medical practitioner involved in the procedure, must be available to the donor to ensure that sufficient information has been given and understood, particularly in relation to discomfort and risk; and that the donor, if she consents, does so with her judgement unimpaired. The counsellor should look for stability of purpose so that neither consent nor withdrawal during treatment would be lightly undertaken.

(b) The donor must know that she is free to withdraw consent to the egg donation at any time without threat of financial penalty and, where appropriate, without impairment of her interest in the successful conduct of the primary operation.

(c) The centre must be prepared to accept, in the event of withdrawal after preparation for egg recovery has begun, the financial loss incurred.

(d) The donor must be informed of the purpose for which her eggs will be used (ie research or donation to another woman for clinical purposes) and the centre at which the eggs will be used. Eggs must not be sold.

(e) The donor must be given a copy of the information booklet provided by the ILA. The consent form at the back of the booklet must be signed by the donor and retained in the records of the centre where the donation took place.

(f) The local Ethics Committee must satisfy itself that the conditions both can and will be met in the centre for which it is responsible.

B The following general conditions must also be taken into account when offering free sterilization (or other related surgery) to women in return for donated oocytes:

(a) Centres wishing to offer free sterilization to women in consideration of their donating oocytes must apply in writing to the ILA for permission. Each centre's application will be judged independently.

(b) The discussion of egg donation must be entirely separate from decisions concerning the management and clinical care of the patient for whom the sterilization or other operation may be indicated. Only when those decisions have been made may the question of egg donation be raised.

(c) The fact of egg donation along should not entitle a patient to transfer to a shorter list or faster lane for sterilization; such a transfer must have its own clinical justification.

Consent form for Egg Donation
To be retained by donor

Name and address of Centre:

I ....(name of woman)

of ....

....

.... (address)

have read the information booklet prepared by the Interim Licensing Authority and I hereby consent to the following:

*1. I consent to the removal of eggs from my ovaries and to the administration of such drugs and anaesthetics and the use of such operative procedures as the medical staff consider necessary.

OR

*1. I consent to the removal of eggs from my ovaries at the operation for ...., and to the administration of such drugs as the medical staff consider necessary.

* delete as required

2. I hereby agree to donate any eggs recovered to the above centre for:
*   (i)   transfer, when fertilized, to a suitable recipient in order to attempt to make her pregnant.
    (ii)   use in research to advance medical and scientific knowledge.
    (iii)   either transfer into a suitable recipient or for use in research.
3. I understand that the choice of recipient will be entirely at the discretion of the medical staff and that I shall not be told the identity of the recipient.
4. I understand that my name will not be disclosed to any person other than the staff at the Centre performing the operation.
5. I hereby relinquish all legal rights and claims over any offspring that may result from the donated eggs.

6.   I understand that I may withdraw consent at any time up to the operation without risk of financial penalty and without prejudice to any primary operation.

7.   I declare that I have not received and do not seek any fee for entering into this agreement.

8.   I have had full discussion with
      .... (Medical Practitioner) and
      .... (counsellor) and I have been given at least 24 hours to consider the contents of this agreement.

9.   The possible side-effects of the medication and the operative procedures have been explained to me.

Dated the .... day
      of..19................

Signed: .... (woman)

           .... (for the Centre)

Witness: ....

* delete as required

Consent Form for Egg Donation
To be retained in the Centre's records

Name and address
of Centre

I .... (name of woman)

of   ....

....

.... (address)

have read the information booklet prepared by the Interim Licensing Authority and
I hereby consent to the following:

*1.   I consent to the removal of eggs from my ovaries and to the administration of
such drugs and anaesthetics and the use of such operative procedures as the
medical staff consider necessary.

OR

* 1.   I consent to the removal of eggs from my ovaries at the operation for
...., and to the administration of such drugs as
the medical staff consider necessary.

2.   I hereby agree to donate any eggs recovered to the above centre for:
*   (i)   transfer, when fertilized, to a suitable recipient in order to attempt to
make her pregnant.
(ii)   use in research to advance medical and scientific knowledge.
(iii)   either transfer into a suitable recipient or for use in research.
3.   I understand that the choice of recipient will be entirely at the discretion of the
medical staff and that I shall not be told the identity of the recipient.
4.   I understand that my name will not be disclosed to any person other than the
staff at the Centre performing the operation.
5.   I hereby relinquish all legal rights and claims over any offspring that may
result from the donated eggs.

6. I understand that I may withdraw consent at any time up to the operation without risk of financial penalty and without prejudice to any primary operation.

*   delete as required

7. I declare that I have not received and do not seek any fee for entering into this agreement.
8. I have had full discussion with
    .... (Medical Practitioner) and
    .... (counsellor) and
    I have been given at least 24 hours to consider the contents of this agreement.
9. The possible side-effects of the medication and the operative procedures have been explained to me.

Dated the .... day
       of................................19......................

Signed: .... (Woman)

          .... (for the Centre)

Witness: ....

Appendix 6: Membership of the Human Fertilisation and Embryology Authority

Professor Colin Campbell
(Chairman)

Vice-Chancellor of Nottingham
University.

Diana Brittan
(Deputy Chairman)

Member of the Equal Opportunities
Commission and Magistrate, City of
London. Chairman of Community
Industry.

Professor Robert Berry

Professor of Genetics, University
College, London.

Professor Ian Cooke

Professor of Obstetrics & Gynaecology,
University of Sheffield. Jessop Hospital
for Women.

Professor Anthony Cox	University of London Professor of Child and Adolescent Psychiatry at the United Medical and Dental Schools of Guy's and St. Thomas' Hospitals.
Jane Denton	Nursing Research Fellow, Multiple Births Foundation at Queen Charlotte's and Chelsea Hospital, London.
Liz Forgan	Managing Director, BBC Radio.
Joan Harbison	Senior Lecturer in Education, Stranmillis College, Belfast.
Dr. Stephen Hillier	Director, Reproductive Endocrinology Laboratory, University of Edinburgh Centre for Reproductive Biology.
Professor Brenda Hoggett	Law Commissioner; Recorder of the Crown Court and Visiting Professor of Law at King's College, London.
The Most Reverend Richard Holloway	Bishop of Edinburgh.
Penelope Keith	Actress.
Angela Mays	Management Consultant.
Dr. Anne McLaren	Principle Research Associate, The Wellcome Institute, Cambridge.
Dr. Jeannette Naish	General Practitioner, Senior Lecturer, Department of General Practice & Primary Care. Joint Medical College of St. Bart's and the London Hospitals , University of London.

Rabbi Julia Neuberger

Chairman (designate) of Camden & Islington Community Health Services NHS Trust.

Professor Robert Shaw

Professor of Obstetrics and Gynaecology, University of Wales College of Medicine, Cardiff.

David Shilson

Senior Official, Bank of England.

Professor Robert Snowden

Professor of Family Studies, Exeter University.

Christine Walby

Director of Social Services, Stafford.

Professor David Whittingham

Professor of Experimental Embryology, University of London and Director of the Medical Research Council Experimental Embryology and Teratology Unit.

Index